Nominalization: Exploring Aspect and Countability

POTSDAM LINGUISTIC INVESTIGATIONS
POTSDAMER LINGUISTISCHE UNTERSUCHUNGEN
RECHERCHES LINGUISTIQUES À POTSDAM

Vol./Bd. 38

Zu Qualitätssicherung und Peer Review der vorliegenden Publikation:

Die Qualität der in dieser Reihe erscheinenden Arbeiten wird vor der Publikation durch einen externen, von der Herausgeberschaft benannten Gutachter im Double Blind Verfahren geprüft. Dabei ist der Autor der Arbeit dem Gutachter während der Prüfung namentlich nicht bekannt; der Gutachter bleibt anonym.

Notes on the quality assurance and peer review of this publication:

Prior to publication, the quality of the work published in this series is double blind reviewed by an external referee appointed by the editorship. The referee is not aware of the author's name when performing the review; the referee's name is not disclosed.

Markéta Blažková

Nominalization: Exploring Aspect and Countability

PETER LANG
Berlin · Bruxelles · Chennai · Lausanne · New York · Oxford

Bibliographic Information published by the Deutsche Nationalbibliothek
The Deutsche Nationalbibliothek lists this publication in the Deutsche Nationalbibliografie; detailed bibliographic data is available online at http://dnb.d-nb.de.

Library of Congress Control Number: 2025035780

This publication was funded by the Faculty of Arts of the University of Pardubice (The Czech Republic).

ISSN 1862-524X
ISBN 978-3-631-93456-2 (Print)
ISBN 978-3-631-93457-9 (ePDF)
ISBN 978-3-631-93458-6 (ePUB)
DOI 10.3726/ b22837

Published by Peter Lang GmbH, Berlin (Germany)

info@peterlang.com

This publication has been peer reviewed.

www.peterlang.com

Contact for General Product Safety Regulation (GPSR): gpsr@peterlang.com

Contents

Preface

This study primarily investigates nominalizations in Czech, with a particular emphasis on the interaction between aspect and countability within them. The arguments presented in this work advocate for incorporating projections that enable and facilitate this interaction.

The research involves a comprehensive analysis of two prominent generative grammar models proposed by respected scholars with extensive research in nominalizations: Artemis Alexiadou and Hagit Borer. After the detailed investigation of functional layers in nominal and verbal domains in Czech, this work puts forward two distinct syntactic structures for two types of deverbal nominals in Czech, namely N/T and B/K nominals. It also shows that Czech nominalizations better comply with ergative patterns as proposed by Alexiadou (2001, 2017d).

Additionally, it confirms the hypothesis put forward by Alexiadou and Borer, asserting that Arguments structure nouns are countable, while refuting Grimshaw's (1990) assumption that Argument Structure nominals are mass nouns. This confirmation is rooted in the parallelism observed between count nouns and telic and perfective events, which are characterized by their bounded nature, drawing upon Jackendoff's (1991) concept of boundedness. The factors that lead to the countability of Czech Argument structure nominals are discussed, noting a decline in the usage of group and kind numerals in oblique Cases and in contexts that express larger numerals.

Furthermore, based on corpus analysis, the study shows that in countable contexts, N/T nominalizations, which may contain a more extensive verbal structure, tend to select telic bases. Conversely, B/K nominalizations form less complex verbal structures and more frequently opt for atelic verbs.All these findings lead to the conclusion that the long-standing presumption of parallelism between the verbal and nominal domains within the framework of generative grammar, as originally proposed by Chomsky (1970) and subsequently reinforced by Abney (1987), is substantiated.

List of Abbreviations

1	First Person
2	Second Person
3	Third Person
A	Adjective
ABS	Absolutive case
ACC	Accusative
ADV	Adverb
AG	Agent
AGR	Agreement
AP	Adjective Phrase
AS	Argument Structure
AS-Nominals	AS nominals (roughly Grimshaw's CENs)
Asp_Q	Quantity Aspect
AUX	Auxiliary
B/K nominals	Czech nominals with the suffixes *-ba/-ka*, and zero-derived nominals
CEN	Complex event nominal
CCS	Categorial Complement Space
CL	Classifier
COUNT	Countable
CP	Complementizer Phrase
D	Determiner
DAT	Dative

DivP	Divider Phrase
DM	Distributed Morphology
DP	Determiner Phrase
e	Open value
EP	Event Phrase
F	Feminine
F^sP	Shell Functional Projection
FUT	Future Tense
GEN	Genitive
GenP	Gender Phrase
HMC	The Head Movement Constraint
HUM	Human
IMPF	Imperfective
INF	Infinitive
INS	Instrumental
ITER	Iterativity
L-D	Lexical Domain
LF	Logical Form
Loc	Locative
M	Masculine
NT	Neuter
N	Noun
n	Nominalizer
NOM	Nominative
NP	Noun Phrase
N/T	Czech nominals with the suffixes *-ní/tí*
#P	Quantity Phrase
P	Preposition
PF	Phonetic Form
PF	Perfective
PL	Plural
POSS	Possessive
PP	Prepositional Phrase
PREF	Prefix
PRT	Participle

QP	Quantifier Phrase
REFL	Reflexive
R-Nominal	Referential nominal
RN	Result nominal
SEN	Simple event nominal
SG	Singular
S-O-Q	Subject-of-quantity
SP	Superlexical Prefix
TH	Theme
TP	Tense Phrase
UNCOUNT	Uncountable
UTAH	The Universal Theta-Assignment Hypothesis
V	Verb
v	Verbalizer
VP	Verb Phrase
XS	Exo-skeletal

Introduction

Survey of Chapter Contents

The primary focus of this study is twofold: firstly, to propose a functional structure that adequately captures the unique characteristics of derived nominals in Czech, and secondly, to employ this structure and analyze the circumstances under which Czech deverbal argument structure Nouns can be made countable.

Previous studies of Czech in more recent frameworks (e.g., Panevová 2000; Karlík 2002; Dvořák 2014) have extensively examined Czech derived nominals, focusing primarily on their morphosyntactic properties, but there has been a lack of in-depth syntactic analysis. While Veselovská's (2018b) syntactic analysis of derived nominals is highly influential in terms of syntax, it does not specifically address individual functional projections with their features in detail or the connection between the verbal and nominal domains. The same holds true for two additional pieces of work operating within a generative framework: Havranová's (2020) dissertation thesis, which explores nominalizations in Dutch English and Czech, and Čakányová's (2022) article focused on the topic of nominalizations in Czech.

According to previous studies, Czech has two types of deverbal nominals traditionally divided into two classes:

Type I has the ending *-ní/tí as in uče-ní* 'teaching', *zkouše-ní* 'examining'.
Type II has a larger variety of suffixes including a zero suffix *výměr* 'measurement' but the most typical are *-ba/ka* as in *mal-ba* 'painting', *stav-ba* 'building'.

They both possess a hybrid nature, combining elements of both nominal and verbal properties. While both types can refer to events, only the Type I nominals have more obvious verbal characteristics and behave as argument structure Nouns. Given that these nominalizations involve both nominal and verbal layers, it is essential to initially analyze the verbal and nominal domains in depth and then scrutinize their interactions within the context of nominalization.

Since Grimshaw (1990) it has been claimed that argument structure nominals are mass and not countable. The similar arguments have been developed for Czech by Veselovská (2019) and Karlík (2019). However, more recent research by Alexiadou et al. (2010c) and Borer (2013) presents evidence that contradicts this claim by exploring the correlation between Aspect and Number in argument structure Nouns. In this study, I will develop a compatible framework to demonstrate that similar arguments apply to Czech argument structure Nouns.

In the second part of the study, I am going to analyze in more detail the countability of argument structure Nouns in Czech to investigate the interactions between nominal and verbal domains. I will show that countability within these structures has been influenced by both aspectual considerations (pertaining to the verbal domain) and the notions of countability (relevant to the nominal domain).

In the generative linguistic tradition, there has been a long-standing assumption of parallelism between these domains, drawing parallels between DP (Determiner Phrase) and TP (Tense Phrase) as proposed by Abney (1987). A key principle will be that when the projections are parallel, it becomes possible to identify a pathway within a derivation where one projection can substitute for the other. This, in turn, plays a role in the relationship between verbal and nominal structures, wherein an increase in verbal structure coincides with a decrease in the prominence of nominal structure.

The approach adopted to address the aforementioned questions will be rooted in generative grammar, which will serve as the theoretical framework for the analysis conducted. Within the realm of generative grammar, two influential models proposed by renowned researchers who have extensively studied nominalizations will be compared. These models include the work of Artemis Alexiadou, who utilizes the Distributed Morphology framework with a primary focus on Greek, and Hagit Borer, who employs the Exo-skeletal model and draws data primarily from Hebrew. In this study, the proposals put forth by the authors will be rigorously examined, specifically with regards to their applicability to Czech data. Additionally, recommendations will be formulated based on the findings.

The outline of this work will be the following. The first and introductory chapter of this thesis will lay the foundation by presenting the fundamental principles of recent generative grammar. It will provide an overview of this linguistic framework and its relevance to the study of nominalizations. Additionally, the chapter will highlight the significant contributions made by influential authors in the field who have focused on the topic of nominalizations within the context of generative grammar. By exploring their works, the chapter aims to establish the theoretical background necessary for the subsequent analysis of derived nominals and their functional structure.

The main focus of the second chapter will be the introduction of two frameworks: Distributed Morphology and the Exo-skeletal model employed by Artemis Alexiadou and Hagit Borer respectively.

Subsequently, the third chapter will delve into the arguments put forth by these authors concerning the nominal domain within the context of their frameworks. Toward the conclusion of this chapter, a comparative examination of both approaches will be conducted, accompanied by their application to Czech data. Throughout this analysis, special attention will be given to the functional layers inside DPs associated with Gender and countability, as these layers are crucial for nominalizations.

In the fourth chapter, I am going to describe and compare the functional layers of verbal domains first as proposed by Alexiadou and Borer and then apply the theories on Czech data. The primary focus of this chapter will revolve around the in-depth evaluation of aspectual issues.

The fifth chapter will describe the integration of the previously discussed domains within nominalizations, while also assessing their applicability to Czech. This chapter will also demonstrate that Czech nominalizations exhibit ergative pattern and are more passive-like or unaccusative, as proposed by Alexiadou (2017d).

Lastly, in the final chapter I am going to examine the circumstances under which Czech argument structure nominals can be made countable. This examination will involve correlating countability with Aspect, thereby shedding light on the intricate interactions between the verbal and nominal domains.

1.1 Generative Approach to Language and Classification of Nominals

This study adopts a generative approach to analyze nominalization. Thus, in this introductory chapter, I will briefly outline the foundational theoretical principles of the current stage of generative grammar, which forms the basis of this thesis.[1] Following this, I will provide insights from prominent generative linguists who have made significant contributions to the study of nominalizations in both English and Czech.

Generative grammarians explain complex linguistic phenomena by means of autonomous grammatical systems that enter into relation with other systems, for example, perception, acoustics etc. This notion, known as the Modularity hypothesis, was extensively advocated by Chomsky (1975). The modularity can be illustrated with a sentence quoted by Newmeyer (1986), which, despite being grammatically correct, is challenging for our perceptual system to process.

(1) *The rat died that was eaten by the cat that the dog chased.*

This example testifies in favor of at least partial independence between different modules.

One crucial module within this framework is *the autonomous grammar module*, also referred to as the language faculty. It is considered by Chomsky (1965) to be innate and associated with a specific part of the human brain. What is more, it is inherently modular, comprising sub-modules that pertain to sound, structure and meaning. Although this model has undergone numerous refinements, and I will discuss the details of its latest version in Chapter 2, it can be broadly represented in the following way:

1 The generative framework of the twenty-first century comprises many not fully compatible branches represented by individual theoreticians. In this study, I will assume the basic Chomskian background shared by most of them; for the specific analysis of nominalizations, I am going to refer to the authors whose theories I found most influential and applicable.

(2) Generative model of grammar

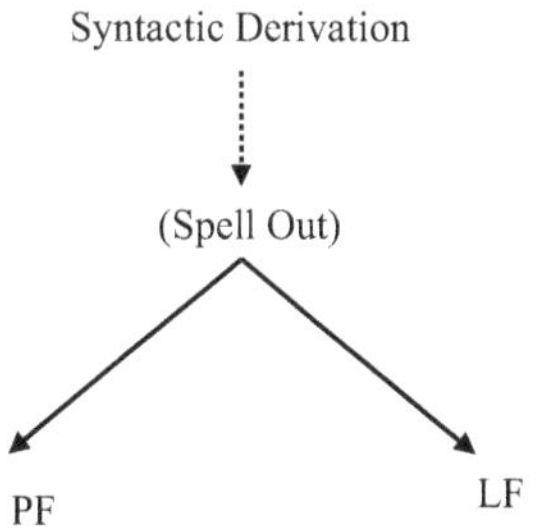

In this model, syntactic structures are computed by means of syntactic operations and the resulting output is sent to both *Logical Form* (LF) and *Phonetic Form* (PF) at spell out. Logical form (LF) is the stage in the derivation where syntactic structures are semantically interpreted. Phonetic form (PF) is the level where structures are assigned a phonetic representation, which is subsequently articulated by the speaker.

The operations in narrow syntax (the level of derivation leading to LF and excluding PF) are typically performed on hierarchical structures, which are then linearized at the PF stage. Numerous tests support this assertion, see Adger (2003, p. 52). I will illustrate it just with a cleft test:

(3) a. *Julie and Jenny arrived first.*
b. ***It was** Julie and Jenny that arrived first.*
c. *****It was** Jenny arrived Julie and first.*

A cleft construction takes a sequence of words and places them after *It was*, serving as evidence that this string of words forms a constituent. This is not possible with other sequences of words as (3c) exemplifies.

Therefore, the syntactic structure is typically represented using a tree diagram. These structures are further organized into phrases based on their selectional properties. For instance, Verbs select objects (4a) and become Verb Phrases (VP), but they do not combine with other lexical Verbs (4b):

(4) a. *kissed Peter*
b. **kissed eat*

When the phrase has no further objects to select, it projects no further and becomes maximal. It can, however, be selected by other phrases as in (5) where the perfective auxiliary *has* selects VP but does not select the NP *Peter.*

(5) a. ***has*** *kissed Peter*
b. *****has*** *Peter*

Furthermore, syntactic phrases are endocentric. They consist of heads and words in pre- and post-modification. The universal structure (6a) captures the fact that there are heads of phrases X^0 that combine with the complement YP. Together they constitute the intermediate projection. On the other hand, the highest level, the maximal projection, subsumes the intermediate projection and SpecX. The X, in turn, can be substituted for by syntactic categories such as N, V, A, P. This structure is called X-bar schema and was introduced in Chomsky (1970).

(6) a. Universal Phrase Structure

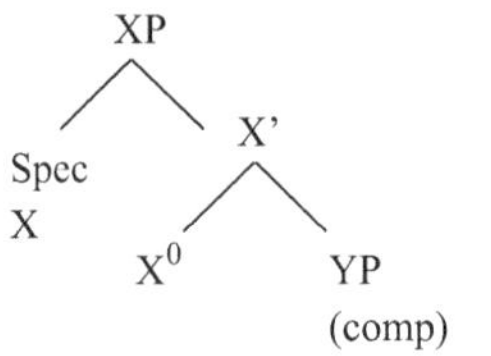

b. Verb Phrase[2]

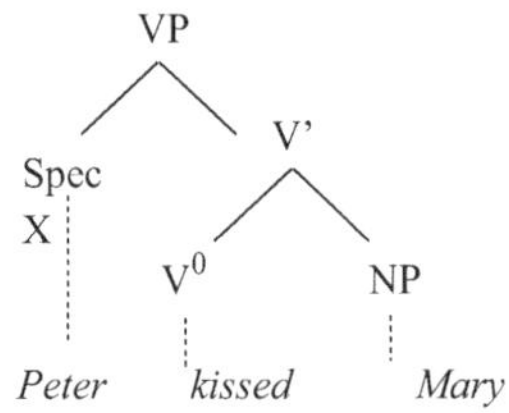

When we describe phrases as headed, we imply that heads select complements and specifiers and that they are selected from outside the phrase (Harris 1957). In our case (5b), the crucial element is the Verb *kiss,* which selects the object. Furthermore, while heads are obligatory, specifiers are usually optional. Complements are more complex: they are obligatory with certain transitive Verbs (7a) but with intransitive Verbs they are not necessary (7c):[3]

2 The structure is simplified. There is no Tense (TP) node represented but it can capture the main idea about Phrase Structure representation.

3 The obligatoriness of NP arguments is more complex and will be discussed later in Chapter 5.

(7) a. **Peter kissed*
b. *Peter kissed Mary.*
c. *Peter ran (the race).*

One crucial advantage of this system is its ability to establish parallelism across syntactic domains. This concept originated with Chomsky's proposal of X-bar theory in *Remarks on Nominalizations* (Chomsky 1970), and since then, there has been a quest for this parallelism. In that paper, Chomsky specifically extends the subject-object asymmetry found at the sentential level to noun phrases:

(8) a. *The enemy* ***destroyed*** *the city.*
b. *The enemy's* ***destruction*** *of the city.*

In examples (8a) and (8b), the NP *the enemy* serves as the subject and Agent whereas *the city* functions as the object and the Theme. For (8) it means that the object (*the city*) is the complement of the head *destroy/destruction*, with the *enemy* acting as its specifier.

Up until now, we have neglected functional categories such as Determiner (D) or Tense (T/I/Aux). In early writings of Chomsky (1965) these categories were considered as marginal, with only lexical categories (N, V, A, P) being eligible to serve as heads of phrases, see below:

(9) AUX in Chomsky 1965

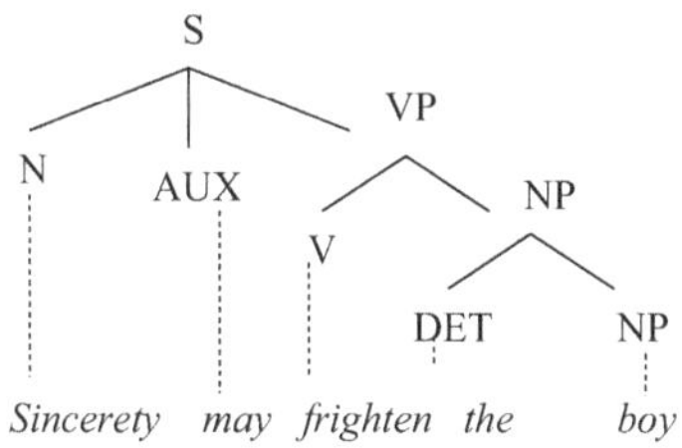

The structure in (9) exemplifies that Aux did not have any special status within the syntactic projection. Later, Stowell (1981) proposed that Aux (now labeled I) is the head of S. Additionally, he added Complementizer node (CP) into the structure to account for elements introducing subordinate clauses.

(10) Stowell (1981)—Functional projection

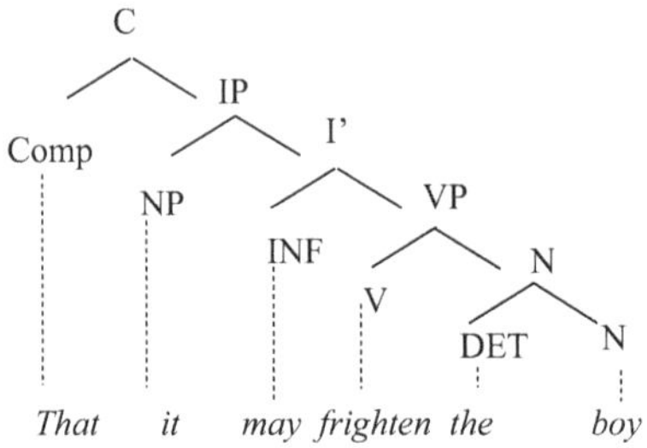

Just as Stowell (1981) argues that AUX/I is the head of its own projection selecting VP, Abney (1987) in his Ph.D. thesis *The English Noun Phrase in its Sentential Aspect* argues that Determiner is the head of its own projection along the nominal spine. Abney also demonstrates that Determiner is the selector. Determiners, like Verbs as illustrated in (7), can take complements obligatorily (11a) or optionally (11b):

(11) a. ***The*** ** (mother) was at home.*
b. ***That*** *(story) frightened the children.*

To represent this parallelism between nominal and verbal domain, compare the pictures in (12):

(12) Lexical heads N and V vs. functional heads T and D

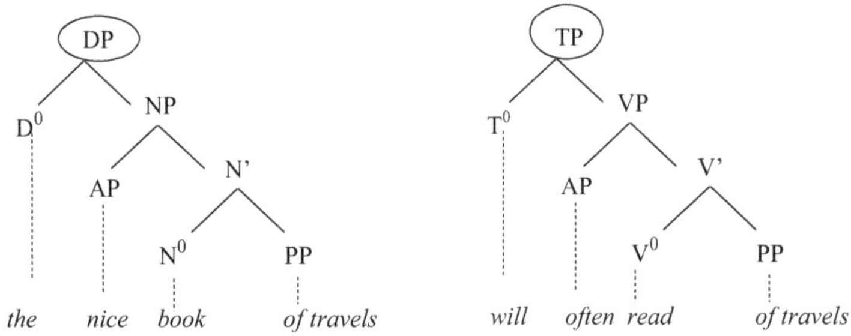

Notice that both contain a lexical head category V or N and a functional category head above the phrases VP and NP.

Abney's (1987) work is influential not only because he proposes a nominal functional head, but he also sets criteria that distinguish functional elements from lexical elements:

- Functional elements functionally select their complement
- Functional categories select unique complement
- Functional elements are closed class
- Functional elements are morphologically weaker, often affixes, clitics, sometimes null
- Functional elements are usually inseparable from their complement
- Functional elements lack descriptive content. Their semantic contribution is second order.

To provide a brief illustration of the aforementioned points, consider the following aspects. Firstly, in terms of unique selection, a CP (Complementizer Phrase) selects a TP (Tense Phrase) instead of a VP (Verb Phrase). This stands in stark contrast to a lexical head, which can select multiple items, such as a Verb selecting NPs (Noun Phrases) or PPs (Prepositional Phrases).

Secondly, closed class items in a language are relatively few in number. These include Determiners, auxiliaries, pronouns, and similar elements. In contrast, open class items like Nouns, Verbs, Adjectives, and Prepositions have a much larger number of members, often in hundreds or thousands. New words continually emerge within the open class items, while closed class items remain relatively stable.

Finally, the semantic content of functional elements is impoverished. Take for example the auxiliary *will* and compare it with the Verb *kiss*. While the auxiliary can convey information about future relevance, it does not describe any action itself, as the lexical Verb *kiss* does.

Since Abney (1987), there has been proliferation of functional categories. Most frequently verbal categories such as Neg(ation) (Pollock 1989) and Asp(ect) (Hendrick 1991), but several studies have shown that nominal structure is also more articulated. To name but a few, there has been the need for additional projections between N and D expressed by several authors, including Ritter (1991) for Hebrew, Giusti (1991) for English and Italian, and Veselovská (2001) for Czech. Picallo (1991) argues on the basis of Romance languages for Gender, and Rappaport (2004) for Possessor Phrase in Slavic.

While parallelism between domains is anticipated, there are also discernible patterns of parametrization. For instance, in English, DP is similar to TP as argued by Abney (1987). In contrast, in other languages such as Greek, DPs resemble CPs, as pointed out by Alexiadou (2001) and Horrock and Stavrou (1987).

1.2 Parts of Speech

The discussion above underscores the profound impact of the generative approach on word categories or parts of speech. Traditionally, the classification of parts of speech has relied on multiple criteria. This is evident in Štícha's (2018, p. 45) analysis of Nouns in Czech, where he proposes several criteria for categorizing Nouns, which can be summarized as follows:

- Morphological
- Semantic
- Syntactic

From a morphological perspective, Nouns in Czech exhibit features such as Number, Gender, and Case. Semantically, they serve as references to people, animals, objects, and actions. In terms of syntax, Nouns primarily function as subjects or objects within a sentence. However, this classification might lead to the assumption that the boundaries between word categories are not rigidly defined and appear to be fuzzy. This would not be a welcome result considering that nominalizations are hybrid categories. Determining whether an expression retains its status as a Noun or a Verb will be of utmost importance.

In contrast, the generative approach resolves these complexities by allowing for a more fine-grained distinction. Since Chomsky's work in 1970, the prevailing view has been that what are traditionally called "lexical" and also many functional categories are in fact complex clusters composed of features or feature complexes. This perspective emphasizes a division of labor between these two types of categories (lexical and functional), which I will illustrate within the verbal domain. A lexical category, such as a Verb, carries substantial content and is responsible for assigning theta roles, as indicated by the category it selects. The following demonstrates this relationship:

(13) *Mary kissed Peter* V, [__NP]

This implies that *kiss* is a transitive Verb which requires an NP complement. In the generative approach, we can assert that the Verb carries an N feature which must be checked (refer to the explanation of the checking mechanism in section 2.1.1). Later, in LF the NP *Peter* will be assigned a theta role and interpreted as the Patient. Functional categories, in contrast, have the task of conveying grammatical information such as Tense, agreement etc. Again, this information is expressed by means of features.

As my research is centered on deverbal nominalizations, which are hybrid categories blending nominal and verbal properties, I will employ the generative approach utilizing features to analyze functional projections in nominal and verbal domains and their interaction in nominalizations. Chapters 3 and 4 will explore features within nominal and verbal layers, while Chapter 5 will delve into their clustering in nominalizations.

1.3 Classification of Nominals in English

Having suggested that nominalizations are of hybrid nature, it is important to analyze how different authors approach their description. Initially, we will closely examine the treatment of English nominalizations in generative writings. Subsequently, our attention will shift to the analysis of nominalizations in Czech. By undertaking this comparative investigation, we can gain insights into distinct approaches and characteristics of deverbal nominalizations in these two languages.

The common denominator of all influential generative theories of nominalizations, for example, Minimalism or Distributive Morphology is that the result object has the feature [+Nominal]. Nominalizations can denote events (14a), arguments (14b) and adjuncts (14c):

(14) a. *collecting/clapping/walking/destruction*
b. *employer/teacher/fire-fighter*
c. *a coffee-grinder/a windshield wiper*

Although many of these Nouns may license arguments, for example, *teacher* which seems to be inherited from the verbal counterpart *He teaches*, only names denoting events can realize both internal and external arguments:

(15) *Caesar's* ***destruction*** *of the city*

In this study, I will mainly focus on the Nouns denoting events. English has three types of such nominalizations at a superficial investigation:

(16)	a.	*The teacher's* ***examination*** *of the students*	**Derived nominal**
	b.	*The teacher's* ***examining*** *of the students*	**Mixed nominal**
	c.	*The teacher's/The Teacher* ***examining*** *the students*	**Gerund**

In this chapter, I will discuss the approaches to these types of nominals in different generative frameworks.

1.3.1 The Early Generative Approach—Robert Lees (1960)

The first generative linguist who systematically analyzed nominalizations in English was Robert Lees in his study *The Grammar of English Nominalizations* (1960). Lees noticed the similarity between the active sentence in (17a) and the corresponding nominal versus the passive sentence in (17b) and the corresponding nominal.

(17) a. *The enemy* ***destroyed*** *the city* → *the enemy's* ***destruction*** *of the city*
b. *The city* ***was destroyed*** *by the enemy* → *the city's* ***destruction*** *by the enemy*

Although Lees noted the differences between gerunds and derived nominals, as gerunds allow for auxiliaries and Adverbs (18c-d) but disallow articles and prenominal Adjectives (as illustrated in (18a-b)),

(18) a. **the* ***performing*** *the song*
b. **his beautiful* ***performing*** *the song*
c. *his* ***having performed*** *the song*
d. *his* ***having performed*** *the song beautifully*

whereas derived nominals (as depicted in (19)) exhibit the opposite pattern, he maintained the assumption that all nominalizations undergo a syntactic transformation from sentences. In other words, according to Lees, all nominalizations are deverbal and desentential.

(19) a. *the (beautiful)* ***performance*** *of the song*
b. **the having* ***performance*** *of the song*
c. **the* ***performance*** *of the song beautifully*

1.3.2 Chomsky (1970): The Impact of Remarks on Nominalizations

Chomsky's (1970) seminal paper *Remarks on nominalization* was a reaction to the early syntactic approach of Lees (1960). Chomsky argued that nominals in (19) and (18) are not equal. In fact, he distinguished between three types of nominals in that paper, corresponding to the categories already illustrated: derived nominals (19), gerunds (18) and an additional type called mixed nominals.

He claimed that derived nominals have more nominal properties as opposed to gerunds that are clearly deverbal. Mixed nominals were assumed to have intermediate properties. Such a conclusion follows from the evidence presented in (19) and (18). Specifically, derived nominals can be modified by Adjectives and Determiners, take a prepositional complement and do not permit auxiliaries nor negation. The last point is visible in (20).

(20) **The <u>not</u>* ***refusal*** *of the offer*

Thus, unlike gerunds, derived nominals are derived as Nouns in the lexicon and are inserted as such in the deep structure.

A second point raised by Chomsky in favor of this hypothesis was that derived nominals do not exist in the same range of constructions as gerundive nominals do. I will illustrate it just with a few examples but see additional examples in Chomsky (1970):

(21)	a.	*John is certain to win the prize.*	**No Tough movement within NP**
	b.	*John's being certain to win the prize.*	
	c.	**John's* ***certainty*** *to win the prize.*	

(22)	a.	*Carly gave Peter the book.*	**No Dative shift**
	b.	*Carly's giving Peter the book.*	
	c.	**Carly's **gift** (of) Peter (of) the book.*	
(23)	a.	*Mary looked the information up.*	**No Particle movement**
	b.	*Mary looked up the information.*	
	c.	*Mary's looking the information up.*	
	d.	*Mary's looking up the information*	
	e.	*Mary's **looking** up of the information.*	
	f.	**Mary's **looking** of the information up.*	

Unfortunately, the rule of Passive was considered as a counterexample to the claim that transformations do not apply in DN's, see (17b). For this reason, Chomsky (1970) argued somewhat inconsistently that Passive applies in the nominal domain.

Chomsky (1970) does, however, note that DNs are related to their verbal correlates in terms of meaning and interpretation of complements. In order to capture this, he introduced X' theory within which the pair *destroy/destruction* is perceived as a category-less entry which can be inserted under the X^0, either N^0 or V^0 and thus acquire its categorial status. In turn, it is the syntactic context of the insertion that determines the phonological form for the entry:

(24) The relationship between *destroy/destruction* in Chomsky (1970)

Notice that the complement is realized in the sisterhood relationship with X^0, thereby demonstrating the parallelism between the verbal and nominal domains. The nominal complement is also depicted here as optional which is the according to Chomsky (1970) the structural difference between Nouns and Verbs.

1.3.3 Grimshaw (1990)

Jane Grimshaw's highly influential study *Argument structure* has brought new light into the research of nominalizations. In her seminal work, she acknowledged Chomsky's (1970) perspective that gerunds are transformed from sentences. However, she emphasized that derived nominals (DNs) do not constitute a homogeneous category, and her findings paved the way for reintegrating derived nominals within the realm of syntax.

In fact, she proposed that DNs can be divided into three main classes which she calls complex event nominals (CENs), simple event nominals (SENs) and result nominals (RNs). Only the former can license Argument structure (AS) while the latter two groups lack it. For the purposes of this thesis, I will sometimes follow Borer (2013) and call them Argument Structure nominals (AS-Nominals) and Referential nominals (R-Nominals). The criteria for distinguishing between those two groups are the following:

(25)		R-Nominals	AS-Nominals
	a.	Non-θ-assigner, No obligatory arguments	θ-assigners, Obligatory arguments
	b.	No necessary event reading	Event reading
	c.	No agent-oriented modifiers	Agent-oriented modifiers
	d.	Subjects are possessives	Subjects are arguments
	e.	*By*-phrases are non-arguments	*By*-phrases are arguments
	f.	No implicit argument control	Implicit argument control
	g.	No aspectual modifiers	Aspectual modifiers
	h.	Modifiers like *frequent*, *constant* only with plural	Modifiers like *frequent*, *constant* appear with singular
	i.	Count Nouns	Mass Nouns

The diagnostics are exemplified for AS-Nominals in (26) and for R-Nominals in (27):

(26) a. *The doctor's (intentional)* ***examination*** *of the patient took a long time/(*was on the table).*

b. *the frequent* ***collection*** *of mushrooms (by students)*

c. *the* ***monitoring*** *of wild flowers to document their disappearance*
d. *the* ***destruction*** *of Rome in a day*

(27) a. *These frequent* ***destructions*** *took their toll.*
b. *the student's* ***examination/exam*** *was on the table/(*took a long time).*

Importantly, mixing of the properties of these nominalizations leads to ungrammaticality as shown in (28). So, for example the Noun *destruction* in (28c) requires an internal argument in the presence of an aspectual modifier *in a day*:

(28) a. **Caesar's frequent* ***destruction***
b. **the frequent* ***examination/exam*** *(by John)*
c. **the* ***destruction*** *in a day*

Grimshaw suggests that the remaining group of Chomsky's Mixed nominals can be best divided into referential nominals (R-Nominals) and complex event nominals (AS-Nominals). The AS of the latter AS-Nominals has to do with their event structure. By event structure, she means a decomposition of a verb into aspectual sub-parts. For example, an accomplishment verb *x construct y* is analyzed as an activity in which some external Agent x engages in activity with the resulting state. This proposal is represented in (29):

(29) Event structure in Grimshaw (1990)

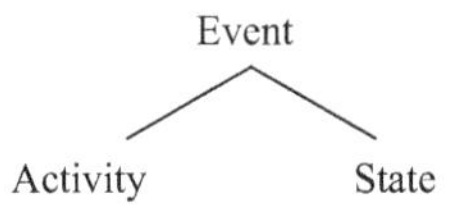

Grimshaw thus hypothesizes that AS-Nominals are amenable to event structure analysis and hence capable of taking arguments. R-Nominals, on the other hand, are without event structure and lack arguments. This distinction is contingent on the presence of an event argument (Ev) for the AS-Nominals vs. a referential argument (R) for the R-Nominals.

Technically, the assignment of the Ev and R arguments is linked to properties of nominalizing affixes. Specifically, - *ING* (always) assigns Ev, Ø-nominalizers only assign R, and *-ATION* may assign either of them. These nominalizing affixes have the ability to assign external roles to the nominal, assuming that the original external argument has been suppressed. To illustrate this, let's consider the verb *observe* in (30a) along with its corresponding argument structure (AS) and the external argument represented by x. Moving on to complex event Nouns, like the example in (30c), we observe that an affix introduces an external role and combines it with the original AS of the verb. As a result, a complex event structure is formed by merging the AS of both elements.

(30) a. *observe*, V, (x,y)
b. *-ation* N, (Ev) or *-ation* N, (R)
c. *observation* N, (Ev)x(y)))
d. *observation* N, (R=X)

However, in Result nominals (30d), the affix assigns an external role without merging with the original AS of the verb. Consequently, the AS is not inherited from the verb, leading to nominals lacking obligatory arguments. For Grimshaw then, argument structure is a property linked to both Verbs and Nouns.

The method and general analysis proposed in Grimshaw (1990), including the criteria in (25), have been accepted and employed in a great number of cross-language studies concerning derived nominals. Together with *the Remarks on Nominalizations*, Grimshaw's study undoubtedly represents another basic step in the generative approach to the phenomena of nominalization, categorial classification and the study of argument structure.

This notwithstanding, many more specific aspects of Grimshaw's model have been challenged and modified as the generative framework developed. These changes include the criteria (25 c, h, i) which are going to be relevant for the topics discussed in this study. The criterion regarding agentive modifier seems to be weak because agentive modifiers can occur with expressions which are clearly not DNs, as seen in examples such as *deliberate strategy, deliberate fire*. Similarly, the existence of expressions such as *frequent/constant joy, frequent fire* weakens the criterion (25h).

Neither is it the case that the distribution of nominals can be accurately characterized solely based on the availability of pluralization. This particular criterion has been challenged by both Borer (2005b) and Alexiadou et al.

(2010c) and was originally discussed in Mourelatos (1978). Mourelatos proposed that atelic CEN/ASNs are categorized as mass Nouns which consequently restricts their ability to pluralize and limits the usage of indefinite Determiners and numerals in English. On the other hand, telic nominalizations allow for pluralization and the use of indefinite Determiners and numerals. He provides examples to illustrate these distinctions:

(31) a. *three late* ***arrivals*** *of the train*
b. *a deliberate* ***capsizing*** *of the boat by Mary*

(32) a. **three deliberate* ***pushings*** *of the carts (by Mary)*
b. **a* ***painting*** *of the nativity (for hours) (by Jones)*

Also, the severance of the argument from the verb presents one of the problems. Additionally, the distinction between complex event nominals (CENs), which are derived from Verbs, and simple event nominals, which represent events but lack argument structure, remains unaccounted for.

The criteria in (25) will be dealt with more detail in Chapter 5 where I will discuss models of nominalizations proposed by Hagit Borer (2013) and Artemis Alexiadou, who challenge these criteria in various ways while still taking them as their starting point.

1.3.4 Emonds (2000, 2022)

A comprehensive analysis of the distinctive properties of nominalizations was conducted by Emonds (2000, 2022) within his *Three Level Insertion Model*. His study is concerned with the polyfunctionality of the English *-ing* morpheme, which not only appears in nominals derived from Verbs (our R-Nominals and AS-Nominals) but also in non-finite clauses (verbal gerunds and participles). Additionally, Emonds extends his analysis to include infinitives, another form of non-finite structures. This section aims to elucidate the main findings concerning derived nominals, particularly as this model was further developed by Veselovská (2018b) for Czech nominalizations.

Within Emonds' Three Level Insertion Model, the Lexicon serves as a repository of purely semantic features, which are exclusively introduced at the initial stage of syntactic derivation and remain unused during syntax.

In contrast, syntactic features originating from the Syntacticon can enter the derivation at three distinct hierarchical levels:

a) together with the semantic features at the very beginning—deep insertion
b) during the syntactic process—late insertion
c) after Spell Out—post syntactic (PF) insertion[4]

Having explained the features, we can demonstrate the derivation of nominals derived from Verbs. Among these, Grimshaw's result nominals, such as *writings* and *buildings*, represent the least verbal type, exemplifying a case of deep insertion of purely semantic features. The more verbal complexes are the so-called complex event nominals as in (33) which start the derivation as Verbs and later/as late as syntax when the suffixes are added they become Nouns. Technically, the suffixes *-ing* and *-ment* can be listed as Ns that subcategorize within N⁰ domain for V.

(33)

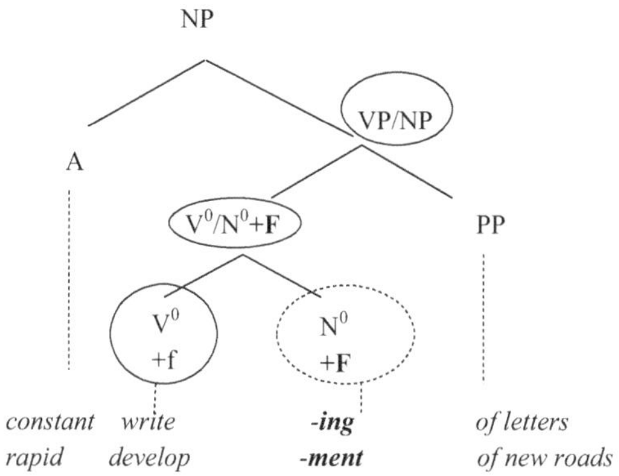

Finally, the most verbal structures are verbal gerunds in (34) features of which can be inserted late. Technically, the *-ing* suffix carries LF cancellation feature Ø which means that the category N of the suffix is uninterpreted. Gerunds

4 PF is associated with purely syntactic features which play no role in LF. These can be alternatively realized features or lack of content features, see Emonds (2000; Ch.4).

thus go through the whole derivation as Verbs, are interpreted as Verbs and take on functions as NPs only externally.

(34)

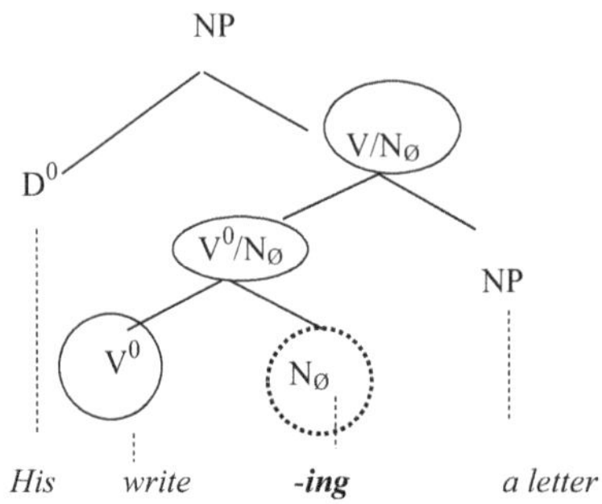

Of particular importance is the distinction between the first two types of nominals, namely result nominals and complex event nominals, which are regarded as derivational, and the verbal gerund which is considered inflectional. Veselovská and Emonds (2016) assert that the nature of derivational or inflectional morphology influences the selection of modifiers within syntactic structures. In the realm of nominalizations, it becomes apparent that the verbal gerund is consistently derived as a Verb, with the *-ing* morpheme primarily determining the Noun category but not actively participating in the selection of modifiers. Consequently, verbal gerunds retain more verbal characteristics, such as lacking the *-of* marking for direct objects and employing adverbial modifiers rather than adjectival ones. In contrast, CENs undergo nominalization in the narrow syntax and thus readily accept Adjectives or *of*-phrases.

Emonds' analysis covers much data concerning nominalizations and it is fully integrated into his theoretical model as summarized in Emonds (2000). Although I will not directly apply his framework in the following sections, I am going to consider his formal methodology and diagnostics.

1.4 Classification of Nominals in Czech

In the preceding sections, we have explored analyses of different deverbal nominalizations with diverse semantic denotations. Our focus has been on the category denoting events, and we have identified three types of deverbal nominals in English: verbal gerunds, mixed nominals, and derived nominals, as depicted in (16). These nominals possess varying degrees of verbal properties. We have outlined their distinctive characteristics, which will serve as a basis for comparison with Czech derived nominals in the subsequent parts of this study.

Similarly, the Czech language features a variety of nominalizations with comparable semantic meanings. Specifically, these encompass designations for events (35a), representations of arguments (35b), and indications of adjuncts (35c).

(35)	a.	*sbírání/tlesknutí/procházka/ chudoba*	'collecting/clapping/a walk/ poverty'
	b.	*zaměstnavatel/učitel/trestanec*	'employer/teacher/convict'
	c.	*rozpouštědlo/vrtačka*	'dissolving agent/drilling-machine'

Again, many of these Nouns may license arguments, for example, *učitel* '*teacher*' which seems to be inherited from the verbal counterpart *He teaches* but only names denoting events can realize both internal and external arguments:

(36)	*maminčino*	*sbírání*	*hub*
	mother$_{\mathrm{POSS}}$	collecting	mushrooms
	'Mother's collecting of mushrooms'		

Our main emphasis in this study will be on the Nouns denoting events. Karlík and Nübler (1998), drawing on Chomsky (1970) and Grimshaw (1990), suggest further subdivision into Type I and Type II categories for these nouns.[5]

Type I nominalizations are derived with the following suffixes:

suffix	Verb		Nominalization
-ěn/en	*znít*	'sound'	*zn-**ěn**-í*
-én/an	*malovat*	'paint'	*malov-**án**-í*
-t	*krýt*	'cover'	*kry-**t**-í*

5 I will refer to the later version of this approach also in section 1.4.2.

Type II nominals comprise various suffixes including zero-derived nominals:

suffix	Verb		Nominalization
-ba	*číst*	'read'	*čet-**ba***
-ka	*procházet*	'walk'	*prochház-**ka***
-0	*lovit*	'hunt'	*lov*
-ost	*žádat*	'walk'	*žád-**ost***

According to Karlik and Nübler (1998) these two types can be distinguished from each other by several factors. I will exemplify only some of them:

a) Productivity: only type I can be formed from all Verbs:

Verb	Type I	Type II
být 'to be'→	*bytí* 'being'	0

b) Suppletion: only Type II is replaced by other forms:

Verb	Type I	Type II
pršet 'to rain'	*pršení* 'raining'	**pršba/déšť* 'rain'

c) Backformation:

Verb	Type I	Type II
hřmít 'to thunder'	->*hřmot* 'roar'->*hřmotit* 'to roar'	->*hřmění* 'thundering'-> 0

In their accepted (non-)lexicalist framework, Karlik and Nübler (1998) expected that Type I nominals are syntactic transforms and Type II nominals have lexical basis. In this thesis I will label the two kinds of Czech nominalizations based on the phonetic realization of their suffixes illustrated in the above tables in the following way:

- the Type I nominals will be labeled as **N/T nominals**;
- the Type II nominals will be labeled as **B/K nominals.**

1.4.1 Veselovská (2018b)

In her studies, Ludmila Veselovská advocates generative approach within Czech linguistics. Besides analyzing many linguistic phenomena, she has dedicated her research to the study of nominalizations in her two articles: Veselovská (2001, 2018b). In these articles, she expands upon Emonds' (2000) Three Level Insertion model, which was introduced in section 1.3.4.

In line with Chomsky's (1970) view, Veselovská acknowledges that English verbal gerunds, which are absent in Czech, undergo syntactic derivation. However, she argues that Czech counterparts of mixed and derived nominals require further division, drawing upon Grimshaw's (1990) insights. This latter group can be classified into two sub-groups: lexically derived (Grimshaw's result and simple event nominals) and syntactically derived (Grimshaw's complex event nominals). At times, I will use Borer's (2013) term R-Nominals and AS-Nominals respectively.

First of all, the author shows that Czech derived nominals have the distribution of NPs. They can be coordinated with prototypical lexical Nouns, see below (the examples will be presented on the scale from the least verbal R-Nominal to the most verbal AS-Nominal):[6]

(37)

R-Nominal			**AS-Nominal**
kniha	*a mal-ba*	*a mal-ov-ání*	*a pře-mal-ovává-ní*
book	and drawing	and drawing	and re-painting

Other nominal environment is the complementation of Prepositions:

(38)

	R-Nominal			**AS-Nominal**
Protestovali proti	*knihá-m*	*malbám na zdi*	*psaní*	*pře-pis-ová-ní*
they protested against	books DAT.PL.F	painting DAT.PL.F	writing DAT.SG.NT	rewriting DAT.SG.NT

6 This terminology is employed in Borer (2013).

The example in (38) shows the nominals in Instrumental environment. Notice that standard Nouns in Czech are countable and Gender marked (both *malba* 'painting' and *kniha* 'book' are feminine). In contrast, nominalizers *-ěn/-en* + *í*, *-án/-an* + *í* (N/T nominals) are all unmarked neuter and have the same form with the exception of Instrumental. This feature deficiency is typical characteristics for AS-Nominals.

The Number deficiency, according to Veselovská (2018b), is also visible in (39) which shows that these nominals do not co-occur with the numeral *dvě* 'two' but are compatible with specific numeral typical for uncountable Nouns *dvojí* 'two$_{\text{KIND}}$'.

(39)

R-Nominal		**AS-Nominal**
dvě malby	*? dvě malování*	**dvě/dvojí přemalování*
two paintings	? two paintings	*two/dual re-paintings

After analyzing the nominal features, we can scrutinize the verbal properties of these nominals. One of the typical verbal characteristics is Aspect. The following examples not only tolerate Aspect sensitive adjectival modification *častý* 'frequent' but also exhibit sensitivity to aspectual Prepositions:

(40)

R-Nominal			**AS-Nominal**
**častá židle*	*? častá malba*	*časté malování*	*časté přemalování*
*frequent chair	?frequent painting	frequent painting	frequent re-painting

(41)

R-Nominal			**AS-Nominal**
**při židli/*po židli*	*při/po opravě*	**při/po opravení*	*při/*po opravování*
*during/*after chair	during/after repair	*during/after repair	during/*after repair

As far as transitivity is concerned, there is a distinct tolerance with respect to complementation. Typical R-Nominals disallow complementation, but AS-Nominals do require it and if they contain aspectual prefixes, then the complementation is obligatory:

(42)

R-Nominal			**AS-Nominal**
*dopis (*textu)*	*psaní (textu)*	***pře**-psaní ? (textu)*	*pře-pis-ová-ní ?? (textu)*
letter (*text$_{GEN}$)	writing (text$_{GEN}$)	rewriting ? (text$_{GEN}$)	rewriting ??(text$_{GEN}$)

The next argument for the presence of verbal properties is demonstrated in example (43). The short clitic reflexive pronoun *se* 'oneself'' that is standard with Verbs is compatible with AS-Nominals but incompatible with R-nominals.

(43)

R-Nominal		**AS-Nominal**	V
**obraz se*	**malba se*	*namalování se*	*namalovat se*
*picture oneself	*painting oneself	re-painting oneself	to (re)paint oneself

Before considering Instrumental Agents in Czech, it is necessary to mention, that they are not seen as a satisfactory proof that passive transformation took place. Instrumental Agents are rather perceived as adjuncts with zero Preposition. Despite that, instrumental Agents are permissible only with verbal elements:

(44)

R-Nominal		**AS-Nominal**	V	
**dopis*	*?psaní*	*/přepisování*	*/přepisován*	*některými studenty*
*letter	?writing	rewriting	rewritten	by some students

Structurally, Veselovská (2018b) explains nominalizations by means of the Three Level Insertion model developed by Emonds (2000). In this model, the categorial head (N) consist of two syntactic heads: a lexical verbal base (V) and a nominalizing suffix (N). There are three levels where the grammatic element N^0 can enter derivation:

A. Initial Numeration
B. Syntax (pre-Spell Out)
C. PF

We can imagine this process as chronological and the amount of "verbalness" of the structure will depend on how far the Verb can project. If the insertion of morpheme N^0 takes place early, that is from the beginning of the numeration, then the nominalization will have a nominal head at all levels during the derivation. This is our picture (45a) where the dotted line might be missing, and the verbal head can be replaced by D. This would be the case of Grimshaw's result and simple event nominals, our R-Nominal.

(45) Insertion of grammatical morpheme N^0 nominalizer

a) Before adding the suffix

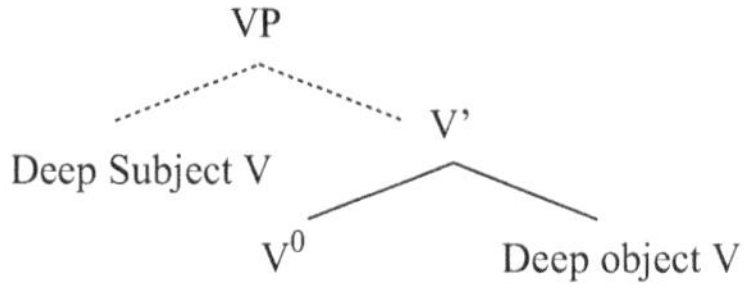

b) After adding the suffix

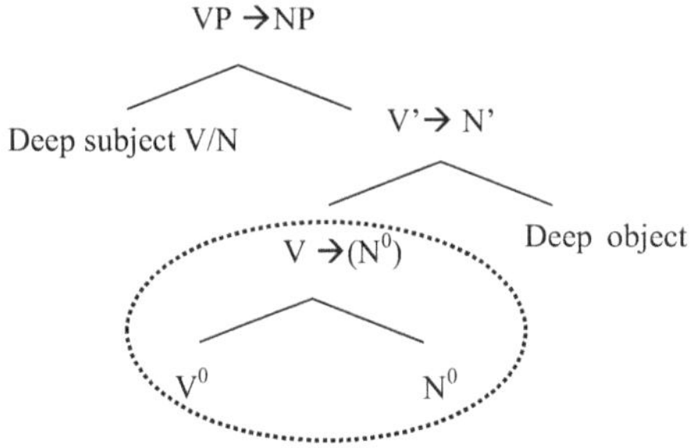

If the insertion of N^0 morpheme takes place late, then the head of the projection in the deep structure is the Verb V_0. The Verb could project some verbal functional heads, for example, Aspect. This would be the case of AS-Nominals. Lastly, the nominalizing morpheme can be inserted into the structure post-cyclically, that is after all transformations have been terminated. For example, English gerunds are formed in this way where V^0 is the head during the whole derivation *cycle*, which explains why Accusative Case can be combined with English gerunds. This was already described in section 1.3.4 discussing Emonds' model.

In Czech, no equivalents of English verbal gerunds can be detected. The combination of POSS and ACC is ungrammatical:

(46)	a.	**Nesnáší*	<u>*moje*</u>	***pře-čt-e-n-í***	<u>*knihu*</u>
		he hates	my	reading	book$_{ACC}$
		*'He hates my reading the book'			
	b.	**Obdivuje*	<u>*moje*</u>	***čt-e-n-í***	<u>*knihu*</u>
		wonder	my	reading	the book$_{ACC}$
		*'He wonders my reading the book'			

Veselovská's (2018b) approach is very useful because it can capture the characteristics of mixed nominalizations, namely the fact that derived nominalizations in Czech inherit some properties from Verbs but are still nominal. I will apply her criteria, but it will be needed to describe features within nominalizations in more detail and combine the criteria in order to get more fine-grained distinctions.

1.4.2 Karlík (2019)

Another Czech linguist who deals with nominalizations is Petr Karlík who analyzed nominalizations within the Lexicalist Framework, that is, inspired by Chomsky (1970). After the above-mentioned study by Karlík and Nübler (1998), Karlík in his nominalization papers (2007b, 2007a, 2008, 2019) applies the same tests as Veselovská (2018b) and reaches the same conclusion that some nominalizations in Czech are syntactically derived while others are lexically derived.

Moreover, Karlík (2019) proposes the following generalization: N/T nominals that are syntactically derived behave as complex event nominals and can become result nominals, B/K nominals behave as simple event nominals and can become result nominals (see Grimshaw's terminology). According to Borer's terminology, B/K nominals can be categorized as AS-Nominals with the potential to transform into R-Nominals. In contrast, B/K nominals correspond to R-Nominals.

The following examples are inspired by Karlík's articles but some additional modifications of mine illustrate the contrast. Unlike N/T nominals in (47a), B/K nominals classified as SENs (47c) can never be negated. B/K nominals can, nevertheless express some eventivity related to duration as the verbal complex *trvat* 'take a long time' signals. The examples (47b) and (47d) provide an argument that both N/T and B/K nominals can become result nominals and consequently do not tolerate negation neither do they express duration.

(47)	a.	***Balení/ ne-bal-e-n-í***	*svačiny*	*do*	*sáčku*	*se mu vymstí.*	CEN
		Packing/non-packing$_{\text{(IMPF).NT}}$	breakfast$_{\text{GEN}}$	into	bag	cause him troubles	
		'Packing/non-packing of breakfast into bag will cause him troubles.'					
	b.	***Balení/ (*ne-bal-e-n-í)***	*léků*	*bylo na stole/ (*trvalo dlouho).*			RN
		package/non-package$_{\text{(IMPF).NT}}$	pill$_{\text{GEN.PL}}$	was on the table/ *took a long time			
		'A package/(*non-package) was on the table/(*took a long time).'					
	c.	***Čet-ba/ (*ne-čet-ba)***	*knih*	*trvala dlouho.*			SEN
		reading/non-reading$_{\text{F.SG}}$	book$_{\text{GEN.PL}}$	took a long time			
		'Reading/(*non-reading) of the books took a long time.'					
	d.	*Obsáhlá*	***čet-ba/ (*nečet-ba)***	*ležela na stole/ (*trvala dlouho).*			RN
		extensive	reading/ non-reading$_{\text{F.SG}}$	was on the table/ took a long time			
		'The extensive reading/(*non-reading) was on the table/(*took a long time).'					

Furthermore, as already demonstrated in Veselovská (2018d), B/K nominals can never be reflexive (48c), similarly to result nominals (48d).

(48)	a.	*Petrovo*	***hol-e-n-í***	***se***	*trvalo dlouho.*	CEN
		Peter$_{POSS}$	shaving$_{(IMPF).NT}$	self	took a long time	
		'Peter's shaving himself took a long time.'				
	b.	*Petrovo*	***hol-e-n-í***	*(*se)*	*leželo na stole/ (*trvalo dlouho).*	RN
		Peter$_{POSS}$	shaving$_{(IMPF).NT}$	self	was on the table/ took a long time	
		'Peter's shaving (*self) was on the table/(*took a long time).'				
	c.	*Petrova*	***mal-ba***	*(*se)*	*trvala dlouho.*	SEN
		Peter$_{POSS}$	painting$_{F.SG}$	self	took a long time	
		'Peter's painting (*self) took a long time.'				
	d.	*Petrova*	*perstrobarevná*	***mal-ba*** *(*se)*	*ležela na stole/ (*trvala dlouho).*	RN
		Peter	colorful	painting$_{F.SG}$ self	was on the table/ took a long time	
		'Peter's colorful painting (*self) was on the table/(*took a long time).'				

It is not possible to deduce Aspect from B/K nominals. In contrast, N/T nominals are aspectually sensitive. Notice that prefix *-při/-pří* is contained in both nominals but its length changes. More will be said about this phenomenon in Chapter 4.

(49)	a.	*Petr*	*začal*	*se* ***stav-ě-n-ím/*při-stav-ě-n-ím/ při-stav-ová-ním***	*domu.*	CEN
		Peter	started	with building$_{\text{(IMPF).NT}}$/ pref$_{\text{PF.}}$building$_{\text{NT}}$/pref$_{\text{PF}}$ building$_{\text{IMPF.NT}}$	house	
		'Peter started with building/(*the extension)/ the extension of the house.'				
	b.	*Peter*	*začal*	*se* ***stav-bou/pří-stav-bou***	*domu*	SEN
		Peter	started	with building$_{\text{F}}$/pref. building$_{\text{F}}$	house	
		'Peter started with building/the extension of the house'				

Interesting are also other aspectual features. B/K nominals do not allow the so-called superlexical prefixes:

(50)	a.	***na**-běh-á-n-í* pref$_{\text{PF.}}$running$_{\text{NT}}$	*kilometrů* kilometer$_{\text{PL.GEN}}$
	b.	*krátké* short	***po**-sp-á-n-í* pref$_{\text{PF}}$.sleeping$_{\text{NT}}$
	c.	*****ná**-běh* *pref.running$_{\text{M}}$	*kilometrů* kilometer$_{\text{PL.GEN}}$
	d.	*krátký* short	*****po**-spánek* *pref.sleeping

Neither can B/K nominals express iterativity:

(51)	a.	*zpív-á-**vá**-ní* singing$_{\text{ITER.NT}}$	b.	*huč-í-**vá**-ní* humming$_{\text{ITER.NT}}$
	c.	**zpěv-**vá*** singing$_{\text{ITER}}$		**hukot-**vá*** humming$_{\text{ITER}}$

Also, B/K nominals do not co-occur with Adverbs:

(52)	a.	*?**Čte-n-í***	*té detektivky*	*rychle*	*je skoro hřích.*
		$\text{reading}_{\text{(IMPF).NT}}$	the detective $\text{story}_{\text{GEN}}$	quickly	is almost a sin
		?'Reading of the detective story quickly is almost a sin.'			
	b.	**Čet-ba*	*té detektivky*	*rychle*	*je skoro hřích.*
		$^{*}\text{reading}_{\text{F.SG}}$	the detective $\text{story}_{\text{GEN}}$	quickly	is almost a sin

On the basis of these investigations, Karlík (2019) suggests two structures for N/T and B/K nominals:

(53)	a.	[functional vP [vP [root]]]	N/T nominals
	b.	[nP [root]]	B/K nominals

This means that lexically derived B/K nominals do not contain any layers associated with verbal projections. They are derived from the root and nominal suffix. Syntactically derived nominals, on the other hand, have at their disposal some larger portion of verbal structure, it might include some aspectual heads.

The question is what licenses optional complements and eventive interpretation of B/K nominals if no functional projections are associated with them. Karlík (2019) claims that eventivity as well as complements of B/K nominals are contained in the root. Also, Karlík (2019) does not mention the borderline cases in the group of N/T nominals which behave as simple event nouns, as will be shown in section 5.4.2.3. I will refine these issues in section 5.4.1 when analyzing Czech nominalizations in more detail.

Nevertheless, Petr Karlík's analyses of Czech nominalizations creatively integrates the semantic aspects of Grimshaw (1990) study.[7] His usage of roots

7 Petr Karlík's concept of argument structure reflects his original proposal of *Modified Valency Framework* that looks at constructions from the perspective of valency frames as described by Karlík (2002, 2003, 2004).

and categorial heads *n/v* at the same time reflects the development of generative grammar with respect to the categorial classification.

1.5 Chapter Summary

To summarize this chapter, I introduced the core concepts of generative grammar used for the analysis of the phenomena of nominalizations. Additionally, I have presented the categorization of nominals in English and Czech as found in relevant literature, demonstrating that English encompasses three types of deverbal nominalizations: derived nominals, gerunds, and mixed nominals with intermediate characteristics. While Chomsky (1970) initially viewed gerunds as derived from sentential structures and derived nominals were confined to the lexicon, Grimshaw (1990) reintroduced some types of derived nominals into syntax and further refined their classification.

Referring to previous studies, I exemplified that the Czech language does not nominalize higher verbal complexes in the same manner as English verbal gerunds. It has, nevertheless, two groups of deverbal Nouns, as described by Karlík (2019) and Veselovská (2018b). Both scholars agree on their classification: Type I (N/T) nominals are syntactically derived, behave as complex event nominal and can become result nominals. Type II (B/K) nominals behave as simple event nominals and can become result nominals (see Grimshaw's terminology). These two groups will be the subject of our study in the upcoming chapters.

In order to propose further refinements of these structures, it is crucial to scrutinize the proposals put forth by two influential authors deeply engaged with nominalizations: H. Borer and A. Alexiadou. Introducing their frameworks and terminology in the subsequent chapter is essential as a preparatory step before elaborating on their specific proposals within the context of nominal and verbal domains, as well as exploring the interplay between these domains in the realm of nominalizations.

Comparing the Frameworks

In this chapter, I will introduce two frameworks and the associated terminology used by Artemis Alexiadou and Hagit Borer. Firstly, I will provide a more general comparison between the model of Distributed Morphology employed by Alexiadou and the *Minimalist model*, which represents the latest line of inquiry in generative grammar and is to a greater or smaller degree shared by most authors working in this field. Therefore, I will first outline the minimalist operations, such as Merge, Agree, and Move that can be performed within this model and its varieties. Subsequently, in section 2.2, I will examine Borer's (2005a) *Exo-skeletal model*, which uses some specific terminology and concepts divergent from the more general generative models.

2.1 Minimalist Program and Distributed Morphology

The generative model of grammar, as presented in Chapter 1, has undergone several revisions, with the Minimalist model representing its most recent version. In this section, I will provide a brief comparison between the Distributed Morphology (DM) model utilized in the works of Artemis Alexiadou and the more general architecture of the Minimalist program.

Both theories, developed around the same time in the early 1990s, are influential within generative framework. Notably, they share a common understanding regarding the structure of grammar, with the syntactic component preceding phonology and semantics, as depicted briefly already in (2) and in more detail in (54) below. Furthermore, there is a substantial agreement between the two branches of the generative framework in terms of the operations they employ, including Agreement, Merge, and Movement. These operations will be further explored in the subsequent sections.

The main divergence between these two theories is related to the treatment of the Lexicon as a repository of language-specific lexical entries. The Minimalist Program model, based on Chomsky's Minimalist Program (Chomsky 1995) is illustrated in (54) below on the right. In this model, there is a concept of language-specific *Lexicon* which includes the clusters of sound and meaning features introduced at the onset of syntactic computation. The presence of arguably universal grammatical features and their linking to the language-specific ones is a matter of discussion.

On the other hand, the DM model, schematically illustrated in (54) on the left, takes a different approach by eliminating the traditional notion of a Lexicon as the starting point of derivation. It replaces it with three separate concepts: (a) the initial list of grammatical features provided by Universal Grammar (which drive the syntactic derivation), (b) Vocabulary comprising language-specific morphemes and (c) the Encyclopedia providing semantic concepts. In the DM model the linking of the three substitutes for the Lexicon is the matter of current discussion and in the scheme below they are in fact not explicitly represented.[8]

(54) The DM model vs. Minimalistic Model, from Embick and Noyer (2005)

Distributed Morphology | Minimalist Program Model

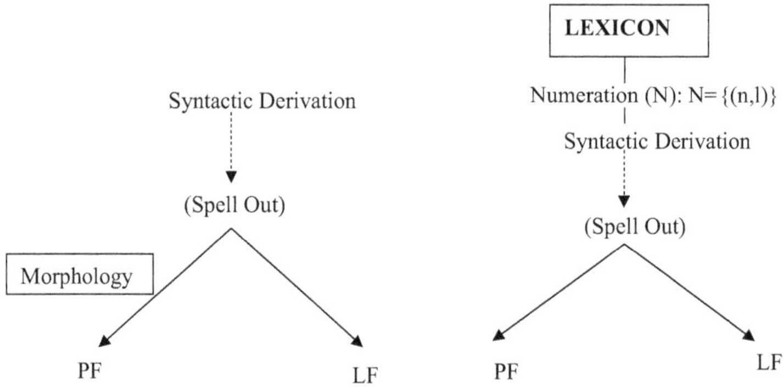

8 I am leaving aside the possible distinction in graphical representation which may result in the usage of distinct labels: T-model and Y-model.

Within the present-day DM model, word formation follows syntactic rules such as Merge, Move, and Agree, which bear significant resemblance to the principles governing syntax.[9] The units that undergo these syntactic operations are referred to as morphemes. These morphemes correspond to terminal nodes in the tree diagram and can be classified into two types: Abstract morphemes and Roots, as depicted in table (55):

(55) Abstract morphemes vs. Roots

	Phonological features	Syntactic-semantic features	Classification:	Example
Abstract morpheme	X	✓	Functional category	[Past], [Plural], [Def]
Roots	✓	X	Open class category	√CAT, √OX

While abstract morphemes consist of syntactic-semantic features drawn from a set made available by Universal Grammar, Roots do not possess any grammatical features and are language-specific combinations of sound and meaning. This distinction aligns with the differentiation between functional categories and open class categories, such as Nouns (N), Verbs (V), and Adjectives (A). It means that the learner of language has to memorize roots such as *√CAT* as well as be aware of the fact that abstract morphemes such as [Plural] are active in their language.

Once the syntactic operations are complete, there is a point at which the derivation splits between PF (Phonetic Form) and LF (Logical Form). At the PF level, certain morphological operations apply. Some of them take place before *Vocabulary insertion* (e.g., Lowering/Merger), while others occur after this stage. Further details about Lowering/Merger will be discussed later in this section.

9 The reader may compare the DM model with the model introduced by Emonds (1991, 2000) and mentioned in section 1.3.4. This model is called the *Three Level Insertion Model* and similarly to the DM Model it rejects the autonomy of morphology with respect to syntax. In this model, purely semantic features are introduced from the beginning of the derivation but are syntactically inert. For the purpose of this study the advantages of one or the other models are rather scholastic.

Vocabulary insertion serves as a mechanism for supplying phonological features to abstract morphemes. For instance, the [Plural] feature associated with the Number head will be phonetically realized as the regular exponent/-z/. This process of Vocabulary insertion is called *Spell Out*. Toward the end of the derivation, specifically after the output from PF/LF, there exists the opportunity to access a repository of specialized meanings known as the *Encyclopedia*. This component is also the locus of, for example, idioms. The whole process described above can be seen in picture (56):

(56) The DM Model of derivation—detailed version as in Harley and Noyer (2000, p. 2)

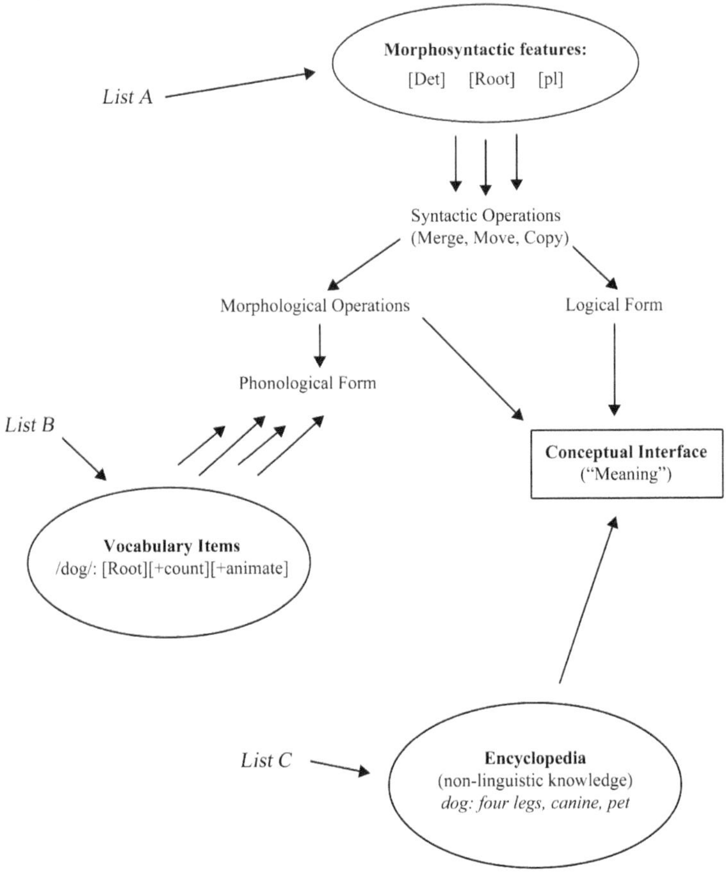

Additionally, assuming that syntax provides the input to semantic interpretation, in any present-day generative model including DM, it is vital to recognize a distinction between *interpretable* and *uninterpretable* features introduced in their first version by Chomsky in his early minimalist paper (see Chomsky 1995). According to this distinction, syntax has the ability to manipulate both types of features, but only interpretable features have relevance to semantic interpretation. For instance, features like Tense [+/- Past] or Aspect [+/-Perfective] fall into the category of interpretable features. On the other hand, uninterpretable features, like, for example, the EPP feature, which triggers subject movement to SpecT, must be checked before reaching the interfaces, otherwise the computation crashes. As for their phonetic realization, both kinds of features can but need not be represented overtly by some kind of morphemes.

The more recent linguistic theory suggests that the classification of features is to be made more complex. Namely that the features cannot be uniquely and universally categorizable as either interpretable or uninterpretable. Instead, a specific feature may be language specific; moreover, it is interpretable in one position but not in another. These proposals will be discussed in more detail in the following section.

2.1.1 Minimalistic Operations: Merge, Agree, Move

In this part I will define three types of syntactic operations that lay at the core of Minimalistic program developed by Noam Chomsky: Merge, Agree, Move. These were integrated to most of present-day generative frameworks including the Distributed Morphology. A more detailed explanation of this concepts is based on representative studies dealing with the phenomena which represent the general accepted state of arts.

- **Agree:** Feature sharing under c-command (Pesetsky and Torrego 2007)
- **Move:** Agree and Merge: It is a combination of operations where Move is pre-empted by Merge. (Chomsky 2000)
- **Merge:** The structure building operation which takes two syntactic objects A and B and forms the new object G={A,B} (Chomsky 1999)

For the operation Agree, I will follow Pesetsky and Torrego's (2007) mechanism:

(57) Agree mechanism as in Pesetsky and Torrego (2007):

(i) An unvalued feature F (a probe) on a head H at syntactic location α (Fα) scans its c-command domain for another instance of F (a goal) at location β (Fβ) with which to agree.
(ii) Replace Fα with Fβ, so that the same feature is present in both locations.

While the initial part of the definition remains consistent with Chomsky's work in 2000 and 2001, Pesetsky and Torrego (2007) present a different perspective on agreement. They propose that agreement is primarily driven by valuation rather than interpretability.[10]

In our previous discussion, we mentioned the concept of interpretability of features. Pesetsky and Torrego propose that features can also have a separate dimension of being valued or unvalued. Accordingly, certain features originate from the lexicon as unvalued and require a value from a valued instance of the same feature found on another element. To compare the proposals, let's first consider the original one by Chomsky (2001):

(58) **Valuation/Interpretability Biconditional** (Chomsky 2001, p. 5)
A feature F is uninterpretable iff F is unvalued.

Chomsky's mechanism of Agree is illustrated in example (59) with the Tense feature. Here the head T has an interpretable Tense feature [+PAST]: iT[past]. (I indicate interpretability and uninterpretability with *i* and *u* written to the left of the feature). The head little *v* contains an uninterpretable (inflectional) feature u[unval]. When T merges with *v*, the Tense feature on T agrees with that in *v* and the latter is thereby valued: uv[past]. In other words, *v* receives a Tense value from T. This operation is called *checking by valuing.*

10 Pesetsky and Torrego (2007) assume a feature-sharing theory of agreement in which the matching feature(s) of the probe and the goal are unified into a single feature. Thus, a feature that undergoes Agree has more than one instance and Agree takes two (or more) occurrences of a feature (e.g., Number on subject DP, T and V-v) and turns them into two (or more) instances/locations of a single feature (e.g., a single feature of Number shared by DP and T-V-v) before the uninterpretable instances delete.

(59) a. *Marie missed John.*
b. iT[past] … u v[unval] → iT[past] … uv[past]

Yet, if unvalued features need to be deleted by the time of Transfer to the interfaces, there is no way to know which features need to be deleted (here it is the originally unvalued feature of *v*) as they are both valued by the time of Transfer. Because there is no link established between features, syntax cannot inspect the feature and see whether the valuation of the feature F2 is due to F1 or conversely.

To solve the problem, Pesetsky and Torrego (2007) propose that valuation and interpretability should be taken as independent. As a result of this separation, four sorts of features are expected. On the left we have the uninterpretable features, on the right the interpretable ones. The features in bold are the types of features not present in the original Chomsky's proposal.

(60)

u F val	**= uninterpretable valued**	i F val	= interpretable valued
u F [ ]	= uninterpretable, unvalued	**i F [ ]**	**= interpretable unvalued**

Moreover, in line with Chomsky's 2001 proposal, Pesetsky and Torrego assert that unvalued features function as probes, but differ in allowing interpretable and unvalued features to act as probes as well (which were absent for Chomsky).

Let's apply Pesetsky and Torrego's (2007) Agree mechanism to our example (59). Now, Tense on the Verb is valued in the lexicon but it remains uninterpretable throughout the derivation. This feature specification allows the finite Verb to serve as a goal. The Tense feature on the T head, on the other hand, is interpretable but unvalued and therefore it acts as a probe, see below:

(61) a. *Marie missed John.*
b. iT [unval] … u v [past] → iT[past] … uv[past]

The situation above thus exemplifies the two types of features that were disallowed in Chomsky's proposal.

In the original Chomsky's feature taxonomy, in addition to having the property of interpretability, features also have a second property, usually known as *strength*. The prominent characteristic of strength is its ability to initiate movement operations. Compare the example in (62a) with a negative sentence that involves a negative *not* and a complete selection of auxiliaries and a modal in (62b):

(62) a. *She has* ***not*** *been reading the book.*
b. *She might* ***not*** *have been reading the book.*

In (62a), the negation *not* precedes the auxiliary, whereas in (62b) *not* follows the modal. To account for these different word order patterns, the first auxiliary *has* in (62a) must have moved to T which is the locus of modals.

Pesetsky and Torrego (2001) put forward the proposal that features have movement properties associated with them. These properties are called EPP (originally the abbreviation referring to the Extended Projection Principle). The EPP characteristic is a trait of a property rather than the feature itself. Technically, this difference is important because Agree is defined as feature sharing and in the EPP case, nothing is shared, EPP is simply parasitic on Agree.

To envision the scenario described in (62), we must consider it as a two-step process. First, there is an agreement between T and a following functional head Perf, resulting in the interpretable unvalued inflectional feature on T being valued. Subsequently, through the process of Agree, the EPP feature on T becomes activated, leading to the movement of the auxiliary to T:

(63) a. iT[][EPP] … uPerf [Perf] → iT[Perf] u[Perf]
b. iT[][EPP] … uPerf [Perf] → iT[Perf] [Perf]

To conclude this part, while Chomsky (2001) ties valuation and interpretability, arguing that all and only uninterpretable features are unvalued, Pesetsky and Torrego (2001) divorce valuation and interpretability which results in a broader range of possible features. I will utilize Pesetsky and Torrego's modified proposal, it will become especially useful in section 3.2.2 where I will discuss Gender features.

2.1.2 Postsyntactic Processes in the DM model

In this section, I will outline the postsyntactic morphological processes to explain the output of syntax. Specifically, I will primarily focus on *syntactic Lowering/Merger* and morphological agreement. The DM model encompasses also various other postsyntactic processes such as Local Dislocation and Fission, which are not going to be discussed here in more detail.

Given the assumption that syntax serves as the input for semantic interpretation, it follows that those semantic features, which correspond to interpretable features, must necessarily be present in syntax. In the mapping to the Phonetic Form (PF), interpretable features are not deleted. Therefore, the features like, for example, Tense or phi- features which are all interpretable and valued can be a target of PF operations.

Let's begin with the concept of Lowering/Merger, focusing on the Tense feature in English. It may seem puzzling that we can observe Tense inflection on Verbs, such as in the sentence *John loved Mary*, if the uninterpretable feature on V is deleted. This becomes even more intriguing when we consider that, unlike in French, English Verbs are known not to raise to T in narrow syntax, as proposed in Emonds (1978). The following examples illustrate the contrast between French and English: the distribution of the negation *pas* and *not* shows that the Frech Verb *aime* can precede it as in (64b), while the English Verb *love* (65) cannot get to the position in front of *not*.

(64) a. *Jean* *n'a* *<u>pas</u>* ***aimé*** *Marie*
John has not loved Mary
'John didn't love Mary.'

b. *Jean* ***n'aime*** *<u>pas</u>* *Mary*
John loves not Mary
'John doesn't love Mary. '

(65) **John **loves** <u>not</u> Marry.*

Reformulating the Affix Hopping of Chomsky (1957), Embick and Noyer (2005) state that in English the morphology signals lowering of the features of T to V post-syntactically.[11] This process involves the lowering of a head to the head of its complement and these heads do not have to be linearly adjacent. In other words, the presence of an intervening adjoined Adverb, such as *loudly* in example (66), does not hinder the process of T lowering to *v*. The effects of such feature movement to the right can be schematically illustrated as below.

(66) *Mary <u>loudly</u> play***ed** *the trumpet.*

(67) Lowering/Merger as in Embick and Noyer (2004, p. 24)

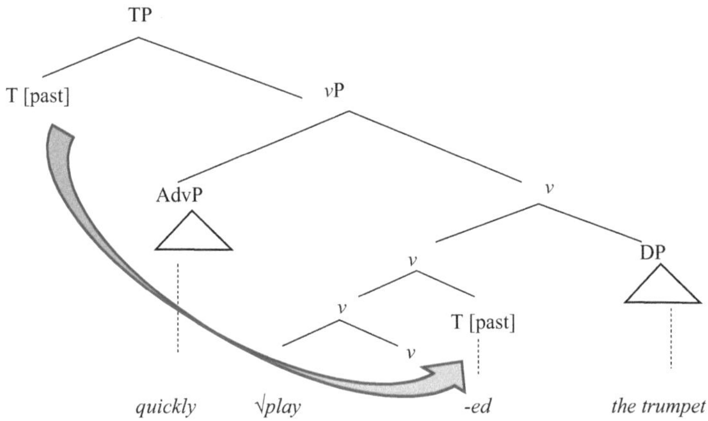

Next, we will discuss the concept of *morphological agreement*. Note here that Agree and agreement are not synonymous. While Agree is a syntactic operation, agreement pertains to the surface morphological properties of the inflectional system. In DM, agreement is specifically confined to the PF level involving assignment of *AGR nodes* and the copying of information onto

11 The same operation is called Merger in Halle and Marantz (1993). Merger like head-to-head movement (e.g., movement of English auxiliary Verbs to T) joins two terminal nodes but keeps them independent. Thus, the newly emerged word will consist of separate morphemes.

these nodes. Furthermore, Embick (1988) assumes that verbal and nominal agreement patterns do not have to be the same. To account for this, two types of AGR nodes are proposed which contain different feature sets:

(68) AGR1: Person, Number
AGR2: Number, Gender

When an element combines with T, it will show the AGR1. Otherwise, it will agree with the AGR2 feature set. The categories that can receive AGR nodes are also specified:

(69)

AGR Node	NO AGR Node
Tense	Verbs
Determiners	Prepositions
Nouns	Adverbs
Adjectives	Particles

The process is described in Embick and Noyer (2005) for Latin Verbs and in the following sections I will apply it to Czech Verbs which contain a root, Tense and agreement morpheme:[12]

(70) **√ROOT – T - AGR**

a. *Ona* *mluvi-l-a.*
$\text{She}_{3.SG}$ $\text{speak}_{PAST.3.SG}$
'She spoke.'

b. *Oni* *mluvi-l-i.*
$\textit{They}_{3.PL}$ $\text{speak}_{PAST.3.PL}$
'They spoke.'

12 The Czech examples in (71) are perhaps more complex than suggested here because they plausibly contain also some null morphemes at the T level. For details, see Veselovská and Emonds (2015) and Veselovská (2022). I will not go into detail here.

The agreement morphemes *-a*, *-i* in (70)—which are added at PF—are called *dissociated morphemes*. The addition of these morphemes follows a step-by-step process. First, an AGR node is inserted at PF and adjoined to T. Second, the information about person and Number from the DP are copied into the AGR, see the process below:

(71) a. The structure without agreement b. The structure with agreement

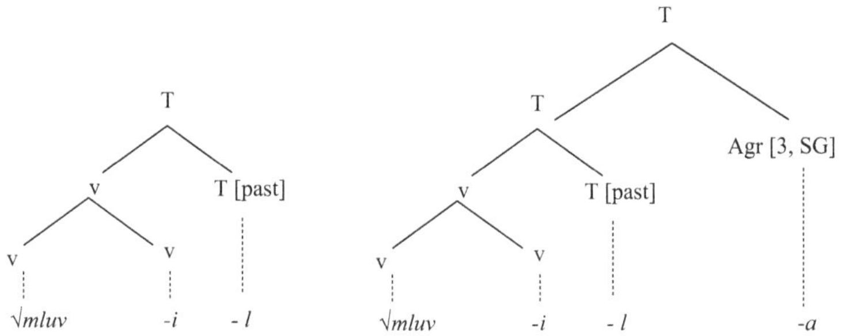

To the best of my knowledge, the process of feature copying and its restrictions have not been thoroughly investigated in Embick and Noyer (2005). In this study the authors do not provide explicit conditions on feature copying. In the earlier study of the agreement Halle and Marantz (1993) argue that these processes are local and adhere to hierarchical structure.

2.1.3 Word Formation—Prefixes and Suffixes

Word formation in Distributed Morphology (DM) involves a traditional process of *head movement* which is the subject of The Head Movement Constraint (HMC) originally proposed by Travis (1984). The following definition is from Chomsky (1986).

(72) **Head Movement Constraint** (Chomsky 1986, p. 71)
Movement of a zero-category b is restricted to the position of a head a that governs the maximal projection g of b, where a theta-governs or L-marks g if a is not C.

In Baker (1988), HMC is reduced to a variety of the Empty Category Principle, that is, related to the requirement for proper government of the trace of the removed element.

(73) **Head Movement Constraint** (Baker 1988, p. 53)
An X^0 may only move into the Y^0 which properly governs it.

In the present-day DM, the head movement entails moving a head to its immediately dominating head, and subsequently moving the resulting complex to the next immediately dominating head. Assuming a structure represented as (74), the ordering of suffixes in a complex head would follow the pattern of √Root-X-Y-Z, as shown in (74b). On the other hand, the structure √Root-Y-X-Z would not be permissible.

(74) a. Assumed projection before the movement

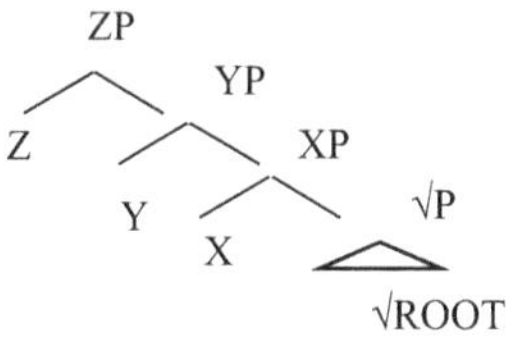

b. Complex structure after the head movement

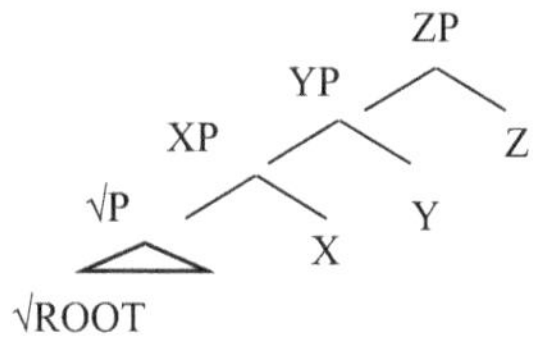

In the framework of DM, prefixes are considered on par with suffixes, allowing for the potential linearization of any of the elements X, Y, and Z as either prefixes or suffixes. Consequently, head movement within DM is capable of generating various linear orders, such as Z-Y-X-√ROOT or Z-√ROOT-X-Y, among others. This leads to the relaxation of left adjunction in head movement as the head was typically positioned to the right. The constraint of no tangling[13] remains, however, operative and the structure such as X-√Root-Z-Y would not be grammatical.

Notice that the ordering of affixes in complex words mirrors basically the ordering of functional heads in syntactic structure. This phenomenon is known as the Mirror Principle (Baker 1988).

13 An assumption that limits the number of possible linearizations by assuming that branches in a tree will never cross each other.

2.2 The Specifics of the Exo-skeletal Model: Borer (2005a)

Hagit Borer, a prominent figure in generative linguistics, has authored multiple books that present innovative ideas within the field. Among her notable works are three books in which she proposes an Exo-skeletal model in different linguistic domains: nominals, event structure, and morphology. In this section, I will provide an overview of Borer's terminology and framework, as presented in her books.

To start with, it has been long recognized that there is a division of labor between the lexicon and syntax. On one end of the spectrum, there are some approaches that associate a linguistic structure with specific linguistic items. In such views, lexical items encompass various properties, including syntactic, semantic, and morphological aspects, such as information about argument structure (e.g., the number of arguments that the Verb takes), syntactic category, and syntactic projection environment. These approaches, characterized by a *detailed lexicon that incorporates multiple properties*, can be referred to as endo-skeletal.

In contrast, H. Borer develops an alternative model known as the Exo-skeletal model. In this model, linguistic structures are relatively independent of the specific items that occur within them. Instead, the items themselves contain only a minimal amount of information. This approach is motivated by the observation that the properties of certain items can be overridden by the syntax. To illustrate this, let's consider the prototypical Noun *siren* in verbal *contexts*:

(75) a. *The factory horns* ***sirened*** *throughout the raid.*
b. *The factory horns* ***sirened*** *midday and everyone broke for lunch.*
c. *The police car* ***sirened*** *the Porsche to a stop.*
d. *The police car* ***sirened*** *up to the accident site.*
e. *The police car* ***sirened*** *the daylight out of me.*

Source: Borer (2005a, p. 8)

According to Borer (2005a), it is not necessary to assign five distinct uses to the verb *siren* in various contexts, such as intransitive (75a), transitive (75b), etc. Instead, these items are inserted into a structure where they become interpretable through coercion by that structure.

In Borer's (2005a) model of grammar, there are *two* main syntactic components: the *functional lexicon*, which includes derivational affixation, and the *Encyclopedia*. Borer's Encyclopedia serves as a reservoir of *listemes*, which are devoid of a specific syntactic category. These listemes are roughly equivalent to roots in the DM Vocabulary. It is, however, important to note that the question of root content is still debated in current linguist theories and varies from author to author. Even in Borer's earlier work, roots included both content and phonological indices while in her later work roots contain phonology but lack content.

At the beginning of derivation, the subset of lexemes is selected from the Encyclopedia to form the *conceptual array*. This subset is then inserted into the *lexical domain*, abbreviated as L-D as shown in (76).

(76) [$_{\text{L-D}}$ *sink, boat, dog*]

The functional lexicon, in contrast, comprises two types of grammatical formatives: independent grammatical formatives called f-morphs (e.g., *the*, *will*) and head features (e.g., past Tense *-ed*). Some grammatical formatives can merge with the lexical domain (L-D) and project in turn functional structures. These functional structures categorize the L-D they dominate.

To illustrate Borer's model of derivation, let's consider the example with the past Tense and focus on the abstract head feature <pst>, equivalent to [+PAST] discussed in the preceding section. The merge of <pst> and L-D would give rise to the following output:

(77) [$_{\text{T}}$<pst> [$_{\text{L-D}}$ *sink, boat, dog*]]

This merging in (77) will make the L-D a VP with the head in T. Subsequently, one listeme may merge a copy and obligatorily raise to T and become its head. The path of this derivation is depicted in (78):

(78) [$_{\text{T}}$[$_{\text{V}}$ *sink*] <pst> [$_{\text{VP}}$ [$_{v}$~~*sink, boat, dog*~~]]] (*sank*)

Of course, any lexeme from the conceptual array in L-D can choose to merge a copy in T and all the representations in (79) are felicitous:

(79) a. [$_T$[$_v$ *boat*] <pst> [$_{VP}$ [$_v$*sink*, ~~*boat*~~, *dog*]]]
b. [$_T$[$_v$ *dog*] <pst> [$_{VP}$ [$_v$*sink*, *boat*, ~~*dog*~~]]]

Borer (2005a, p. 31) writes that "it only remains to be hoped that some post-derivational phonological area will be capable of dispensing a well-formed phonological representation." In the study itself, no more information is given for the exact execution of this process, and it leads to a massive overgeneration of structures which is the main drawback of this model, acknowledged by the author herself.

We can now continue with the derivation with an f-morph *will* as in future Tense. Again, the f-morph *will* will merge with an L-D. Since *will* functions as a T element,[14] it enables the categorization of the L-D as a VP. In this scenario, head movement is not needed and in case of *will*, it is in fact blocked.

(80) [$_T$<*will*, fut> [$_{L-D}$ listeme-1 listeme-2 listeme 3]]

In addition, Borer states that the f-morphs can be bound and free. For example, the English progressive marker *-ing*, is considered an f-morph rather than an abstract head feature. It requires the support of a stem and involves the movement of an L-stem. Categorizing suffixes such as *-ation* are also subsumed under bound f-morphs.

To provide a schematic representation of the syntactic derivation in Borer's Exo-skeletal model, we can depict it using the following diagram:

(81) Exo-skeletal model

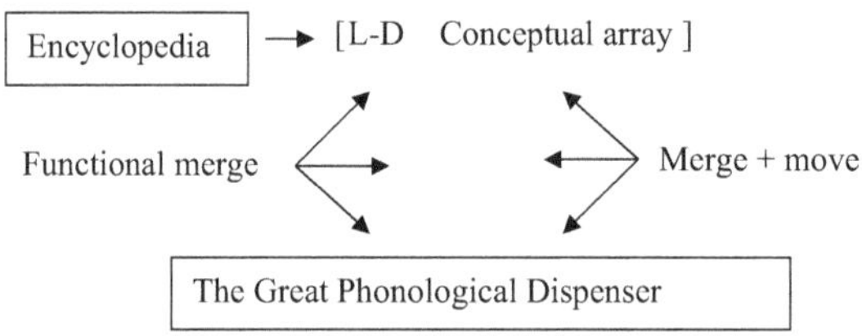

Source: Borer (2005a, p. 33)

14 See the discussion below in (87) for the explanation of how functional elements with the same semantic specification work and assign range to functional heads.

We can now turn to a more comprehensive exploration of functional structure within the Exo-skeletal model. In this model, functional heads possess open values that necessitate the assignment of range through various means. The open value is not entirely unrestricted, it is associated with a categorial label that constrains the class of elements capable of assigning range to it. To illustrate this concept, consider the Quantity Phrase, which functions as a nominalizer and is headed by an open value marked categorically as #. The range for the open value in the Quantity Phrase can only be assigned by quantity expressions, not by Tense. The syntactic representation of this configuration is provided in (82).

(82) $[_{\#}$P <e># $[_{NP}$]]

In the given representation (82), the symbol <e> denotes an open value, and the subscript # indicates its categorial membership. Specifically, in the context of English, this open value can be assigned range by an f-morph such as *most*, *much*, *two* and so on.

In addition to direct range assignment, which involves both an assignment by an f-morph and a head feature, there is another mechanism known as *indirect range assignment.* This type of range assignment can occur either through specifier-head agreement or with the help of an Adverb of quantification. Let me illustrate the latter type with definiteness spreading as described by Borer (2005b) for English.

(83) a. $[_{DP}$ $[_{DP}$ *the dog's* <e>$_{d}$ $[_{NP}$ *ear*]] definite
b. $[_{DP}$ $[_{DP}$ *a dog's* <e>$_{d}$ $[_{NP}$ *ear*]] indefinite

As demonstrated in example (83), the Possessor is situated in SpecDP and can exhibit either definite or indefinite properties. Consequently, it has the capability to assign range to <e>$_{d}$, on the condition that it enters into a specifier-head relationship with it.

Now, we can proceed to discuss the second type of indirect range assignment, which involves the use of an Adverb of quantification:

(84) a. Adverb $_{Q}[_{\# P} <e>_{\#} [_{NP}$ N]]

b. $[_{DP} <e^{i}>_{d} [_{\# P} <e^{i}>_{\#}$ [*hummingbirds*]]] *often*^{i} *breed in the summer.* (under the reading where most hummingbirds breed in the summer)

An Adverb of quantification can bind $<e>_{\#}$ in DP. The rationale behind calling it indirect is clear. It is not specified in the functional lexicon as range assigner for a particular open value. Additionally, indirect range assignment does not require movement of the L-head, although it does not prevent it either.

2.2.1 S-Functors and C-Functors

In her later work, *Taking Form* (Borer 2013), the author focuses on nominalizations. She introduces the distinction between two types of the so-called functors: S-functors and C-functors. *S-functors* subsume range *assignors*, such as Determiners or past Tense markers, which correspond to f-morphs and abstract head features, respectively.

C-functors, on the other hand, involve derivational morphemes like *-able*,-*ment*, and *-tion*. Chapter 5 specifically addresses the topic of nominalizations, with a particular emphasis on C-functors.

The distinction between S-functors and C-functors is closely tied to the differentiation between inflection and derivation. Therefore, before explaining the rationale behind the distinct treatment of these two types of functors, it is necessary to explore Borer's approach to inflection and the motivation behind it.

Borer (2013) states that neither inflection nor derivation can be solely characterized by the predictability of form based on function. To illustrate this, let's consider inflection and take for example the plural morpheme as shown in (85). It is evident that the forms used to indicate plural are clearly distinct:

(85) a. *table* → *table-s*

b. *goose* → *geese*

In a similar vein, when considering derivation, whose main function is to determine a categorial label, it does not ensure predictability of form:

(86) a. *torture → tor-ment*
b. *destroy → destruct-ion*

In contrast to inflection, derivation is not as erratic when it comes to determining the function based on form. While the inflectional morpheme *-s* in English can serve multiple functions such as indicating plurality, case, or verbal inflection, the derivational affix *-tion* predominantly attaches to words with the category V (verb), with only a few exceptions where the base morphemes may lack a clear category, as seen in examples like *nation*.

However, if we restate the function as abstract function, then inflection is more regular than derivation. The combination of a Verb (V) with the past Tense marker (PAST) is not only predictable from a syntactic perspective but also carries semantic predictability. In contrast, the combination of a Verb with the derivational affixes *-ation*, *-ance* or *-able* do not possess the same level of semantic predictability.

Having discussed the properties of inflection and derivation, let us return to the definitions of C-functors and S-functors, which include both inflectional and derivational morphemes. S-functors are responsible for determining the *relationship* between a semantic range and a syntactic position that contains an open value, where the semantic range is realized. For example, the numerals *three* or *four* are S-functors that assign range to a syntactic position marked by #, which stands for Quantity. Their semantic relatedness is reflected in the fact that they are operators ranging over the same open value.[15]

C-functors, on the other hand, function as *modifiers* within the structure. As a result, the heads of extended projections appear in pairs, where one member projects and provides an open value, while the other member (the S-functor) supplies the assigned range for that value. This relationship is schematically represented in (87). In this head pair, the open value e acquires the value S (by assumption the semantic range S). Besides, it acquires a categorial label (X) which is for Borer (2013, p. 38) "a syntactic way of encoding the fundamentally semantic common determinator of the array of S-functors that may assign range to it."

15 More details on this can be found in section 3.1.

(87) The head pair

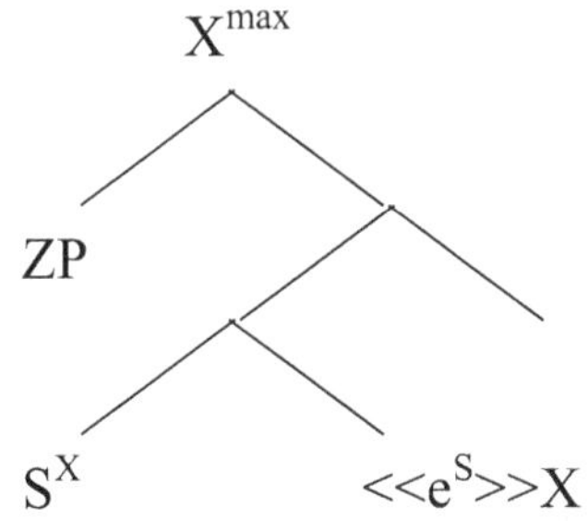

The syntactic function of the C-functors is associated with the projection of a categorial node and the selection of a specific *Categorial Complement Space* (CCS) corresponding to categories such as N, V, A, and P. While C-functors may have a semantic function, it is not always necessary nor sufficient for their role in syntax. To exemplify this, the C-functor [V] *-able* projects the category A and defines its CCS as V.

2.2.2 Prefixes and Suffixes

In contrast with the DM, Borer (2013) assumes that prefixes and suffixes have a different syntactic status. While prefixes are instances of min/max and cannot project, derivational suffixes (C-functors) are (non-maximal) min which forces them to project. To fully understand their role in the syntactic structure we must explain two additional conditions on movement. Borer stipulates that moved constituents are always linearized to the left of their merger target in English. Moreover, there is a Uniformity Condition proposed in Chomsky (1995):

(88) **Chain Uniformity Condition:** A chain is uniform with regard to phrase structure status. (p. 253)

The direct entailment of this maxim is that whatever re-merges and is linearized to the left may not project.

Consequently, derivational suffixes will never move, for any such movement would, by definition, force them to be a maximal, non-projecting instantiation. This is depicted in structure (89b) and further described in Borer (2013, p. 299). Derivational suffixes are, however, instances of (non-maximal) min, effectively forcing them to project as (89a) shows.

(89) a. *verb-al*

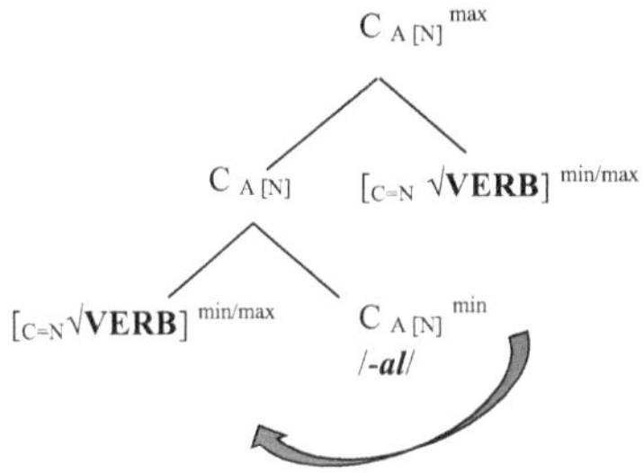

b. **al-verb*

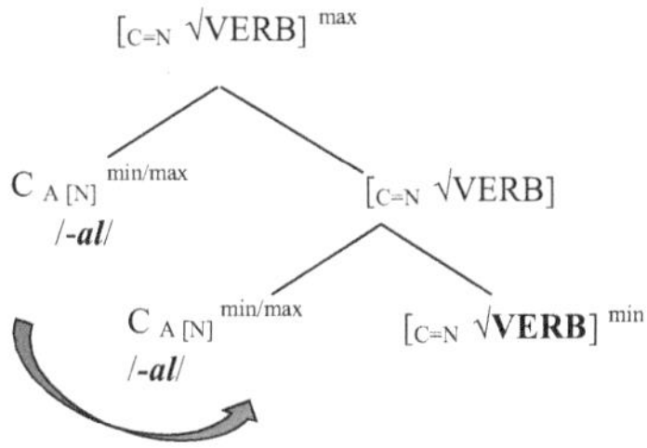

The movement of heads within extended projections, on the other hand, is possible because in those cases heads re-merge and then re-project. I will not go into detailed description and the reader can refer to Borer (2013, p. 298) for more information.

Another instance of head movement that conforms to Uniformity is possible with prefixes. These are instances of min/max, can move and incorporate to the left giving the resulting structure in (90) for the Noun/verb *input*, as was depicted in Borer (2013, p. 300):

(90)

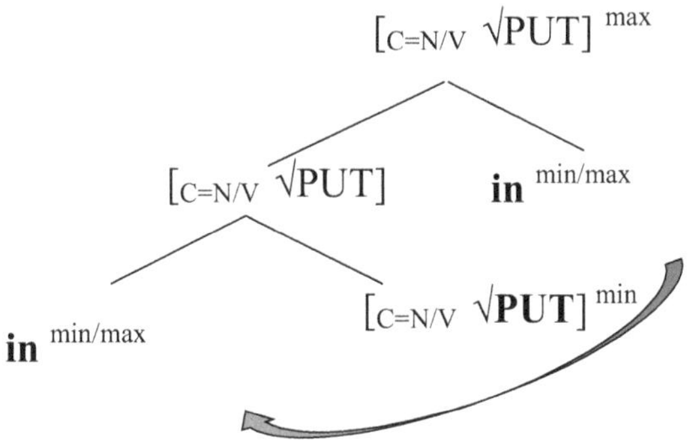

Also, the instances of min/max must move because otherwise the elements would be in symmetrical c-command relationship and violate Kayne's original LCA (1994) proposal for asymmetrical c-command condition in linearization.

Consequently, the right-headedness in Borer results from the nature of C-functors and leftward condition on linearization. Right-headedness can be also applied to English compounds where one of the roots moves and becomes a maximal category while the unmoved root projects and is thus a head.[16]

(91) a. *head-arrow* b. *arrow-head*

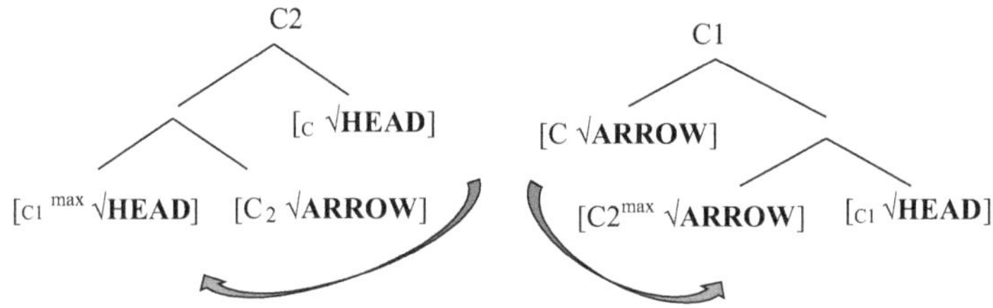

Lastly, to derive the structures of forms such as *break*-in, *blackout*, it is necessary to take the structure in (90) formed by the incorporation to give rise to the additional movement of $[_C$ √**BREAK**$]^{min}$as in (92).

16 The phenomenon of Right-headedness has been known since seminar works of Lieber (1983), and Williams (1981). While Williams (1981) proposes the well-known Right-hand Head Rule for the domain of morphology, Lieber (1983) assumes with her Feature percolation mechanism that affixation in morphology is symmetric (to account for cases such as [V *en* [A *dear*]], [V *en* [A *noble*]]) and compounds are asymmetric with arrangement of their heads on the right. See the criticism of these proposals in Emonds (2013) who claims that the default right-headedness can be applied both in morphology and syntax, especially in domains which are non-free. In free domains, which compounds are instances of, the ordering is derived from the stress placement. Consequently, contra Borer (2013) some primary compound in English can be left-headed. For example, in (i):

(i) *Put the supplies* $[_{PP}$ *back* $[_P$ *downstairs/inside/upstream*] *when you can.*

(92) The structure for the form *break-in*

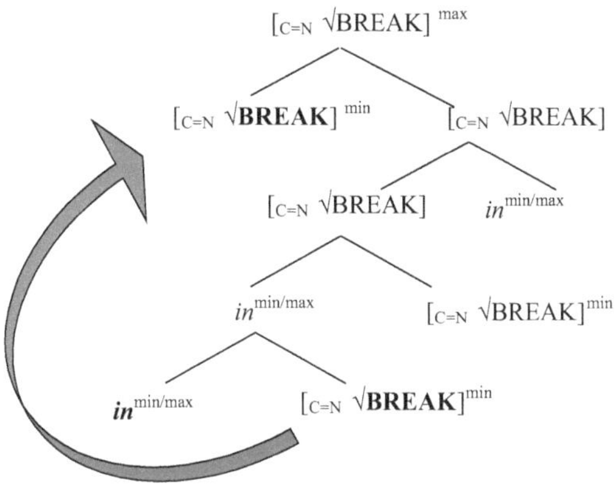

This additional step is necessary because Prepositions/particles are non-projecting heads and must move. By the movement they would be linearized to the left and we need to derive the structure where they are on the right.

To conclude this part, we have seen that prefixes and suffixes have a different treatment in Borer's XS model than in the DM model where they are treated on a par. Moreover, the left adjunction for prefixes in the DM model is relaxed which eliminates the additional derivational steps for the form such as *break-in* as in (92). I will return to this issue when discussing Slavic prefixes in section 4.4.2.1 that are capable of inducing telicity.

2.2.3 Meaning and Content

According to Borer (2013), meaning construction consists of two components. The first of these corresponds to Frege's *Bedeutung* and what Borer terms as *Semantic meaning* which is built of non-spelled out representations and computed from fundamentally abstract properties of functors and syntactic structures. In contrast, Borer's *Content* corresponds to Frege's *Sinn* and is not grammatically constructed but rather grammar defines a domain into which Content can be inserted from a distinct cognitive domain. It is matched with structures on the basis of spell out and is thus sensitive to phonological realization.

Extremely expressed, Borer adheres to some version of the T-model where Content interacts with PF and Semantic meaning with LF. Insofar as, for example, *many students ate the potatoes* has semantic meaning, it is by virtue of having syntactic structure as well as functors such as *many*, *the* which are oblivious not only to the phonological representation but also to the Content of *potatoes*. The Content *potato*, on the other hand is oblivious to the fact that it is a direct object or plural. We note now that the construction of meaning requires a conjoined set of representations.

After the explanation of the terminology ('nuts and bolts') of the Exo-skeletal model, in the next chapter, I am going to concentrate on implementing this framework within the nominal domain.

Nominal Layers and Their Relevance for Nominalization

In this chapter, I am going to concentrate on the analyses of a nominal functional projection. I will introduce and discuss the two contrasting models described in the preceding chapter, that is, the concept proposed by Hagit Borer and Artemis Alexiadou. In spite of the fact that they both share a background in generative grammar, the two linguists have developed more or less independent frameworks that both deserve a more thorough examination. While summarizing the basic concepts that the authors apply for the analysis of the nominal projection, I will concentrate on the structural levels related to Number feature(s). Then I am going to utilize these theoretical frameworks to analyze Czech data. In this regard, I will complement my findings with the insights provided by a Veselovská and Karlík as mentioned in sections 1.4.1 and 1.4.2.

3.1 Borer: Nominal Functional Projection

In her book, *In Name Only*, Borer (2005a) proposes the following layers for nominal functional projections:

(93) $[_{DP} \langle e \rangle_{d} [_{\#P} \langle e \rangle_{\#\,(DIV)} [_{CL}^{max} \langle e \rangle_{DIV(\#)} [_{NP}]]]]$

The ordering of these layers can be seen in graph (94) below. It starts with the *Classifier Phrase* (CL^{max}) which is the layer where division of mass Nouns is carried out. It hosts plural and feeds the projection of the *Quantity Phrase* aka Number Phrase (#P) with Numerals and Quantifiers. The DP (*Determiner Phrase*) is associated with definiteness. In the upcoming section, I will provide a detailed discussion of each of these components.

3.1.1 The Classifier Phrase: Mass vs. Count and Numerals (# P)

As for the traditional concept of a possible nominal feature of Countability, according to Borer's (2005a) perspective, the explanation for the mass/count distinction should not be sought in the inherent denotation of Nouns, as *all* Nouns are inherently mass. The transformation of Nouns into count Nouns occurs through the projection of specific syntactic structures.

As depicted in picture (94) taken from Borer (2005a), the primary difference between mass Nouns and count Nouns lies in the absence of a Classifier in the Classifier Phrase (CL^{max}). This projection plays a crucial role in dividing the mass entity, enabling it to establish a relationship with the count system. The feature <div> in the graph below is an abstract head feature on a moved N-stem which is spelled out as a plural marker *-s*.

(94) a. Count Noun structure

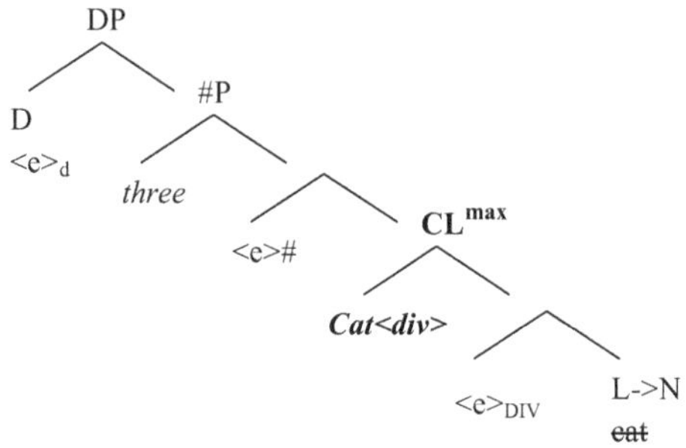

b. Mass Noun structure

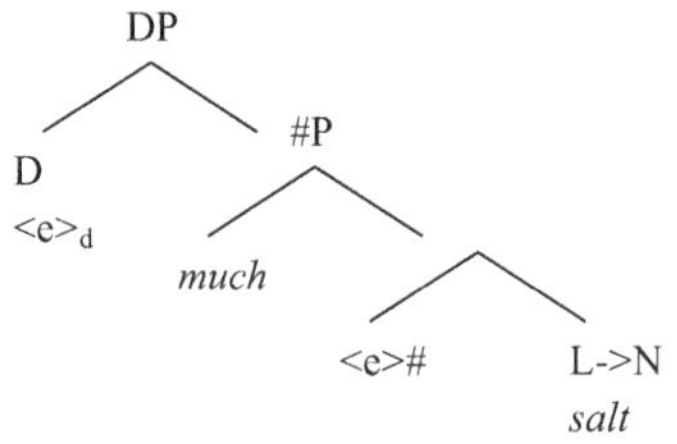

The assumed advantage of this system is that mass/count languages are structurally parallel to existing classifier languages. In English, the Classifier is instantiated by the plural Number marker. Borer (2005a) argues that plural inflection can be viewed as a form of classifier inflection, given its complementary distribution with Classifiers in Chinese. She claims that there is, in fact, no language where they coexist in a single structure although both plural and Classifier may be present as two different strategies in a language.

We can imagine a dividing function, which is to say, the assignment of range to $<e>_{DIV}$, as the superimposition of an infinite set of webs, or *reticules* on a mass denotation. These reticules include various configurations: a reticule without any divisions, reticules without complete cells, or reticules which create cells that do not correspond to a canonical singular. The #P counting function (which is to say, the assignment of range to $<e>_{\#}$ by a counter) then selects the reticule which matches the properties of a particular Determiner. For example, the cardinal *three* will select a reticule with three cells while the Determiner *zero* will choose the reticule without any cells.

As previously mentioned, the absence of CL^{max} results in the emergence of a mass nominal. Since it remains undivided, it cannot be subjected to counting by Numerals. However, it can still be subjected to quantification:[17]

(95) a. **three salts*
b. *much salt*

When there is no plural morpheme *-s*, no division of stuff can be performed and the ungrammaticality results:

(96) **three cat*

A Noun which is divided by plural can be further quantified:

(97) a. *several boys*
b. *a few boys*

These Quantifiers in (97) as well as the Quantifier *much* from (95b) appear in the same position as numerals.

17 *Three salts* in (95a) is grammatically possible with a different interpretation, namely *three packs of salt*. This is due to the coercion which is easily achieved for listemes. In contrast, expressions that are marked syntactically such as *much wine* are hard to be coerced into count expressions.

Consequently, as we have seen, Quantifiers in Borer (2005a) are classified with two dimensions, [± COUNTER] and [± DIVIDER]. While *counters* assign range to $\langle e\rangle_{\#}$, *dividers* assign range to $\langle e\rangle_{DIV}$. Some Quantifiers are portmanteau elements and can have both functions.

Turning now to the issue of singular. In Borer's (2005a) framework, singular is realized by an indefinite article such as *a* in the phrase *a cat*. In cases where the Noun appears in its bare form without a division, the indefinite article serves the dual function of both a divider and a counter. The indefinite article then originates in CL^{max} and subsequently undergoes movement to #P.

Upon closer examination, it becomes evident that bare plurals are not derived from singular forms. Rather bare plurals follow from the plural morpheme *-s* which functions as a divider. Furthermore, bare plurals lack the projection of #P and therefore have non-quantity interpretation. Due to their undetermined quantity as depicted in structures (98) both bare plurals and mass Nouns fail to show telicity of the event (99).

(98) a. $[_{DP} \langle e\rangle_{d} ([_{\#P} \langle e\rangle_{\#}) [_{CL}{}^{max}\ \mathit{cats}\ \langle e\rangle_{DIV} [_{NP}\ \mathit{\not{cats}}]]]$
b. $[_{DP} \langle e\rangle_{d} ([_{\#P} \langle e\rangle_{\#}) [_{NP}\ \mathit{salt}]]]$

(99) a. *Mary drew* ***circles*** *(the whole afternoon)/(*in five minutes).*
b. *Mary ate* ***rabbit*** *(the whole afternoon)/(*in five minutes).*

After presenting an overview of how the mass-count distinction can be mediated structurally, we can continue with the higher level in the nominal projection which is the Determiner Phrase (DP).

3.1.2 The DP Layer

The DP layer in Borer (2005a) is associated with definiteness only. The indefiniteness is not determined at the D level, but rather at the #P level. The author argues that the so-called *strong Quantifiers* (see (101)) have the ability to raise to D and assign a range to $\langle e\rangle_{d}$.[18] In contrast, *weak Quantifiers* (see (101)) and *Numerals* raise to D optionally, resulting in the ambiguity between

18 The DP is headed by an open value which needs to be assigned range. The subscript d indicates the affinity with the category D.

what Borer (2005a) calls a strong and a weak reading. Let me provide an illustration, as quoted in Borer (2005a) of the strong reading for the weak Quantifier *a* (p. 145):

(100) *Each teacher overheard the rumor that* ***a*** *student of mine had been called before the dean.*

In this particular reading in (100), there is a specific student of mine such that each teacher overhead the rumor that he was called before the dean. In this interpretation, the use of a student is akin to referring to a specific individual, similar to how one would interpret a proper name or a definite description.

The division of Quantifiers into these two classes is depicted below:

(101)	Strong Quantifiers	*the*, demonstratives, universal Quantifiers (*each, every, all, both* (*some, any, no*))
	Weak Quantifiers	*a*, Numerals, *many, few, much, little, several*

This division actually reproduces Jackendoff's (1977) observation about two closed class of modifiers of N. The fact that some element can co-occur while other are mutually exclusive, see (102), led Jackendoff (1977) to group the D words (Borer's strong Quantifiers) together.

(102)
a. **the every boy*
b. *the three cats*
c. **the all boys*
d. *the little bread*

Structurally, raising of weak Quantifiers to D is described in Borer (2005a) as in (103):

(103)
a. [$_{DP}$ *one/a* <e>$_{d}$ [$_{\#P}$ ~~*one/a*~~ <e>$_{\#\,(DIV)}$ [$_{CL}$^{max} ~~*one/a*~~ <e>$_{DIV(\#)}$ [$_{NP}$ *meat/boy*]]]]
b. [$_{DP}$ *ten/few* <e>$_{d}$ [$_{\#P}$ ~~*ten/few*~~ <e>$_{\#}$ [$_{CL}$^{max} *meats/boys* <e>$_{DIV}$ [$_{NP}$ ~~*meat/boy*~~]]]]

Another question that needs to be addressed is how the <e>$_d$ is licensed within the structure when the reading is weak. The <e>$_d$ needs to be licensed because it functions as mediating predicates and arguments. The author brings attention to observations made in Italian where nominal expressions functioning as arguments have to be introduced by a lexically filled D (as noted by Longobardi 1994):

(104) a. *(Un/Il) grande amico di Maria mi ha telefonato.*
'A/The great friend of Maria telephoned me.'
b. *Gianni e Amico di Maria.*
'Gianni is a friend of Maria's.'
c. *Maledetto tenente!*
'Damn lieutenant!'

The expressions in (104b) and (104c) are not arguments and rather serve only as a predicate and an expletive respectively. Therefore, D do not need to be filled.

The situation becomes more complex when it comes to Nouns which can be in a bare form in argument positions. This is especially true for mass Nouns and bare plurals:

(105) a. *Cats are great.*
b. *Bread is on the table.*

Interestingly, such Nouns are ungrammatical in preverbal contexts in Italian (106a), but they are acceptable when used in postverbal positions (106b), see some examples taken from Borer (2005a, p. 65):

(106) a. **Acqu viene giu dalla colline.*
'Water comes down from the hill.'
b. *Viene giu acqua dalle colline.*
'come down water from the hills'

To put the pieces together, we can conclude that unlike singular expressions, bare mass Nouns and plurals have a null Determiner. Nevertheless, preverbal positions in Romance languages are not lexically governed. Consequently, these null-Determiner nominals may only receive an existential interpretation in postverbal position in Italian.[19] Generic interpretation is not available in Romance languages for bare nominals.

Structurally, Borer (2005a) proposes that $<e>_{d}$ can be bound in either of two different ways. Firstly, it can be bound by *Existential closure* which is contingent upon the c-commanding domain of the verb and results in an existential reading (107a). Secondly, it can be bound by the Generic operator GEN with a generic reading in (107b):

(107) a. I $\exists$ [$_{V}$ *raised*] [$_{DP}$ $<e^{i}>_{d\ldots}$ [*cats/a cat/three cats/several cats/some cat(s)*]

b. GEN^{i} [$<e^{i}>_{d}$[$_{\#P}$ $<e^{i}>_{\#}$ *cats*]]] … [*eat mice*]

In example (107a), the phrase *cats* is interpreted existentially, conveying the meaning that there are some cats, and they are located on the roof. On the other hand, in (107b), the phrase *cats* is interpreted generically, expressing the idea that for any typical cat, it eats mice. Both existential closure and generic operators have the status of (covert) Adverbs, licensed by the discourse. Notice also that the GEN not only binds $<e>_{d}$ but also $<e>_{\#}$ which consequently excludes a generic reading for nominal expressions that are modified by an f-morph such as a *cat, three cats* etc.

Now, we have an answer to the puzzle regarding weak Quantifiers not raising to D but still functioning as an argument. We have seen that the Existential operator and the Generic operator can take over this job by turning predicates into arguments.

We also need to resolve why (108a) is grammatical but (108b) is not:

(108) a. *the cat*

b. **the a cat*

Borer (2005a) claims that the complementary distribution between indefinite and definite article is not due to their competition for D, but rather their competition for #P. She also posits that the definite article functions as "a discourse anaphor of sorts, which picks up its reference from a previously established discourse antecedent" (p. 161). In her theory, this implies that

19 English subjects are subject to existential closure due to lowering or some similar operation.

the inherits the mass-count properties of its antecedent which can force or alternatively bar the projection of CL^{max}. When the Noun is mass, Borer (2005a) describes the structure as in (109):

(109) [$_{DP}$ <e>$_{d}$ *the* [$_{\#P}$ ~~*the*~~ <e>$_{\#}$ [$_{NP}$ *salt*]]]

In the case of the singular count restriction, the definite article *the* inherits the properties from singulars which are by definition dividers and counters:

(110) [$_{DP}$ *the* <e>$_{d}$ [$_{\#P}$ ~~*the*~~ <e>$_{\#(DIV)}$ [$_{CL}^{max}$ ~~*the*~~ <e>$_{DIV(\#)}$ [$_{NP}$ *cat*]]]]

When the restriction is count and non-singular, there is little reason to assume that the definite article inherits the dividing properties of its antecedent. Instead, it behaves more like *several* which is only a counter. In this case, the structure involves the head feature <div> on the moved head:

(111) [$_{DP}$ *the* <e>$_{d}$ [$_{\#P}$ ~~*the*~~ <e>$_{\#}$ [$_{CL}^{max}$ *cat*. <div> <e>$_{DIV}$ [$_{NP}$ ~~*cat*~~]]]]

3.1.2.1 Head vs. Specifiers

If the definite article is a range assigner to <e>$_{\#}$, it raises the question of how to explain the grammaticality of constructions like (112), where other Quantifiers are capable of assigning range to <e>$_{\#}$ as well.

(112) *the three/many medals*

According to Borer (2005a), while definite and indefinite articles must be heads,[20] other Quantifiers might be heads or specifiers. In the case of the

---

20 See Emonds (2012) for a different view. He puts forward several arguments to show that unlike D, the complement of Q passes some tests for maximal projection. This is visible in (ii):
(ii) *Try to sell* [$_{FP}$ [$_{FP}$ *these two big beds*] *and* [$_{FP}$ *few antiques*]
(Not interpreted as) *Try to sell these few antiques.*
We didn't buy [$_{QP}$ *many* [$_{NP}$ *books on culture*] *or* [$_{NP}$ *guides for tourists*]]
If D were a functional head its complement (Q+ NP) should constitute a maximal projection and coordinate, and yet D in (iia) is not understood as modifying the second conjunct. In contrast, complements of Q in (iib) do.

definite article, it inherits the quantificational properties of its specifiers through Spec-head agreement. By inheriting the quantificational qualities from the specifier, no double marking of <e>$_{\#}$ arises, see below.

(113) Head vs. Specifiers

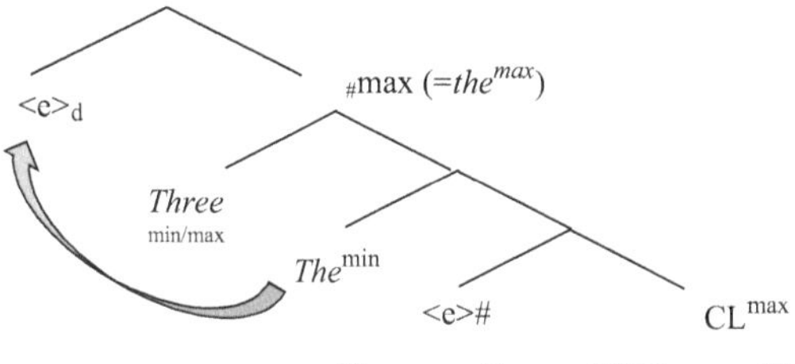

(Source: Borer 2005a, p. 171)

Nevertheless, *the* continues to be the first and foremost range assigner to <e>$_{d.}$ In the case of the example provided, *the* merges as a head while *three* as a specifier. Subsequently, it can move and assign range to <e>$_{d}$. The ungrammaticality of (114), when *the* occurs with strong Quantifiers, then follows from their competition for the D slot.

(114) **the each/every boy*

Finally, let's compare Borer (2005a) with Chierchia (1998) regarding their views on mass Nouns. Chierchia (1998) argues that mass Nouns are inherently plural, while Borer (2005a) proposes that mass interpretation of Nouns arises from a default setting associated with the absence of dividing structure. One of the arguments which Borer presents against the plurality of mass Nouns is the impossibility of interpretive coercion. For example, the Noun *rabbit* can be interpreted either as count or mass. However, when the Noun is grammatically marked as plural, such as *rabbits*, it cannot be coerced into a mass interpretation.

(115) a. **There is **rabbits** in my stew.*
b. *There is **rabbit** in my stew.*

Borer (2005a) argues that when we analyze the findings from coercion in the context of Chierchia's framework, it leads to the conclusion that there exists a distinction between lexical marking and grammatical marking of plurality. If there truly existed a fundamental difference between lexical and grammatical marking of plurality, it would not align with the behavior of Pluralia tantum words. Pluralia tantum are Nouns that are inflectionally plural but semantically singular, such as *trousers* or *scissors*. Despite their inflectional plural marking, these Nouns cannot be coerced into a mass context:

(116) *My trousers tear (*s) easily.*

The above observations make Borer (2005a) conclude that the mass/count distinction cannot be attributed solely to the listemes (roots) themselves.

3.1.3 Gender

Borer (2005a) accepts the traditional view that Gender is a syntactic feature. Since roots cannot have any syntactic features, it follows that Gender must not be on the root. The author, however, does not suggest any specific proposal about the location of Gender.[21]

Nevertheless, Borer (2005a) does mention Gender agreement in the context of N-to-D movement in Hebrew, where the definiteness feature on N triggers movement (2005a, p. 223). In this context, the Quantifier in (117) agrees with the head N in terms of definiteness, Number, and Gender.

(117)	*ha.prax.im*	*ha.rab.im*
	the.flowers.$_{M}$	the.many/much.$_{PL.M}$
	'Many flowers'	

21 The widely accepted proposal concerning Gender in a generative framework can be found in Ritter (1993). Since then, the syntactic models have been entertained in which Gender and Number are represented separately. Ritter argues that in languages where Gender is grammatically relevant, for example, Hebrew, Gender is a feature on N and Number is a separate projection because it serves as a landing site for movement. In Romance languages where the syntactic class is relevant, this property is a feature on Number.

Borer (2005a) provides an explanation for this process by noting that the Quantifier in Hebrew does not have inherent quantificational properties, much like the definite article in English. As a result, it does not assign range to <e>$_{\#}$. Instead, the abstract head feature <def> together with its supporting L-head can move. This movement is expected to trigger specifier-head agreement in terms of Gender, Number, and definiteness. The entire process initially described in Borer (2005a, p. 223) for the example (117) can be visualized in (118):

(118) [$_{DP}$ *praxim*. <def> <e>$_{d}$ [$_{\#P}$ *ha*$_{AGR}$. *rabim* [$_{\#P}$ ~~*praxim*~~.<def> <e>$_{\#}$ [$_{CL}$ ^{max} ~~*praxim*~~ <e>$_{DIV}$ [$_{NP}$ ~~*perax*~~]]]

3.1.4 Borer's Proposals and the Czech Nominal

In this study, I will adopt certain proposals put forward by Borer (2005a) as discussed in the previous sections. Specifically, I will accept Borer's hypothesis that Nouns initially exist as mass entities and require division in order to be quantified. Consequently, I will incorporate Borer's CL^{max} projection, with some modifications. However, I will not assume that plural serves as a dividing element and I will explore this issue further when introducing Alexiadou's framework, which distinguishes different types of plural. Additionally, I will adopt Borer's ideas regarding root categorization and the distinction between weak and strong Quantifiers. Finally, I will not assume that the presence of abstract head features needs to be accompanied by N-to-D movement.

3.2 Alexiadou: Nominal Functional Projection

Artemis Alexiadou is a widely accepted author known for her extensive work which includes numerous cross-linguistic articles and books. One notable publication that provides a comprehensive overview of nominal projection is the book *Noun Phrase in the Generative Perspective*, which was co-authored by Alexiadou in 2007 along with other researchers. The cross-linguistic perspective on the nominal projection can be found in her article about nominalizations in Alexiadou (2020).

In her analysis of nominals, Alexiadou combines insights from Borer (2005a) on countability and Kramer (2015) on the morphosyntax of Gender. To further explore the topic of Gender, Alexiadou provides decisive arguments about Gender in two of her articles from (2004) and (2017b). As these issues were not analyzed in depth in Borer (2005a), this will help us deal with them in Czech where Gender is reflected in morphology. The topics concerning countability and Number are described in four articles by Alexiadou (2017a, 2019a, 2019b, 2021). Determiners are discussed in the (2014a) book *Multiple Determiners and the Structure of DPs*.

In her approach to nominal projection, Alexiadou adopts the framework of Distributed Morphology (DM), as outlined in section 2.1. The specific assumptions she made regarding nominal projection will be presented in the following section. The proposed layers for nominals functional structure in Alexiadou (2020) are the following:

(119) [$_{\text{DP}}$ [$_{\#\text{P}}$ (quantity) [$_{\text{DivP}}$ plural marking [$_{n\text{P}}$ Gender [Root]]]]]

Roots combine with the nominalizer *n* which carries Gender information. Plurality is realized under DivP. The layer of quantity introduces counting function and facilitates the realization of Numerals. The Definiteness is associated with the D layer. Adjectives can appear between DP and *n*P and on *n*P itself.

3.2.1 Root Categorization in DM

Alexiadou's approach is rooted in Marantz's (1997) DM where roots need to be categorized by immediately adjoining categorial nodes. The nominalizer and verbalizer for nominal and verbal functional projections respectively can be seen below:

(120) Root categorization

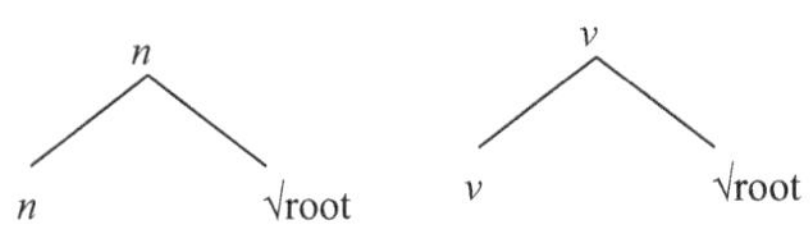

The nominalizer carries Gender and inflectional class in languages that have such features.

3.2.2 Gender

As can be seen in structure (119), there is no separate functional projection for Gender in Alexiadou (2020). Rather she argues that Gender is a syntactic feature on the nominalizer *n*. In her earlier work, Alexiadou (2004) presents arguments against positing a distinct functional projection for Gender which will be further explored in the upcoming section. Following this discussion, it will be illustrated how Gender can be integrated into syntactic derivation.

Alexiadou (2004) claims that the introduction of a separate functional head is justified if it fulfills two main criteria. Firstly, it should have syntactic effects, such as participating in agreement or serving as a landing site for movement. Secondly, it should have an impact on interpretation and pronunciation, involving the semantic and morphological interfaces.

As far as the syntactic activity is concerned, Gender is in striking contrast with Number which is the landing site for movement. This line of this argumentation is advanced in Ritter (1992) who suggests that Gender marking is derivational and involves affixation in the lexicon while Number is considered to be inflectional because it requires head movement.

Consequently, the only syntactic effect of Gender is agreement. Alexiadou (2004) analyzes Romance languages (Spanish, Italian) and Greek and Hebrew and identifies a common feature among them regarding Gender. Specifically, she observes that in these languages, Adjectives agree with Nouns in terms of Gender.

Similarly with semantic effects, Number features have clear semantic implications as they determine whether the Noun is interpreted as singular of plural. On the other hand, Gender does not have consistent interpretation associated with biological sex. This might be possible in some languages, for example, in Tamil where feminine Nouns refer to human females, masculine Nouns to human males and neuter to non-human entities. However, other languages, assign grammatical Gender to inanimate Nouns. For example, the Czech word *židle* 'chair ' is classified as feminine Gender.

Moreover, some nouns in human languages are not even specified for Gender and need to enter into an agreement relationship with a human referent to be assigned this value. This is typical for nouns which are marked as [+HUMAN]. Alexiadou (2017b) supports this view by analyzing the behavior of Nouns under ellipsis, leading her to classify them into three distinct classes.

To begin, let us examine the variation within Class I of [+HUMAN] Nouns in elliptical contexts. Notice that in (121a) the masculine Noun is capable of licensing feminine ellipsis. However, the reverse is not true, as seen in (121b) where the feminine Noun cannot license masculine ellipsis.

(121)	Class I										
a.	*O*	*Petros*	*ine*	*kalos*	*dhaskalos*	*ala*	*i*	*Maria*	*ina*	*mia*	*kakia.*
	the	Petris	is	good$_M$	teacher$_M$	but	the	Maria	is	a$_F$	bad$_F$
	'Peter is a good teacher but Maria is a bad one.'										
b.	**I*	*Maria*	*ine*	*kali*	*dhaskala*	*ala*	*o*	*Petros*	*ine*	*enas*	*kakos.*
	the	Maria	is	good$_F$	teacher$_F$	but	the	Petros	is	a$_M$	bad$_M$
	*'Mary is a good teacher but Peter is a bad one.'										

Source: Alexiadou (2017b, p. 14)

Alexiadou (2017b) argues that the above phenomenon can be explained by the presence of derivational Gender morphology in feminine Nouns, which cannot be overridden by ellipsis. On the other hand, the default inflection of masculine Nouns allows for such licensing.

In contrast to the Class I group of Nouns, the Class II Nouns exhibit a different pattern. In this case, neither element can serve as an antecedent for ellipsis in relation to the other:

(122)	Class II										
a.	**O*	*Petros*	*ine*	*kalos*	*adherfos,*	*ala*	*i*	*Maria*	*ine*	*mia*	*kakia.*
	the	Peter	is	good$_M$	brother$_M$	but	the	Mary	is	a$_F$	bad$_F$
	*'Peter is a good brother but Maria is a bad one (sister).'										
b.	**I*	*Maria*	*ine*	*kali*	*adherfi,*	*ala*	*o*	*Petros*	*ine*	*enas*	*kakos.*
	the	Mary	is	good$_F$	sister	but	the	Peter	is	a$_M$	bad$_M$
	*'Maria is a good sister but Peter is a bad one (brother).'										

Source: Alexiadou (2017b, p. 14)

For this second group of Nouns, Alexiadou (2017b) proposes that they are *inherently* marked for Gender and formed in a similar manner as the feminine Nouns in Class I, that is on the basis of derivational affixes.

In addition, there is a third type of Nouns in Greek where either element can antecede each other.

(123) **Class III**

a.	*O*	*Petros*	*ine*	*kalos*	*jatros,*	*ala*	*i*	*Maria*	*ine*	*mia*	*kakia.*
	the	Peter	is	$good_{M}$	$doctor_{M}$	but	the	Mary	is	a_{F}	bad_{F}
	'Peter is a good doctor but Maria is a bad one.'										
b.	*I*	*Maria*	*ine*	*kali*	*jatros,*	*ala*	*o*	*Petros*	*ine*	*enas*	*kakos.*
	the	Mary	is	$good_{F}$	doctor	but	the	Peter	is	a_{M}	bad_{M}
	'Maria is a bad doctor but Peter is a bad one.'										

Source: Alexiadou (2017b, p. 15)

In this third class of Nouns, Alexiadou (2017b) proposes that Gender is assigned structurally in the nominalizer *n* through agreement with a human referent in D.

To repeat the facts that have been discussed. We have identified three classes of human Nouns with Gender features that are not equal (although they can be phonetically identical):

- Class I (*dhaskal-a/os* '$teacher_{F/M}$'): Feminine [iGENDER] surfaces as derivational affix, masculine is the default inflectional Gender on *n*.
- Class II (*adherf-os/i* 'brother/sister'): All [iGENDER] located on *n*.
- Class III (*jatros* '$doctor_{F/M}$'): Structural assignment via *n* and D agreement.

The above-mentioned arguments highlighting the inconsistent interpretation of Gender and the absence of clear syntactic effects led Alexiadou to the conclusion that a separate Gender projection is not well-motivated.

In literature, there have been some attempts to introduce a separate functional projection for Gender, for example, in Picallo (1991). She argues that Gender has an effect at the interpretative component (LF). She also observes that Catalan Nouns are inflected for Gender:

(124)	a.	*el*	*gos-ø*	b.	*els*	*goss-o-s*
		the_{M}	dog_{M}		$the_{M.PL}$	$dog_{M.PL}$
	c.	*la*	*goss-a*	d.	*les*	*goss-e-s*
		the_{F}	dog_{F}		$the_{F.PL}$	$dog_{F.PL}$

Source: Picallo (1991, p. 280)

However, Alexiadou (2004) argues that the presence or absence of post-stem vowels in Nouns expresses *inflectional class* rather than Gender. The members in this class share nothing more than the property of having a particular *class marker* and the choice of vowel does not correlate with Gender. Words can have feminine *a*-vowel and trigger masculine agreement.

If Gender is not projected as its own functional category, it must be associated with another head that can accommodate the Gender feature. Ritter (1992) proposes that Gender is located on the Num head. She observes that in certain languages, Number and Gender are expressed by portmanteau morphemes. This phenomenon is also present in Czech where it is not always clear whether suffixes on Czech Nouns express Number, Case or Gender, see the examples below:

(125) **PLURAL**

	NEUTRUM		**MASCULINE**		**FEMININE**	
NOM	*měst-A*	*moř-E*	*muž-I*	*stroj-E*	*růž-E*	*žen-Y*
	$\text{city}_{\text{NT.PL}}$	$\text{sea}_{\text{NT.PL}}$	$\text{men}_{\text{M.PL}}$	$\text{machine}_{\text{M.PG}}$	$\text{rose}_{\text{F.PL}}$	$\text{women}_{\text{F.PL}}$

SINGULAR

NOM	*měst-O*	*moř-E*	*muž*	*stroj*	*růž-E*	*žen-A*
	$\text{city}_{\text{NT.SG}}$	$\text{sea}_{\text{NT.SG}}$	$\text{man}_{\text{M.SG}}$	$\text{machine}_{\text{M.SG}}$	$\text{rose}_{\text{F.SG}}$	$\text{woman}_{\text{F.SG}}$

The portmanteau morphemes, however, according to Alexiadou (2004) cannot serve as conclusive evidence for the co-occurrence of Gender and Number on a single functional head. In the framework of Distributed Morphology, there is the concept of a *Fusion* operation, which allows for the fusion of two functional heads into a single morphological node.

If Gender can fuse with Number, it indicates their close proximity within the functional projection. Hence, Alexiadou (2017b), building on Kramer's (2015) work, assigns the location of Gender features to the nominalizer *n*. This methodology will be thoroughly discussed and examined in the upcoming section.

3.2.2.1 Semantic vs. Grammatical Gender

Kramer's approach highlights a distinction between semantic and arbitrary gender, which helps to resolve inconsistencies in gender interpretation.

Semantic gender is rooted in specific semantic properties, like male/female or animate/inanimate distinctions, while arbitrary gender lacks such semantic grounding. Kramer's cross-linguistic analysis delves into this differentiation by proposing interpretable and uninterpretable versions of gender features for each gender category, such as masculine and feminine. In this framework, natural gender is viewed as an interpretable feature associated with the nominalizer *n*, whereas arbitrary gender is seen as its uninterpretable counterpart.

Kramer (2015) also supposes that arbitrary Gender is valued and does not need to be checked neither enter into Agree relation. She stresses that it is unvalued features that cause a crash while uninterpretable valued features are simply ignored by the semantics, see the discussion regarding the types of features and their checking in section 2.1.1. In that section, it was proposed that valuation and interpretability can be independent and in fact Pesetsky and Torrego (2007) have questioned in their footnote 15 the assumption that uninterpretable features must be checked/deleted/eliminated before the syntax-semantics interface.

Let's examine the application of this framework to the Greek language, as discussed by Alexiadou (2021). She adopts a feature specification originally developed by Markopoulos (2018) for Greek. In this specification, the [+/-HUMAN] dimension corresponds to the interpretable Gender features and the [+/-FEM] dimension pertains to uninterpretable Gender features:

(126)		Adapted from Alexiadou (2021, p. 11)	
	a.	n [+human, +feminine]	→ FEMININE
	b.	n [+human, –feminine]	→ MASCULINE
	c.	n [+human]	→ MASCULINE
	d.	n [-human]	→ NEUTER
	e.	n	→ NEUTER
	f.	n [+feminine]	→ FEMIMINE
	g.	n [–feminine]	→ MASCULINE

Structurally, in the case of Nouns such as *woman* with the features [+HUMAN] and [+FEM], they will be introduced into the structure with two *n* heads. The *n* head with the feature [+HUMAN] will select the root √woman, and then the *n* head with the feature [+FEM] will select for the *n* head with the feature [+HUMAN]. On the other hand, Nouns with grammatical Gender will have only one *n* head, either with the feature [-HUMAN] or [+/-FEM]. These different 'flavors' of the *n* head can be seen below:

(127) Flavors of *n* head (adapted from Markopoulos 2018)

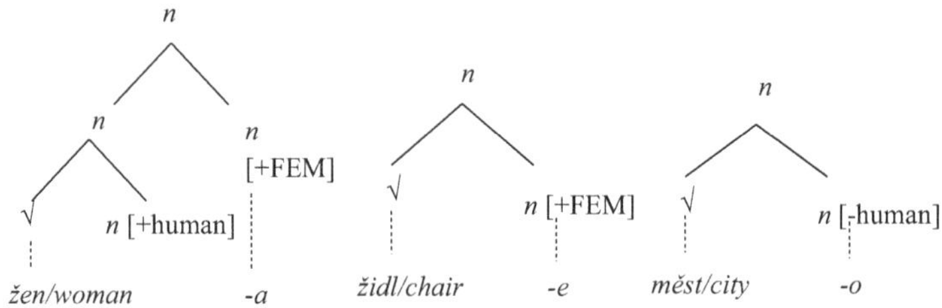

In this system, there are two possibilities for neuter defaults. It can be a plain head which is completely underspecified for humanness. Alternatively, neuter defaults can arise when non-human Nouns are *underspecified* with respect to the feature [+/-FEM]. Markoupoulous (2018) shows that [-HUMAN] Nouns are deverbal Nouns and refer to inanimate objects, it is therefore reasonable to assign them the feature [-HUMAN].

A similar kind of underspecification can also be observed in the masculine Gender. The masculine Gender of a human Noun may derive from either a *n* [+HUMAN] [-FEM] or a *n* [+HUMAN] head. This distinction captures the different behavior exhibited by Nouns like *aðerfós* 'brother' and *ðáskalos* 'teacher' in elliptical structures in Greek.

3.2.3 Outer vs. Lexical Plurality

Alexiadou (2020) respects the arguments presented by Borer (2005a) regarding the Division and Number layers. However, she introduces further distinctions within the category of Plural. She distinguishes between *outer* plurality and *lexical* plurality. Lexical plurality is instantiated by Pluralia tantum Nouns such as *scissors*, and it is located on the nominalizer *n*. On the other hand, outer plurality can be further divided into the dividing function and counting function of plural. The dividing plural corresponds to Borer's concept of division in the Classifier CL^{max}, where the mass stuff is divided in order to be counted in NumP (#P). In Borer's framework, plural is not simply a multiplication of singulars, and it can create divisions that do not align with a canonical singular form, see Borer's (2005a, p. 120) example below:

(128) *My kid sister drew* ***circles*** *(all morning)/(*in half an hour).*

The interpretation of (128) is consistent with the fact that no single circle has been drawn. It also triggers *atelic* effects. The counting plural, on the other hand, is a multiplication of singulars.

The concept of the three types of a plural and their different syntactic positions is assumed to be represented in the structure below. Notice that in contrast to Borer in the above scheme (94) where plural morpheme in English is positioned in the Classifier Phrase (Alexiadou's DivP), Alexiadou (2021) establishes two structural positions for English plural morpheme *-s*, namely NumP and DivP:

(129) Structural positions of plurals

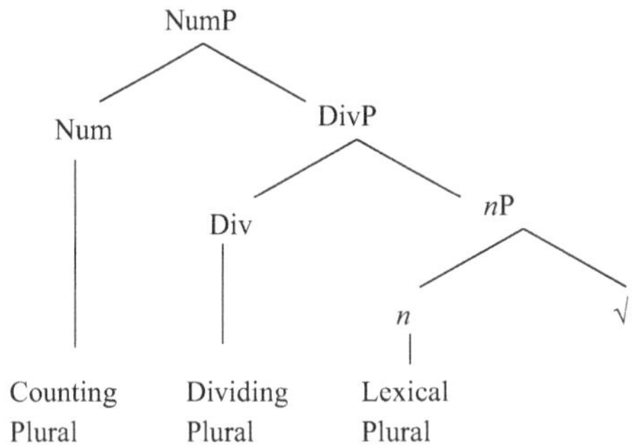

More linguistic data that support the division into Counting and Classifying plurals can be found in Mathieu (2014). He calls counting and classifying plurals as exclusive and inclusive plurals respectively. He correlates exclusive plural with cardinals, particularly in his analysis of plurals of singulatives in Arabic. In this language, collective Nouns need to be turned into individuals before they can be pluralized. Singulative morphology is in DivP while plural morphology is in NumP. Importantly, while exclusive plural can be interpreted as two and more, inclusive plurals as one or more entity. This aligns with the interpretation illustrated in (128), where *circles* can be understood as instantiating a particular object type.

The exclusive/counting and inclusive/dividing plurals are represented for English below and are taken from Alexiadou (2019a, p. 126–127).

(130)	a.	*Mary saw horses.*	Exclusive
	b.	*Every guest who brought presents left early.*	Inclusive

If we allow the possibility of double realization of plurality, we might wonder why we do not come across occurrences like the following:

(131) **international waters-s*

In her article, Alexiadou (2021) puts forth the argument that the absence of double realization of plurality can be attributed to the principle of economy. Additionally, she claims that English appears to have only lexical plurals in the nominalizer *n* and dividing plurals in DivP, while the inclusive reading of counting plurals may arise through pragmatic reasoning.

3.2.4 The DP Layer

The feature [+/-Def] is standardly related to the category D which is the natural host of the article. For Alexiadou et al. (2007), the functions of this category are as follows:

- Assigner of argumental status to its complement NP (see Abney 1987)
- Grammatical category which in some languages grammaticalizes the semantic notion of definiteness

The argumentative status of articles has been previously briefly addressed in section 3.1.2, demonstrating that articles are not optional elements within phrases, as proposed in Jackendoff's (1977) approach. To reiterate this claim, consider example (132) where singular count Nouns typically cannot occupy thematic positions (such as being subjects or objects of Verbs) unless they are subordinated to an article.

(132) a. **He found cat on the doorstep.*
b. **Cat arrived last night.*

In English, DPs marked as definite can serve various semantic and pragmatic functions, including anaphoricity, familiarity, identifiability, uniqueness, referentiality, general knowledge, and situational contexts. While these notions are relevant, they are not the focus of my study here and I recommend further reading in Alexiadou et al. (2007) for a more comprehensive exploration of these concepts. In this thesis, definiteness appears to be taken as a superordinate term comprising these distinct semantic/pragmatic concepts associated with it.

3.3 Language Specifics vs. Language Universals

In the introductory chapter, we have established that proponents of generative grammar adhere to the notion of an autonomous grammar module that is innate. By introducing the extended nominal projection within the frameworks of Hagit Borer and Artemis Alexiadou, we can further discuss what aspects are expected to be universal and what aspects are language specific.

Both authors argue that the extended projections are fixed and universally available in all grammars. This includes the functional layers within these projections, such as DP or NumP/#P, and their relative merge positions. For instance, D is expected to merge above NumP/#P and not above other layers. However, not all projections need to be present in every language, as some languages may be underspecified in certain projections. The absence of certain functional elements within a language's grammar can have significant implications for interpretation. This is evident in the case of Quantifiers, as demonstrated in previous section, particularly with Quantifiers like *much*. These Quantifiers lack a dividing function which hinders their ability to count discrete entities. However, despite this limitation, they still retain the capacity to express quantification.

On the other hand, language-specific effects arise due to specific options related to language-specific items or morphemes. As will be demonstrated in section 3.5.3, cardinal numbers serve as dividers in Hungarian but not in English.

3.4 Summarizing the Distinctions Between Borer and Alexiadou and Considering Czech Data

In this part, I will present a comparison between Borer's and Alexiadou's model for nominal functional projection and identify the relevant arguments that will be employed in my study.

To begin with, the table below outlines the labels used in both Borer's and Alexiadou's models for nominal functional projection. It will help us identify the corresponding elements in each framework:

(133)	**Alexiadou** (2020)	**Borer** (2005a)
	DP	DP
	#P/NumP	#P
	DivP	CL
	n	
	ROOT √	ROOT √

Each projection will be discussed separately, beginning with the categorization of roots and then moving on to higher levels within the structure.

Regarding the categorization of roots, Alexiadou's approach builds upon Marantz's (1997) Distributed Morphology (DM) framework, which emphasizes the need to categorize roots. In this framework, categorial nodes are directly attached to roots as the graphs below illustrate:

(134) Root categorization in DM

Borer (2005a) argues that such categorization is superfluous. I will adopt her perspective, which suggests that the categorization as N or V can be achieved through merging with additional nominal or verbal functional projections, such as D or T. This means that the lexical projection can be categorized through the functional structure itself. Additionally, Borer does not exclude the possibility of categorization through derivational nodes and introduces the concept of C-functors, as described in section 2.2.1.

Also, roots in DM are not assigned a specific syntactic category and remain category-less in the syntactic structure. In contrast, Borer's framework categorizes roots as V-equivalent in syntax through their merger with either the Extended projection or C-functors. This mechanism is visible in the schemes in (135) below.

(135) Root categorization in Borer (2005a)

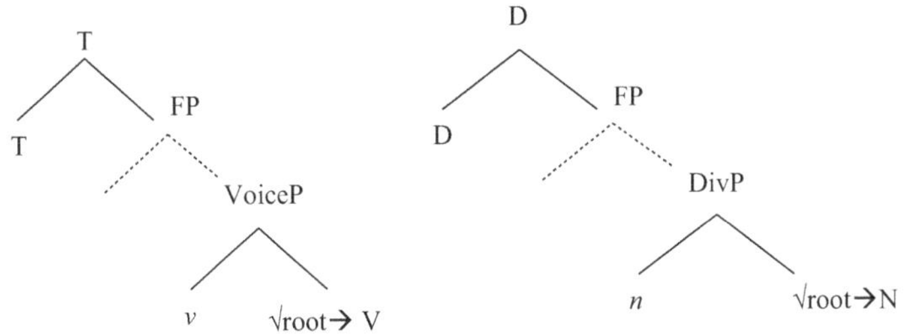

In our next discussion, it is imperative to consider Gender, which some authors, for example, Ritter (1993), posit as closely tied to the root. Neither Alexiadou nor Borer include a separate projection for Gender in their respective models. Borer does not elaborate Gender in depth and does not specify the locus of a Gender feature. On the other hand, Alexiadou (2020) proposes that Gender is a feature associated with the nominalizer *n*. In my analysis, I will diverge from both authors and argue for the inclusion of separate Gender projections in Czech. However, I will draw on Alexiadou's (2017b) insights and diagnostic tools to examine the behavior of [-HUMAN] Nouns in elliptical contexts and utilize her featural descriptions of Gender [+/-HUMAN], [+/-FEM].

As far as mass-count distinction is concerned, Borer (2005a) argues that Nouns initially exist as mass and then undergo division to become countable. She introduces a Classifier phrase (CL) and a Number phrase (#P) projection to account for these two functions. Alexiadou (2020) adopts this view but labels these projections differently, referring to the Classifier as DivP and the Number phrase as NumP.

In addition to this, both authors introduce various positions for plural morphology. In Borer's framework, plural is located in the Classifier phrase and functions to divide entities. However, Alexiadou identifies another type of plural called counting plural, which represents a multiplication of singulars. Accordingly, counting plural is located within the Number phrase. This differentiation between the two types of plural morphology is exemplified in (136).

(136) a. *Mary drew **circles**.*
b. *Mary saw **horses**.*

Example (136a) is compatible with the interpretation where no single circle has been drawn, while (136b) implies the presence of more than one *horse*. Alexiadou (2019a) argues for a unified position for plural morphology. In her analysis, she proposes that English has a dividing type of plural located in DivP, whereas the other type of plural results from pragmatic reasoning. The structural positions of counting and dividing plural are depicted in syntactic tree (129).

I will take over the structural descriptions for mass-count nominals, acknowledging the need for a unified position for plurals in languages. In the context of Czech nominalizations, I will argue that the data support locating the plural feature within the QP. To substantiate this assertion, I will draw on Jackendoff's (1991) concept of boundedness suggesting that the plural can introduce unboundedness even within structures that are already bounded in the DivP projection. Additionally, I will propose that this modeling of plural based on boundedness offers distinct advantages, as it extends beyond the nominal domain and can be applicable across verbal and other domains as well.

For the DP layer, both Alexiadou and Borer anticipate that the DP layer is the assigner of argument status to its complement NP and serves as the position for articles. While the precise implementation for the DP layer is outside the scope of this thesis, I will not discuss it in much detail. I will follow Borer's analysis that Determiners can have a portmanteau function, serving as both Quantifiers, dividers and markers of Definiteness. This means that some Determiners can obligatorily raise to D while other have the option to do so. This is corroborated by the data in (137), which has previously been observed by Jackendoff (1977):

(137) a. **The every boy*
b. *The three cats*

Lastly, Borer envisaged the operation of N-to-D movement, which involves the simultaneous projection of the abstract head feature and the movement of a listeme. For instance, the projection of plural, considered an abstract head feature, involves partial N-to-D movement. In contrast, Alexiadou operates within a different framework where the projection of head features need not be tied with movement. According to Alexiadou, plural is simply a feature on the terminal node. I also share the view that partial N-to-D movement is not fully justified for Czech, and I will provide further details on this topic in section 3.5.5.

3.5 Nominal Projection in Czech

Following the theoretical discussion in previous chapters and based on Czech data, I am proposing the structure for a Czech nominal projection as in the following scheme (138). Additionally, I am specifying the assumed feature content and provide examples of potential entries in this diagram.

(138) The nominal projection in Czech

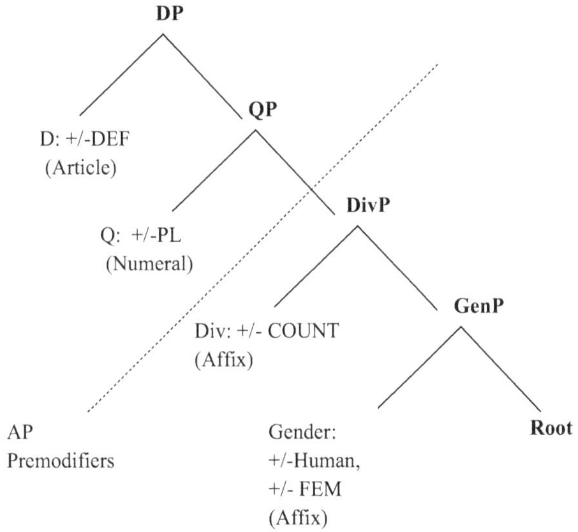

The features that are associated with individual projections are the following:

- **The GenderP** is related with the features [+/-HUMAN], [+/-FEM].
- **The DivP** layer introduces properties related to boundedness and turns the undivided mass Nouns into count Nouns.
- **The QP** in turn deals with features [+/- PL] and is realized by Numerals, Quantifiers and Plural.
- **The DP** layer functions as the locus of definiteness.
- Pre-modifying **Adjectives** can be introduced to the left of the root in the specifiers of functional projections but their specific position relative to DivP is uncertain. In Czech, there is no clear distinction in the positioning of Adjectives with respect to Gender and countability, as indicated in the diagram (138) with a dotted line for premodifiers.

Having outline the syntactic structure in Czech, I will deal with each individual functional projections in the Czech separately. At the end of the section, I will elaborate some processes within the Czech nominal projection, namely covert and overt N-to-D movement.

3.5.1 Gender Projection

The notable distinction in the Czech model proposed in (138) and the models used by Borer and Alexiadou—as they were discussed in the preceding chapters—is the absence of a categorizing nominalizer projection. I will argue that this category is superfluous and needs to have some additional functional role. Given that the nominalizer *n* in the Alexiadou's (2020) projection contains the feature of Gender, in my proposal this nominalizing function can be taken over by GenderP. One may wonder whether the inclusion of a separate GenderP projection in Czech is motivated and meaningful and therefore I am listing the reasoning for my proposal below.

The main argument in favor of taking Gender a separate functional projection is the role of the feature in the system. The systematic relevance of Gender for nominalizing the structure can be seen in various instances where it not only nominalizes roots but also other categories, that is, Verbs,

Adjectives. For example, German derived nominals with certain verbal layers are feminine. However, this is not an argument easily transferred into Czech where such examples have default neuter:

(139)	a.	*zniče-ní*	*města*	b.	die	*Zerstör-ung*	*der Stadt*
		destruction$_{NT}$	city$_{GEN}$		the$_{F}$	destruction$_{F}$	city$_{GEN}$
		'destruction of the city'					

As the analysis of the *-ní/tí* nominals in Veselovská (2001) and Karlík (2019) demonstrate, the default neuter in Czech as in (139a) often indicates that the structure is more verbal than other deverbal nominals. The less verbal nominalizations with the *-ba/ka* suffixes as in (140) have a marked feminine. This proves that the feature of Gender is contributing to the categorizing of the root.

(140)	a.	*stav-ba*	*stavět*	b.	*kres-ba*	*kreslit*
		construction$_{F}$	to construct$_{INF}$		drawing$_{F}$	to draw$_{VERB}$

As for de-adjectival Nouns, we can find examples such as (141). These are usually also feminine and share the root with Adjectives:

(141)		**ADJ**	**→ NOUN**		**ADJ**	**→ NOUN**
	a.	*krás-ný*	→ *krás-a*	b.	*slabý*	→ *slab-ost*
		beautiful$_{ADJ}$	→ beauty$_{F}$		weak$_{ADJ}$	→ weakness$_{F}$

Another argument in favor of Gender dominating immediately the root is the close proximity of Gender morphology to the Noun itself. For example, English as well as Czech Noun *actr-ess-es* 'her-eč-ky' where feminine suffix *-ess/eč* is closer to the Noun than the plural suffix *-es/ky*.

A significant aspect of Gender in Czech is its relevance for the choice of the nominal Case paradigm. Moreover, it is overtly present in the Czech fused agreement morphology. In the nominal domain Gender is overtly reflected on agreeing premodifiers (142a) and postmodifiers (142b) (Adjectives, possessive pronouns and Determiners) agree with the Noun in the same morphology including the Gender feature. Gender is also overtly visible in the morphology of participles, especially in the very productive preterite participle as in (142c).

(For the space reasons I omit the other agreement features of Number and Case in the glosses below).[22]

(142)

a. *ta/ten/to* *krásná/krásný/krásné* ***kočka/stůl/dítě***
that$_F$/that$_M$t/that$_{NT}$ niced$_F$/nice$_M$/nice$_{NT}$ **cat$_F$/table$_M$/ child$_{NT}$**
'your beautiful cat/table/child'

b. ***kočka/stůl/dítě*** *stejně krásná/krásný/ krásné* *jako ta ten/to*
cat$_F$/table$_M$/child$_{NT}$ equally niced$_F$/ nice$_M$/nice$_{NT}$ that$_F$/that$_M$/that$_{NT}$
tvoje/tvůj/tvoje
your$_F$/your$_M$/your$_{NT}$
'the cat/table/child as nice as the yours'

c. ***kočka/stůl/dítě*** *zmizel-a/-0/-o*
cat$_F$/table$_M$/child$_{NT}$ disappered$_F$/nice$_M$/nice$_{NT}$
'the cat/table/child disappeared'

Given the free constituent order in Czech, the fused agreement morphology inside both the nominal and verbal domains makes Gender a feature of vital importance for the analysis of the syntactic relations.

22 Czech is an inflecting language, and agreement can be found inside both nominal and verbal domain. The Czech examples, if containing all features of each lexical entry in the gloss, would be very long. Moreover, the labels of some features and feature clusters may be theoretically controversial. Therefore, in the glosses, I am going to provide only the features relevant for the present discussion.

3.5.1.1 Grammatical vs. Semantic Gender

Czech Gender has also an impact on interpretation, and it can be divided into grammatical and semantic Gender. The semantic Gender pertains to [+HUMAN] Nouns and reflects the biological sex.[23]

Apart from the Nouns high in animacy, the grammatical Gender in Czech is not intrinsically related to any specific (semantic) feature. It is a formal feature which assigns words to particular declension types. [-HUMAN] Nouns can then be masculine, feminine and neuter. To illustrate this, the word *Mary* would be interpreted at LF as feminine due to her biological Gender while the word *židle* 'chair' would be feminine too, although this feature does not carry any specific interpretation.

Alexiadou (2017b) observes that human denoting Nouns reveal the most mismatches between form and meaning. Let's consider the classes of [+HUMAN] Nouns in Czech based on their behavior in elliptical contexts, as described in section 3.2.2. Applying this analysis to Czech, we find that Czech has only the first two classes as seen in (143) and (144). Examples belonging to Class III, which are grammatical in Greek, are not possible in Czech (145).

Class I

(143)	a.	*Petr*	*je*	*dobrý*	*učitel,*	*ale*	*Marie*	*není*	*dobrá.*
		Peter	be$_{AGR}$[24]	good$_{M}$	teacher$_{M}$	but	Mary	not be	good$_{F}$
		'Peter is a good teacher but Mary isn't a good one.'							
	b.	**Marie*	*je*	*dobrá*	*učitelka*	*ale*	*Petr*	*není*	*dobrý.*
		Mary	be	good$_{F}$	teacher$_{F}$	but	Peter	not be	good$_{M}$
		*'Mary is a good teacher but Peter isn't a good one.'							

23 I am leaving aside many lexical entries denoting young HUMANs and other animates—like *děcko/dítě* 'child', *děvče* 'young female', or *hříbě* 'colt', *kotě* 'kitten'—which are assigned a neuter Gender. The way (and reason) for the underspecified Gender here is beyond the scope of this work.

24 For the space reasons I am not going to mark the subject-predicate agreement features in my Czech examples. The so-called verbal agreement features of Person and Number are in Czech marked by a morpheme on the initial part of the possibly analytic predicate, while Gender (and Number) are features overtly realized on the following 'adjectival' participles. Those interested in exact distribution of agreement features in Czech can see Veselovská (2022).

Class II

(144) a. **Petr je dobrý bratr, ale Marie není dobrá.*
Peter be good$_M$ brother$_M$ but Mary not be fine$_F$
*'Peter is a good brother but Mary isn't a good one.'

b. **Marie je dobrá sestra ale Petr není dobrý.*
Mary be good$_F$ sister$_F$ but Peter not be bad$_M$
*'Mary is a good sister but Peter isn't a good one.'

Class III

(145) a. **Petr je dobrý doktor, ale Marie není dobrá.*
Peter be good$_M$ doctor$_M$ but Mary not be good$_F$
*'Peter is a good doctor but Maria isn't a good one.'

b. **Marie je dobrá doktor, ale Petr není dobrý.*
Mary be good$_F$ doctor but Peter not be good$_M$
'Maria is a bad doctor but Peter isn't a good one.'

The data presented in (143)–(145) can be interpretated in such a way that the feminine Nouns in Class I and both masculine and feminine in Class II must have derivational Gender morphology, while the masculine Nouns in Class II show a *default* inflection. This is evident from the fact that derivation cannot be overridden by ellipsis whereas inflection can.

I interpret the outcomes of the above discussion into the analysis in the following way: the derivative morphology will be represented by the head GenderP [+HUMAN, +/-FEM] while the inflectional default morphology will correspondent to the head with features GenderP [+HUMAN].

After examining various types of Nouns, we can finally outline the system of Gender licensing in Czech and summarize the options in (146).

(146) Gender features in Czech

[+human, +feminine]	→ FEMININE (Class I)	e.g., *žena* 'woman'
[+human, –feminine]	→ MASCULINE (Class II)	e.g., *muž* 'man'
[+human]	→ MASCULINE (Class II)	e.g., *doktor* 'doctor'

[-human]	→ NEUTER	e.g., *město* 'city'
	→ NEUTER	e.g., *stavění* 'construction'
[+feminine]	→ FEMIMINE	e.g., *růže* 'rose'
[–feminine]	→ MASCULINE	e.g., *stůl* 'table'

The [+/-HUMAN] dimension is associated with *interpretable* Gender features while the [+/-FEM] dimension is linked with *uninterpretable* Gender features. We can see that the situation described in table (146) is similar to the situation in Greek, where there are two defaults for masculine and neuter Gender. Also, similar analysis for Czech can be found in Veselovská (2018a) where the feature [+/-HUMAN] and its location either on N or D can account for the Czech Gender system.

To conclude this section—I propose that the overall function of the Gender feature in Czech, especially as a part of the complex fused morphology of the system of agreements, can be used as an argument in favor of taking Gender as a separate functional projection. It is often not of linear order, but the above agreement morphology reflects the underlining syntactic structure in Czech. This, I believe, provides a solid reason for designating the functional head responsible for noun categorization—specifically, the Gender functional head.

3.5.2 Division Projection (Countability)

I accept the idea proposed by Borer and Alexiadou (see sections 3.1 and 3.2) who assume that the root is not inherently marked for countability. It is rather related to a specific head and feature, which I will designate as a DivP. Following this framework Countable Nouns project the DivP that carries the feature [+COUNT] which subsequently feed Number projection (QP). On the other hand, mass Nouns project a [–COUNT] and such a feature will prevent the counting function in the QP. The Div projection is by default singular (i.e., non-plural); plural is added under the QP.

3.5.3 QP

In my analysis of Czech data, I will follow Borer's (2005a) theory and consider Determiners as lexical entries containing the features [+/-DIVIDER] and [+/-COUNTER]. These features are located around the projections DivP, QP and DP[25]

The table (147) below illustrates the three possible combinations of the [+/-DIVIDER] and [+/-COUNTER] features for Czech Determiners. The place they initiate their derivation reflects their feature content in the following way:

DivP generated entries:

Cardinal numerals as in (147a) initiate their derivation within the DivP projection and subsequently raise to the higher QP position within the nominal structure. This means that they can function as both dividers and counters.

In contrast, Determiners such as *jedna* 'one' (147c) function solely as dividers and do not raise to the QP projection; instead, they remain in situ.

QP generated entries:

Determiners defined as [+COUNTERS], [-DIVIDER] such as *mnoho* 'much' originate in the QP layer and check the feature [+/-PLURAL]. Interestingly, in this scenario, the divider is absent, leading to an effect predicted by Borer (2005a). Without DivP, mass nominal emerges which cannot be counted but can be quantified. Subsequently, the output in (147b) will be interpreted as a large amount of stuff.

(147)	a.	Cardinals	***tři***	*stoly*	[+COUNTER]	[+DIVIDER]
			three	table_{PL}		
	b.	***Quantifiers***	***mnoho***	*soli*	[+COUNTER]	[-DIVIDER]
			much	$\text{salt}_{\text{UNCOUNT}}$		
	c.	***Cardinal one***	***jedna***	*kniha*	[-COUNTER]	[+DIVIDER]
			one	book_{SG}		

Some Quantifiers, such as *mnoho* 'much/many' have a dual function. Besides serving as a [+COUNTER], [-DIVIDER] as in (147b), they can also function

25 In traditional taxonomy, there are no Determiners in Czech—assuming Determiners are in fact articles. Note, however, that many Czech items can also appear in the DP position, similarly to English articles. They also exhibit strict ordering unlike adjectival modifiers which do not obey any conditions on their linear order.

as a [+COUNTER], [+DIVIDER] and originate in DivP as the following example demonstrates:

(148)	***Mnoho***	*chlapců*	[+COUNTER]	[+DIVIDER]
	many	boys$_{PL}$		
	'Many boys'			

It is worth noting that in the above-mentioned examples, there is agreement between the Nouns and the Determiners in terms of Number. I propose that the feature [+/-PLURAL] can be realized on the Noun post-syntactically through the Agreement process, as outlined and explained in section 2.1.2. We can compare the grammatical example in (147) with the ungrammatical examples in (149) to illustrate the phenomenon where agreement does not apply.

(149)	a.	**tři*	*stůl*	b.	**jeden*	*stoly*
		three$_{PL}$	table$_{SG}$		one$_{SG}$	tables$_{PL}$
		*'three table'			*'one tables'	

When it comes to bare Nouns, the dividing and counting function is carried out by the positively valued features which are realized on the root of the Noun post-syntactically by lowering as singular or plural morphemes.

(150)	a.	*knih-a*/book$_{F.SG}$	[-COUNTER]	[+DIVIDER]
	b.	*knih-y*/books$_{F.PL}$	[+COUNTER]	[+DIVIDER]

One may wonder why the Quantifiers *mnoho* 'many/much' in (151a), (151b), and the cardinal *tři* 'three' (151c) do not exhibit the same subject-verb agreement when they both check the feature [+PL].

(151)	a.	***Mnoho/Pět***	*chlapců*	*bylo*	*ve škole.*
		Many$_{SG}$/Five$_{SG}$	boy$_{PL.COUNT}$	be$_{3.SG}$	at school
		'Many/Five boys were at school.'			
	b.	***Mnoho***	*soli*	*bylo*	*na stole.*
		Much	salt$_{UNCOUNT}$	be$_{3.SG}$	on the table.
		'Much salt was on the table.'			

c. ***Dva/Tři/Čtyři*** *chlapci* *byli* *ve škole.*
Two_{PL}/Three_{PL}/Four_{PL} $\text{boy}_{\text{PL.COUNT}}$ $\text{be}_{\text{3.PL}}$ at school
'Two/Three/Four boys were at school.'

The morphological distinction between the Quantifiers described above is analyzed in detail in Veselovská (2018a). The author used the labels Partitive and Agreeing Quantifiers. Following Pesetsky's (2013) analysis of Russian, the author argues that both kinds of Quantifiers can participate in Q-to-D movement, Partitive Quantifiers can undermerge to D, Agreeing Quantifiers standardly do overmerge there. I will briefly explain these operations and refer to Veselovská for further reading.

The undermerge operation, originally introduced by Pesetsky (2013) involves the right adjunction of Q to D, followed by the application of the Right-hand Head Rule (Williams 1981), resulting in the relabeling of D as Q. This undermerge operation blocks the features of Q. When D has deficient phi features, the S-V agreement can only be default. In contrast, in the overmerge operation, Q left adjoins D without the need for relabeling and no blocking occurs. Schematically, both processes are outlined in picture (152) and further described in Veselovská's (2018a) work (p. 118).

(152) Overmerge (Right adjunction, Standard incorporation) vs.
Undermerge (Left adjunction)

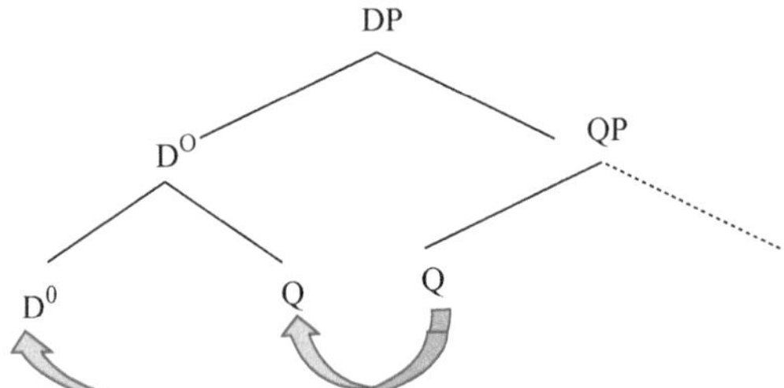

Also, Borer (2005a) predicts that [+/-DIVIDER] and [+/-COUNTER] functions cannot be assumed to be universal. An example that supports this view is seen in Hungarian, where cardinals seem to have a dividing function:

(153) *a két fekete kalap (-ot)* [+COUNTER] [+DIVIDER]
the two black hat(-ACC)

Similarly, Czech cardinal *jedna* 'one' has two specifications. It must be [-COUNTER] [+DIVIDER] as in the example (154c) on one hand, and [-COUNTER], [-DIVIDER] in example (154b).

(154)		CZECH		ENGLISH	
	a.	**dvě*	*listí*	**two*	*foliage*
	b.	*jedno*	*listí*	**one*	*foliage*
	c.	*jedna*	*židle*	*one*	*chair*

As can be observed, English cardinal *one* is not specified for the other reading [+COUNTER], [-DIVIDER] as demonstrated by the ungrammatical expression **one foliage*.

3.5.4 The DP Layer

In contrast to the belief held by some linguists, such as Bošković (2005, 2008) and others, I will assume in this study that Czech—although it does not have articles—does have the functional projection which can be labeled DP. This claim is defended in detail in Veselovská (2018a), and a part of the argumentation concerns the fixed ordering of the Determiner field, illustrated in (155).[26]

(155)	a.	*Všichni*	*ti*	*čtyři*	*chlapci*
		all	the	four	boys
	b.	**čtyři*	*ti*	*všichni*	*chlapci*
		four	the	all	boys

According to Borer (2005a), the definite value and mutual exclusivity of certain elements, as illustrated in (155), are attributed to the distinction between *strong* and *weak* Quantifiers, which can optionally or obligatorily raise to D and compete for this position. Borer explains the ungrammaticality of such combinations in English by the double marking effect that would arise if these elements were to co-occur in the Determiner slot (D). I will exemplify that this distinction can also be applied to Czech, although some

26 I will not repeat all the arguments in favor of the DP hypothesis here and refer the reader to the cited literature and studies summarized there.

modifications will be necessary since we cannot assume that all features of Determiners are universal.

(156)		CZECH	ENGLISH
	a.	-	**a the boy*
	b.	*nějaký ten chlapec*	**some the boy*

The elements mutually exclusive in English, that is, those which plausibly occupy the (obligatory and unique) central Determiner slot, can co-occur in Czech (156b). Nevertheless, there are some other elements, namely Universal Quantifiers, which might qualify for strong Determiners in Czech. Let us analyze their properties. First of all, Veselovská (2018a) shows that universal Quantifiers must precede numerals in Czech:

(157)		CZECH	ENGLISH
	a.	*všechny/každé tři jahody*	*all three boys*
	b.	**tři všechny/každé jahody*	**three all boys*

Also, universal Quantifiers cannot co-occur, which would be a signal of their competition for a single slot:

(158) **všechny* *každé* *jahody*
all each strawberries

Moreover, Borer (2005b) categorizes universal Quantifiers in Czech as strong Determiners due to the fact that they exhibit telicity effects and are not grammatical in perfective structures. Unlike cardinal numerals and partitive Quantifier such as *mnoho* 'many' in (159c) which can have a weak reading interpretation and occur in perfective contexts, universal Quantifiers (*každý* 'every', *všechen* 'all') in (159a-b) possess only a strong reading and are excluded in perfective structures:

(159) a. *Natrhala* ****každou*** *jahodu.*
pick$_{PAST.3.SG}$ every strawberry$_{SG}$
'She picked (*every) strawberry.'

b.	*Nadělal*	***všechny**	*dluhy.*
	$_{PF}$do	all	debts
	'He made (*all) debts.'		
c.	*Natrhala*	***tři/mnoho***	*jahod(y).*
	$pick_{PAST}$	three/many	$strawberry_{PL}$
	'She picked three/many strawberries.'		

Let me propose a structural explanation for this phenomenon. Borer (2005b) presents the verbal projection, as shown in (160), which can help us understand the data in (159).[27] In perfective contexts, prefixes like *na* assign range to the DP in [Spec, AspQ]. However, in our examples, the Quantifiers *tři* 'three', *každý* 'every', *and všechny* 'all' assign range to $<e>_{\#}$ in DP. This means that the prefix cannot assign range to the same element, as it would result in double marking. Instead, the perfective prefix can be realized as range assignment to $<e>_{d}$. Yet, the strong Determiners such as *každý* 'every' or *všechny* 'all' do not have this slot open, which renders it ungrammatical in this context.

(160) Telicity effects

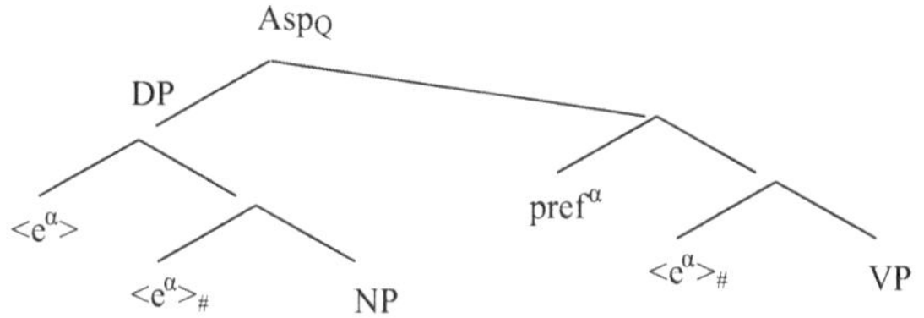

Source: Borer (2005b, p. 175)

Considering all these factors, we can conclude that the situation in Czech is in fact similar to English. Just like in English, strong Quantifiers in Czech must raise to D obligatorily, while weak Quantifiers have the option to do so.[28] The distinction lies in what qualifies as a strong Determiner in Czech, as the Czech counterpart of the English Determiner can have a different function and behavior in the syntactic structure.

27 This structure and the analysis of telicity/quantity will be the subject of Chapter 4.

28 The weak Quantifier *mnoho* 'many' undermerges to D. Thus, it does not involve the typical head-to-head movement due to reasons related to definiteness.

Additionally, similar to English, certain elements in Czech can serve as heads while others act as specifiers. In Czech, cardinal Numerals and universal Quantifiers must function as heads, whereas general Quantifiers serve as specifiers. The following graph illustrates these points and the possible derivations in Czech:

(161) Head vs. Specifiers in Number

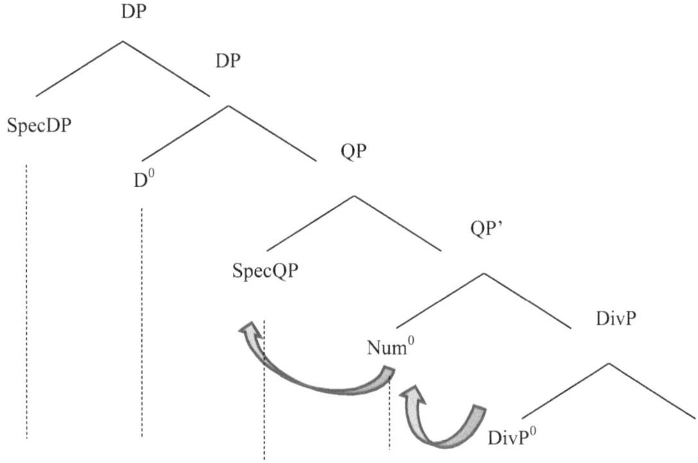

a.		*tři*/three	*ti*/the	~~*tři*/three~~	~~*tři*/three~~	
b.		*ti*/the		*tři*/three	~~*tři*/three~~	*chlapci*/
c.		*všichni*/all		*tři*/three	~~*tři*/three~~	boys
d.		*všichni*/all		~~*všichni*/all~~	~~*všichni*/all~~	
e.	*ti*/the	*všichni*/all	~~*ti*/the~~	~~*všichni*/all~~	~~*všichni*/all~~	
f.		*všichni*/all	*ti*/the	*tři*/three	~~*tři*/three~~	

Let us start with the derivation of *všichni tři chlapci* 'all three boys' in (161c). This example contains elements that must function as heads and its derivation proceeds as follows. The numeral *tři* 'three' originates in DivP and raises to QP. However, it cannot raise any higher because the position in DP is already occupied by the Quantifier *všichni* 'all' which requires the D position. Subsequently, the combination **tři všichni chlapci* '*three all boys' is ungrammatical.

Now compare the previous examples with the grammaticality of the following structures '*ti všichni chlapci* ' in (161e) and *všichni ti chlapci* 'the all boys' in (161f) . This time, the general Quantifier *ti* 'the' may precede a universal Quantifiers, indicating that it can occupy a specifier D position. In contrast, cardinals and universal Quantifiers do not have this option as was suggested above.

This analysis can also account for the co-occurrence of elements in (162a), which is permissible in Czech but not derivable within Borer's syntactic structure:

(162)		CZECH	ENGLISH
	a.	*všichni ti čtyři chlapci*	**all the four boys*
	b.	**čtyři ti všichni chlapci*	**four the all boys*

(163) *[$_{DP}$ *all* [$_{D}$ *the* [$_{\#P}$ ~~*all/three*~~ [$_{\#P}$ ~~*three/the*~~ [$_{NP}$ *tables*]]]]

Borer (2005a) explains the ungrammaticality of the English examples in (163) as a structural constraint. According to her analysis, *all, the, and three* must all merge in the #P projection. However, there are only two available slots in #P projection: one created through merger as a head and another through merger as a specifier. This lack of available slots prevents the co-occurrence of these three elements in the structure, as demonstrated in (163).

The fact that these elements can co-occur in Czech also suggests that Determiners, when they do co-occur, can be generated directly in the D position. This allows for their simultaneous presence in the structure without violating the structural constraints observed in English.

3.5.5 Processes Inside the Nominal Structure

In this section, I will direct primary attention toward the processes occurring within the nominal structure because those can be used as direct indicators of a specific configuration within the functional domain, namely of the presence of specific functional heads. The main emphasis will be on the consequences of both overt and covert N-to-D movement.

3.5.5.1 Overt N-to-D Movement

In her analyses, Borer (2005a) posits that the merging of abstract morphemes, such as the plural marker <pl>, requires overt head movement. The motivation behind introducing the N-to-D rule is rooted in the parallelism observed between the nominal and verbal domains. In the verbal domain, Emonds (1978) convincingly showed that the distinct positions of Verbs in English and French can be best accounted for by head movement (V-movement). For the nominal domain, arguments in favor of similar head movement inside one extended projection were provided by Longobardi (1994) and Cinque (1995) using Italian data. By drawing an analogy, Borer (2005a) anticipates that English plurals will undergo raising to SpecDivP (her SpecCL).

The N-to D movement could according to Borer (2005a) be realized either covertly or overtly. Should it be the case that the movement is covert, it would require a convention which would allow plural to be phonologically realized. However, Borer does not provide further details or specify the mechanism involved in this process.

If the movement is realized overtly, it would necessitate an additional constraint stating that Adjectives in English must never project between N and DivP.[29] As for Czech, I am not aware of any evidence that could prove this point. As demonstrated with the example (164), there is no difference in the surface position of Adjectives and Nouns regarding countability.

(164)	a.	*Mnoho*	*sypkého*	*písku*	
		much	loose	$\text{sand}_{\text{UNCOUNT}}$	
		'much of loose sand'			
	b.	*Ty*	*dvě*	*krásné*	*kočky*
		the	two	nice	$\text{cat}_{\text{PL.COUNT}}$
		'the two nice cats'			

Cross-linguistically, the N-to D movement is fully justified in Hebrew where Adjectives occur post-nominally and definiteness agreement between Adjectives and functional heads can be detected. Therefore, Borer (2005a) suggests for Hebrew abstract head feature [+Def] on N which triggers movement. Yet, no such signals are available in English and Czech. Free postnominal

29 In Borer (2005a), Adjectives are represented as adjunctions rather than specifiers as in Cinque, although within a bare-phrase-structure approach, the distinction, especially if we take into account the existence of multiple specifiers, is not significant.

order of Adjectives is not permissible. Adjectives in English and Czech can occur post-nominally only if they are part of a more complex structure, such as when they are modified by a participial clause (165):

(165) a. *Dostal jsem k Vánocům <u>ilustrovanou</u>* ***knihu***
got AUX for Christmas illustrated book
'I got for Christmas an illustrated book.'

b. *Dostal jsem k Vánocům* ***knihu*** *<u>ilustrovanou</u> akademickým malířem*
got AUX for Christmas book illustrated academic $painter_{INS}$
'I got for Christmas a book illustrated by a trained artist.'

There is some evidence for a partial N-to-D movement in Romance languages. Cinque (1994) presents data supporting this phenomenon in Italian (166), where N can undergo movement, but not as far as to D. A comparison between Italian, Czech, and English is visible in the examples below:

(166) a. $[_{DP}$ *ta* $[_{FP}$ *italská* $[_{NP}$***invaze***N [*Albánie*]]]]
b. $[_{DP}$ *the* $[_{FP}$ *Italian* $[_{NP}$***invasion***N [*of Albany*]]]]
c. $[_{DP}$ ***l' invasione***N $[_{FP}$ *italiana* t_N $[_{NP}$ t_N [*dell'Albania*]]]
Adapted from Veselovská (2018a)

In Cinque's analysis, the Adjective phrases (APs) are situated in the specifier position of functional heads. And we can see that in Italian the head N moves from its base position through the head hosting the first Adjective to a higher head, still however following the D^0. However, Cinque (1994) does not operate with DivP, and he deals only with the combination of the following elements: DEM, NUM (our QP), N, A. Thus, we do not have data from other languages that would support the movement to DivP.

As discussed by Veselovská (2018a), there is no compelling evidence for N-to-D movement in standard nominal structures in Czech although some examples can be provided using the contrast between the prenominal position of the Adjectives and the constructions involving Adjectives combined with indefinite pronouns *někdo/něco* ‘somebody/something’ as in (167). These cases, however, seem to exhibit characteristics more in line with certain nominal functional heads rather than simple N-movement:

(167)	a.	*někdo*	*velký*	b.	*něco*	*velkého*
		someone$_{NOM}$	big$_{NOM}$		something$_{NOM}$	big$_{GEN}$
		‘someone big’			‘something big’	

To conclude, I propose to separate the realization of an abstract feature on nodes from movement. As far as the plural is concerned, I will adopt the perspective of Alexiadou, who operates within the Distributed Morphology (DM) framework and who claims that the plural is a feature on the terminal node and can be realized on N post-syntactically, as explained in section 2.1.2. In this approach, the appearance of abstract features on terminal nodes is not accompanied by movement. Even though the realization of abstract features on terminal nodes might not involve movement, there could still be other reasons why N needs to undergo covert raising to D. These potential reasons will be explored and exemplified in the subsequent section.

3.5.5.2 Covert N-to-D Movement

In syntactic literature, the DP layer has traditionally been considered the domain responsible for encoding definiteness and specificity. However, in the case of Czech there exists a unique phenomenon where bare singular stems can function as both definite and indefinite Noun phrases, see (168).

(168)	*Petr*	*jedl*	*jablko.*
	Peter	east$_{PAST}$	apple$_{DEF/INDEF}$
	‘Peter ate an/the apple.’		

Additionally, Czech exhibits a restriction against N-to-D movement, further complicating the assignment of definiteness within the DP layer. The fact that the definiteness feature must be on the Noun is demonstrated in (169) with parallel grammatical and ungrammatical structures in English. Sometimes, definiteness can be overtly realized by demonstratives *ten/ta/to* which are regarded as equivalents of the definite article in English

(169) a. *Koupil jsem si nové (*to) auto. To/(*) auto je zelené.*
bought myself new the car the car is green
'I have bought a/(*the) new car. The/(*) car is green.'
b. *I have bought a/(*the) new car. The/(*a) car is green.*

I propose that when a Noun appears without an overt determine such as *ten/ta/to* 'the' or other Quantifiers (*mnoho* 'much', *tři* 'three' etc.) that could raise to D and check the feature [+/-definite], then the data argue in favor of only LF movement of a head Noun into the D position. This perspective is also advocated in Veselovská (2018a).

3.6 Chapter Summary

To sum up, this chapter has involved an application of the previously introduced theoretical models proposed by H. Borer and A. Alexiadou. I have explored how these models can be applied to Czech data. In this section, I will summarize the main findings and highlight the main distinctions in these models.

I proposed that Czech complex nominal projection DP contains four functional layers, namely GenderP, DivP, QP, and DP as illustrated in (138) and repeated below for convenience together with the proposed features of individual functional domains.

(170) The nominal projection in Czech

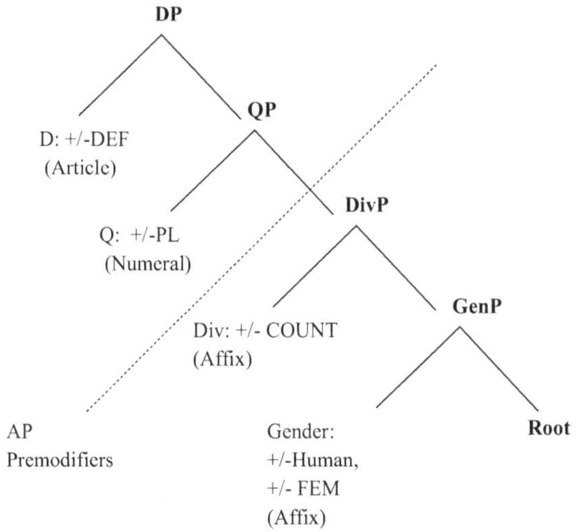

The core element of the above structures is the *root* embedded under functional layers that supply it with features and categorize it. In the preceding chapter I discussed also the features which are associated with individual functional layers:

- **The GenderP** is associated with the features [+/-HUMAN], [+/-FEM].
- **The DivP** layer introduces properties related to boundedness, with countable Nouns carrying the feature [+COUNT] and mass Nouns being [-BOUND]. The DivP also turns the undivided mass Nouns into count Nouns, and it feeds the Number layer where bounded Nouns can be pluralized.
- **The QP** in turn deals with features [+/- PL] and is realized by Numerals, Quantifiers and Plural.
- **the DP** in Czech is present despite the fact that Czech is an articleless language. The DP layer functions as the locus of definiteness, with certain Determiners optionally or obligatorily raising to this level.
- Pre-modifying **Adjectives** can be introduced to the left of the root in the specifiers of functional projections but their specific position relative to DivP is uncertain. In Czech, there is no clear distinction in the positioning of Adjectives with respect to Gender and countability, as indicated in the diagram (170) with a dotted line for premodifiers.

The table below provides a comparison between these labels and the ones proposed by Borer (2005a) and Alexiadou (2020):

(171)	The comparison of labels in the three models		
	Czech model	**Alexiadou (2020)**	**Borer (2005a)**
		DP	
(iii)	QP	#P/NumP	#P
(ii)	DivP	DivP	CL
(i)	GenderP	*n*	-
	√root		

The main distinctions in these models can be outlined as follows. Diverging from the perspective of both authors, I argue for the inclusion of separate

Gender projections in Czech as Gender in Czech is reflected in morphology and has an impact on interpretation. Additionally, I adopt the structural descriptions for mass-count nominals employed by both authors, which are realized through two projections labeled as DivP/CL and QP/#P/NumP. However, a noteworthy difference arises: unlike Borer's CL which hosts plural morphology and does not correspond to a canonical singular, the DivP in Czech model is by default singular. The DivP feeds the QP which hosts the plural morphology in Czech. Similar scenario as in Czech is envisaged by Alexiadou (2021) with the Counting Plural in her NumP. Besides, she introduces the concept of Dividing plural situated within the DivP which is employed in her subsequent analyses.

I believe that the positioning of plural morphology within QP aligns with Jackendoff's (1991) notion of boundedness. According to Jackendoff, the plural function has the potential to introduce unboundedness even within structures that are inherently bounded within the DivP projection.

Moreover, I diverge from Borer (2005b) and do not expect N-to D movement. It is not supported by the ordering of Adjectives within Noun phrases.

The above structure and characteristics of the distinct functional layers will be instrumental in exploring the countable properties of nominalizations. They will help us explain some characteristics of derived nominals, namely how nominalizations can be pluralized and interact with the verbal domain. For this purpose, a detailed analysis of the verbal nominal projection will be presented in the next chapter in a similar manner to the previous examination of the nominal projection, that is, considering the same two influential frameworks.

Verbal Layers and Their Relevance for Nominalization

In this chapter, I will describe the structure of a complex verbal projection as it was proposed by the two authors whose frameworks I adopted in the preceding chapters, namely Hagit Borer and Artemis Alexiadou. While providing a comprehensive overview of all layers of the verbal projection, I will pay particular attention to the projections associated with Voice and Aspect as these two layers are crucial for analyzing Czech nominalizations, which will be discussed extensively in Chapter 5.

The studies I will summarize below are *The Normal Course of Events* by Borer (2005b), and *Number/Aspect interactions in the syntax of Nominalizations* by Alexiadou et al. (2010c). Additionally, I will refer to other articles, especially those dealing with the concept of Voice, above all Alexiadou et al. (2006, 2015) and Alexiadou (2012, 2014b).[30] Following a thorough comparison of the theoretical frameworks suggested by these authors, I will apply their models to Czech data.[31]

30 Alexiadou backs up her aspectual analyses with thorough investigations of these issues in Slavic and English language by Borik (2006).

31 Previous examinations of nominalizations within a generative framework have recognized that Czech deverbal nominals exhibit compatibility with both verbal and nominal characteristics, albeit without making an effort to pinpoint the placement of individual features within particular functional layers. While Veselovská (2018b) and Čakányová (2022) address nominalizations within their articles, Havranová's (2020) dissertation represents an extensive work where such analysis is not included. Despite the description of verbal and nominal diagnostics, the localization of verbal and nominal attributes is confined to the VP and NP layers, with no specific projections and features attributed to them. Rather, the author employs *the Switch Categorizer Hypothesis* as formulated

4.1 Borer—Verbal Functional Projection

In her monograph *The Normal Course of Events* (Borer 2005b) the author proposes the following three layers for the verbal functional projections Event (EP), Tense (TP), Aspect ($Asp_Q P$) and a root labeled as Verb (VP).[32] The extended verbal projection is thus as in (172).

(172) $[_{EP} <e>_E [_T [_{AspQ}{}^{max} <e>_\# [_{VP}]]]]$

The projection of *Aspect* (Asp_Q) will give rise to a quantity event with telic interpretation discussed in detail in the following sections. The TP layer is associated with the feature of *Tense* and the *Event* (EP) layer hosts the event argument.

4.1.1 Asp_Q—Inner Aspect Layer

The functional node Asp_Q represents inner Aspect and is associated with telicity. The absence of this level results in atelicity. It's crucial to delve into the intricacies of telicity further, particularly as it will be discussed in the realm of nominalizations, where it intersects with their ability to pluralize.

4.1.1.1 Telicity as Quantity

In Borer (2005b), telicity is linked to the notion of quantity, where atelic events are characterized as being *non-quantitative* and *homogeneous* in nature. Her definitions of homogeneity and quantity are in (173):

---

by Panagiotidis and Grohmann (2009). However, it is only applied to specific types of nominalizations when it could potentially have broader applicability. Consequently, her structures of nominalizations lack consistency. I also disagree with some conclusions in this dissertation. For example, she claims that B/K nominals can be interpreted as complex event nominals when they have argument structure and take place over time (p. 113).

iii. *zkouška* *studentů* *zabrala* *skoro hodinu*
exam $students_{GEN}$ $take_{3RD.SG.FEM.PAST}$ almost hour
'The examining of students took almost an hour.'

Nevertheless, the arguments in her examples could be omitted and nothing testifies in favor of AS status of B/K nominals. They are rather interpreted as simple event nominals as described in section 5.4.2.1.

32 Recall that for Borer, the functional structure has the effect of categorizing the L-domain. Thus, the root projection will be Verbalized, that is, categorized as VP in the presence of TP.

(173) a. P is homogeneous iff P is cumulative and divisive

i. P is divisive iff $\forall x\,[P(x) \rightarrow \exists y\,(P(y) \wedge y < x)] \wedge \forall x,y\,[P(x) \wedge P(y) \wedge y<x \rightarrow P(x\text{-}y)\,]$

P is divisive iff for all x with property P there is a y, proper subset of x, with property P, such that subtracting y from x yields a set with the property P.

ii. P is cumulative iff $\forall x\,[P(x) \wedge P(y) \rightarrow P(x \cup y)]$

b. P is quantity iff P is not homogeneous

This perspective suggests that telicity can be viewed as an equivalent to the distinctions attested in the nominal domain between quantity and non-quantity nominals. Recall that neither bare mass Nouns nor bare plurals are quantities. Instead, they are homogeneous and do not project a Quantity Phrase (#P). Thus, #P in the nominal domain and Asp_Q in the verbal domain can be interpreted as parallel syntactic nodes devoted to quantity interpretation.

We can now elaborate further on Borer's (2005b) definition of homogeneity which encompasses both cumulativity (sums) and divisiveness (parts). If either of these requirements fails the expression is considered quantity. For example, *three apples* are not cumulative (*three apples* plus *three apples* does not give *apples*) as well as non-divisive (subtracting *three apples* from *three apples* does not yield *three apples*). By definition, then *three apples* is quantity. Note here also, that *books* are divisive and thus non-quantity because plural is not multiplication of singulars in Borer. In other words, there are no parts of *books* which are not *books*, *a single book* no longer being part of *books*.

Similarly in the verbal domain, *John read books* is cumulative because *read books* and *read books* is *read books*. It is also divisive because part of *read books* is *read books*. The predicate *read books* then is atelic.

It is also worth noting that Borer (2005b) does not predict that telic events must have an end-point, which diverges from many other approaches to telicity. Rather there is some kind of threshold beyond which the event can continue. Borer illustrates this with an example *fill the room with smoke* where the process of filling may continue after the room is full of smoke. Therefore, establishing telicity in Borer merely requires referring to some initial or final sub-interval within P which is not P. Clearly, *build a house* (under non-activity interpretation) will involve some sub-events which are not *build a house* and can be obtained by subtracting from *build a house*.

Having introduced the definition of quantity, let us demonstrate how quantity can be computed in syntactic structures. As mentioned earlier, the node that is responsible for this computation is Asp_Q. In languages such as English, Asp_Q typically receives the value indirectly through specifier-head agreement, transferring the value of the DP in $SpecAsp_Q$. Refer to the structure (174) as presented in Borer (2005b, p. 77):

(174) Asp_Q—Spec-Head Agreement

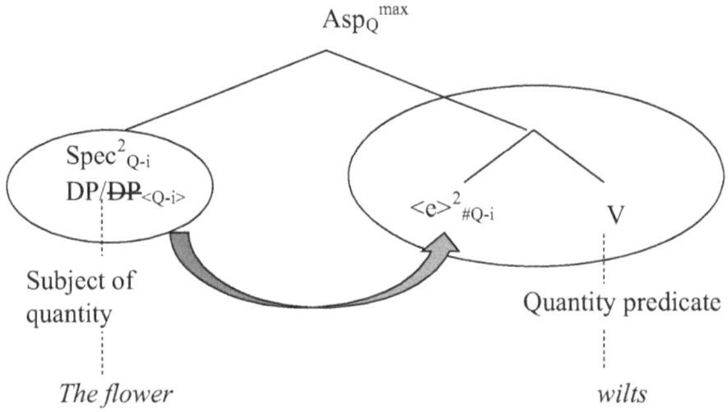

More specifically, the DP (*the flower*) designed as quantity with a value Q-i is assigned to [Asp $<e>_{\#}$] via Spec-head agreement. As can be seen. the presence of a quantity nominal can give rise to a telic event, thereby conforming Verkuyl's generalization in (175):

(175) **Verkuyl's Generalization (taken from Borer, 2005b):**
Telic interpretation can only emerge in the context of a direct argument with property α.[33]

Nevertheless, Verkuyl captures only a part of the generalization. Telicity in English can emerge even without the presence of a quantity DP. Thus, Verkuyl's generalization only applies to indirect range assignments. It does not account for assigning the range *directly*: via prefix, Adverb or PP adjuncts. These cases will be elaborated more in detail below.

33 Verkuyl is not specific about the nature of this property and its precise characterization has not been agreed upon. In Borer (2005b), it correspondents to quantity.

Locative prefixes in English as well as perfective prefixes in Czech, themselves historically locative Prepositions as Filip (2000) observes, are quantificational in nature and can assign range to Asp$_Q$ <e>$_{\#}$ directly (p. 70). I will discuss Czech perfective prefixes later in section 4.4.2.1, but for now the reader should be aware of this connection illustrated in (176):

(176) a. *Robin took* ***off*** *(in two seconds).*
b. *The army took* ***over*** *(in two hours).*

The sentences (176) are telic and no DP which would trigger telicity is present. Hence, locative particle must assign range to Asp$_Q$ <e>$_{\#}$, see below:

(177) [$_{AspQ}$ *up* <e^{up}>$_{\#}$ [$_{L\text{-}D}$ *take* ([~~*up*~~ <e^{up}>])]]

Adverbs or PP adjuncts can also be direct range assigners to Asp$_Q$:

(178) a. *Robin danced* ***twice*** *in two hours.*
b. *John ran* ***to the store*** *(in two hours).*
c. *John ran (*in two hours).*

The examples (178a-b) have telic interpretation not only by the availability of *in-X-time* phrase but also because they are not homogenous. In (178a) there is at least one sub-event (singular dancing) which does not fall under the predicate *dancing twice*. It cannot be thus considered divisive. Neither is it cumulative, *danced twice* and *danced twice* is not *danced twice*. Likewise, in (178b), we can imagine the path of running from home to the store and take some sub-event, for example, from home to the middle of the way on this path. Clearly, this sub-event will not be equal to *run to the store*.

To make matters more complicated, in Borer's framework it is not possible to determine when a certain adjunct functions as a modifier and when it is a range assigner. For example, the delimiters such as *to the store* in (178b) function as a range assigner while in the following example (179) the delimiter *to New York* should be viewed only as an optional modifier of Asp$_Q$.

(179) *Kim pushed carts* ***to New York*** *(for several hours)/(*in several hours).*

In this example, the quantity nature of the DP *carts* continues to play a crucial role in spite of the delimiter. Borer (2005b) acknowledges the complexity of aspectual issues and leaves these matters for further research. The quoted examples serve to illustrate the intricate nature of aspectual considerations.

While the level of inner Aspect computed in Asp_Q has been analyzed in detail in Borer's writings, the level of outer Aspect, which will be the subject of the next section, has not been explored to such an extent.

4.1.2 Outer Aspect—Grammatical Aspect

Upon examining verbal functional projections as outlined in 4.1, one might wonder if there is any other projection related to aspectual issues beyond Asp_Q. In fact, Borer assumes the presence Grammatical Aspect, which she labels G-ASP (Grammatical Aspect). It is the type of Aspect that is computed at the higher level above the Asp_Q in the sense of Verkuyl (1972).

In her later book *Taking form* (Borer 2013), she speculates about the semantic dependence between Tense and Aspect, with Tense exerting dominance over Aspect rather than the other way round. She proposes three different models for this scenario. First, G-ASP could be a complement of T. Second, G-ASP could be specifier of T and T could raise higher. Third, there could be a relationship between the head of the Tense Phrase and the head of the G-ASP Phrase, involving head-to-head movement or Agree without a complementation relationship.

Borer assumes that English progressive and time duration adverbials such as *for X-time* are instantiations of the outer Aspect (G-ASP). The idea is that they function as operators on existing structure rather than as their determinants. Thus, the *for X-time* phrases take structures without Asp_Q as their input and return a bound event, but which nevertheless leave argument assignment intact within the inner aspectual domain. To illustrate this, the sentence in (180a) is an activity and it remains so within the scope of the *for X-time* phrase in (180b):

(180) a. *Kim ran.*
b. *Kim ran for three hours.*

In contrast, the nominalizer *-ing* (181a), which will be analyzed more in detail in Chapter 6 and contrasted with progressive and gerundive *-ing*, as in (181b) does not operate on existing structures but prevents Asp_Q from ever emerging.

(181) a. *Pat's **forming** of a complex event (for three minutes)/(*in two minutes).*
b. *Kim **formulating** government policy (for several weeks)/(in two weeks).*

The fact that Asp_Q is excluded in sentence (181b) is corroborated by the ungrammaticality of the *in X-time* phrase which is a modifier of Asp_Q and requires its presence. Unlike, the *for X-time* phrase, the *in X-time* phrase cannot affect a change in event structure and it does not function as an operator but rather only as a modifier of quantity.

4.1.3 Event Phrase

In order to understand the motivation behind the postulation of an Event phrase we need to start with Davidsonian[34] approach which introduces an event argument as an additional part of verb semantics. For example, a verb such as *buy* is considered a three-place predicate. Apart from an event argument, it has an argument denoting Agent and one denoting what was bought (the Theme).

Borer (2005b) builds upon the Davidsonian approach, separates the event argument from other arguments and proposes the Event Phrase to host it. This has implications for Argument structure as will be demonstrated in the next section. Subsequently, the event structure correspondents to syntactic functional structure, which at least always contains the EP.

The main function of the EP is to establish a *predication* relationship between the EP and the following functional head. In this sense the verbal structure represents a parallel with the nominal domain introduced in 3.1 where we can find the same predication relationship between the DP and the following functional head. Just like range assignment in $<e>_d$ maps predicates to referential expressions, the range assignment to $<e>_E$ turns predicates to events. For instance, when the predicate is Asp_Q, it will be understood as a quantity event.

34 See Davidson (2007).

Moreover, EP projects above TP or independently of TP altogether (as we will observe in complex event nominals), that is, the EP can be licensed autonomously, not necessarily contingent on the presence of Tense in the structure. The head of Event, however, must be *existentially closed* and this closure is accomplished by a spatial rather than a temporal *operator*. Referential DPs (strong DPs) contain spatial illocutionary force and are thus capable of licensing EP, alternatively EP can be licensed by locative expressions.

4.1.4 The Projection of Arguments

Many authors within the generative framework, including Alexiadou, adopt the concept of Voice as developed in Kratzer (1996) which introduces external arguments and separates them from other arguments of verbs. Thus, a verb like *buy*, previously considered as a three-place predicate, would now be viewed as a two-place predicate. Borer (2005b) goes one step further and separates not only external argument but also internal argument from the verb.

Consequently, lexical entries (Verbs) do not contain any information about the projection of arguments as traditionally assumed.[35] For illustration, consider the following verbs in (182), which are typically associated with specific arguments in conventional frameworks. In Borer's model these arguments are licensed solely by the functional structure. To be more specific, the Verb *break* in the context of a structure like (182) licenses arguments, that is, it is transitive, but in the structure with no argument it can be intransitive. Hence, the Verb (L-head[36]) is just a *modifier* of the structure, alternating *only its semantic value* without impacting other structural properties.[37, 38]

35 In generative framework, the number of arguments that the verb selects is called *subcategorization* or the c-selection frame.

36 For the description of L-head, see section 2.2.

37 The modifier in this context is *not* to be equated with a specifier position

38 Functional heads, for example, are seen as pairs in which one member provides an open value, while the other provides the range assigned to that value. The latter is optional (adjunct-like) in the sense that *may* and *must* can both assign range to the same open value. This duality amounts to separating the syntactic portion of the structure from its semantic function. For Borer, L-heads do not have open values and are not assigned range, but distinct Verbs will have distinct semantic content. Thus, they rather modify than determine the structure.

(182) *John gave Mary a book.* *Mary broke her promise.*
give [V; NP, NP] *break* [V; NP]

In this model, arguments are merged as specifiers of functional projections, and their interpretation is regulated by particular syntactic positions. This idea of tying particular position with interpretation aligns with the UTAH (*The Universal Theta-Assignment Hypothesis*) proposed by Baker (1988).

(183) **The Uniformity of Theta-Assignment Hypothesis.** (UTAH, Baker 1988)
Identical thematic relationships between items are represented by identical structural relationships between those items at the level of D-structure.

Borer's concept of the AS is, however, not identical with the above. For Baker's UTAH, the argument structure is a property of lexical items: If a verb assigns a Theme in a particular position, this Theme role will be realized in this position throughout the derivation. Within this system, all instantiations of the verb, for example, *drop* must have the same thematic and syntactic configuration. Consider the instantiations below:

(184) *drop*$_{\text{TRANS}}$ *drop*$_{\text{INTRANS}}$ [$_{\text{N}}$*drop*] [$_{\text{A}}$*dropped*]

As thematic roles cannot be eliminated, Verbs such as *drop* which alternate between transitive and intransitive variants, must start as intransitive and the external argument is added through cause-type head. Yet, adjectival passives (*dropped*) are unergative and the nominal *drop* does not allow any argument, which causes complications for the proponents of UTAH.

In Borer, no complications with interpretations arise as the Verb entry is devoid of any information about the AS and the relation between Verb and its argument is not fixed. The Verb stem is simply embedded under one of the structures below. If a listeme is embedded under (185a), it will be unaccusative, if (185b) unergative and (185c) transitive.[39]

39 As far as intransitive Verbs are concerned, Borer (2005b) provides several arguments that unaccusative-unergative distinction is syntactic. The former includes an argument occupying the same syntactic position as a direct object, while the latter has an argument in the same syntactic position as a subject of a transitive.

(185)

a.	$[_{\text{AspQ}}$ [SUBJECT-OF-CHANGE	$<e>_{\#}$			$[_{\text{VP}}[_{\text{V}}$ *drop*]]]]
b.	$[_{\text{EP}}$ [SUBJECT-OF-PROCESS	$<e>_{\text{E}}$			$[_{\text{VP}}[_{\text{V}}$ *drop*]]]]
c.	$[_{\text{EP}}$ [SUBJECT-OF-PROCESS	$<e>_{\text{E}}$	$[_{\text{AspQ}}$ [SUBJECT-OF-CHANGE	$<e>_{\#}$	$[_{\text{VP}}[_{\text{V}}$ *drop*]]]]

In the remainder of this section, I will focus on derivation of the syntactic structures mentioned earlier and explain how arguments are integrated into them.

We start by examining structures that involve the projection of only one argument. In the first scenario, Asp_Q is projected, and the argument merges with it, but no Case is available in this configuration. Consequently, the subject-of-quantity (s-o-q)[40] DP *the flower* must move to a position where it can receive Nominative Case, likely to SpecTP. The resulting structure resembles that of unaccusative Verbs as in (186).

(186) Unaccusatives (see Borer 2005b, p. 84)
a. *The flower wilted in a day.*
b.

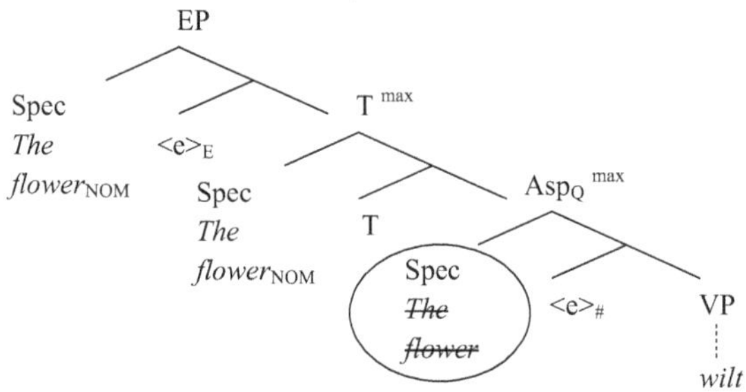

As for unergatives, they are the result of the following derivation: there is no projection of Asp_Q and the DP in need of case must merge directly with T as in (187). This structure is interpreted as atelic by default because atelicity emerges in the absence of telicity.

40 A role that is associated with an object which undergoes a quantifiable change. It is assigned to a DP if it merges with ASP_Q.

(187) Unergative (see Borer 2005b, p. 84)

a. *The flower wilted for several hours (and then I watered it and it recovered).*

b. 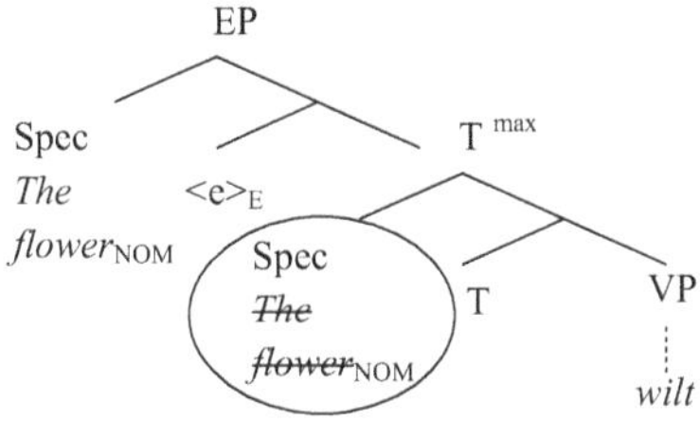

Finally, the transitive structure such as *Anna read the book* is depicted in (188). Here, the two arguments must merge as functional specifiers. Asp$_Q$ is projected and assigns Accusative Case which results in telic interpretation.

(188) Telic transitive structure (see Borer 2005b, p. 85)

a. *Anna read the book in two hours.*

b. 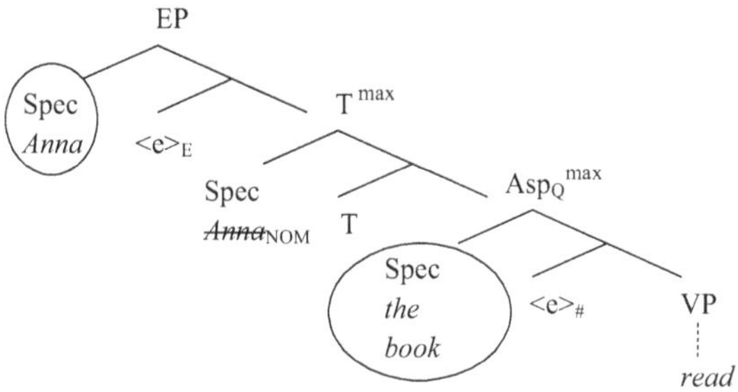

The remaining question is which structure is available for atelic transitives as in (189):

(189) *Kim built houses.*

Interestingly, the languages such as Finnish that distinguish atelic and telic direct objects morphologically, use the partitive case for the latter. Therefore, Borer claims that Case may be the determining factor in licensing the semantically vacuous layer which is not headed by <e>$_{\#}$.

This layer, which remains present for phonological reasons, is referred to as the shell FP (henceforth F^{s}P) by Borer (2005b, p. 109). She also postulates that the partitive case is generated on N, must be checked in SpecF^{s}P and cannot be checked in Asp_Q. Subsequently, telicity is blocked, and atelicity emerges.

(190) Atelic transitive structure

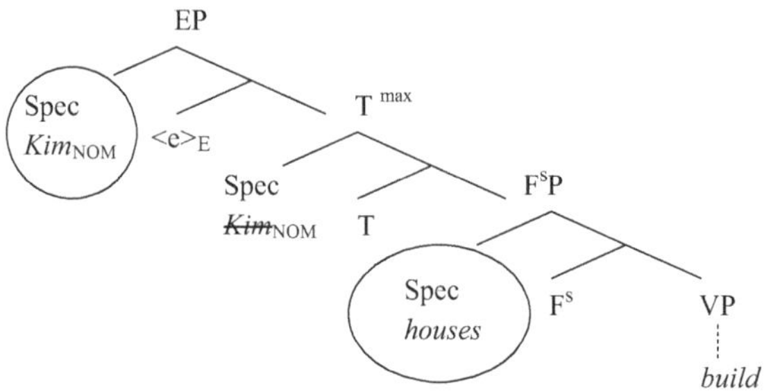

The preceding discussion has been focused on active structures; the upcoming section needs to concentrate on Borer's analysis of passives. This focus is essential as it will be necessary for understanding nominalizations, some of which, according to Borer, are constructed using passive structures.

4.1.4.1 Passive Structure

The *analytical* form of the passive Voice in English is according to Borer (2005b) *bi-clausal*. In this construction, there exists an active sub-event *e* embedded under an operator π, call it Passive Voice. This operator (π) is associated with the elimination of objective Case. Furthermore, the emergence of the participial morphology is not due to any absorbing the external thematic role; rather, it occurs because *e* cannot merge with T. The auxiliary is required to support T, and the morphological form of the Verbs emerges in the context of this auxiliary. This means that the participial morphology and the auxiliary are altogether disassociated from the properties of passive.[41]

Independent support for the separation of passives from morphology can be found in French causatives. In French causatives (191), the diagnostics

41 Similar analysis for Czech analytic passives is presented in Veselovská and Karlík (2004). The authors propose that the adjectival PF morphology of Czech passive participles is to be related to the Merge of the passive Aux inside the verbal extended projection which has morphosyntactic characteristics of a copula (and blocks the Merge of Agent).

of the passive are present, indicating a passive-like structure, but both the auxiliary and participial morphology are absent.

(191)	*Marie*	*fera*	*laver*	*le chien*	*(par Jean).*
	Mary	make$_{FUT}$	wash	the dog	(by Jean)
	'Mary will cause the dog to be washed (by Jean). '				

The emerging structure for passives is visible in (192):

(192) [$_{E}$ DP1 aux [$_{T}$ ~~DP1~~ aux [$_{\pi}$ ~~DP1~~ V$^{e\ \pi}$ [e DP2 [e ~~V~~^{e} [$_{ASPQ}$ ~~DP1~~ ~~V~~]]]]]]
Ext. arg + Originator   int.arg + S-O-Q

Neither DP1 nor DP2 has access to Case. Moreover, the passive operator π binds DP2 in (192) preventing it from moving and requiring its realization as pro$_{indef}$. Alternatively, it can be phonologically realized if a preposition such as *by* is available to assign inherent case to it. The Object (DP1) must raise to T in order to receive Nominative Case, then presumably to SpecE. The verb (V) also undergoes movement as anticipated and ultimately lands in the position occupied by π.

Passive constructions, along with a variety of structures that can be generated through the inner aspectual projection Asp$_{Q}$, will be subjected to deeper examination within the context of nominalizations that are built upon these foundations.

After demonstrating the functional structure of verbal projection as in Borer (2005b), we can now move on to Alexiadou's framework in the following section 4.2, to be able to compare and apply the corresponding parts of the two frameworks on Czech data in section 4.3.

4.2 Alexiadou—Verbal Functional Projection

Artemis Alexiadou (2020) in her article *D vs. n nominalizations within and across languages*) proposes the following structure comprising a Root and five functional heads to delineate the verbal domain:

(193)	[$_{CP}$ [$_{TP}$ [$_{AspectP}$ [$_{VoiceP}$ ***external argument*** [$_{vP}$ ***internal argument*** [Root]]]]]

In (193) the Root is dominated by the layer *vP* which functions as the categorizing head, that is, the verbalizer. This head induces event implications. The layer of *Voice* is responsible for introducing the external argument. *AspectP* serves as the layer of outer Aspect while TP handles *Tense*. The top, CPs projection, plays a role in discourse linking functions and resemble the DPs in some languages, in others they are like TPs.

In the following part, these projections will be investigated in more detail. The emphasis will again be on the lower functional projections that can be found within nominalizations, particularly Aspect and Voice.

4.2.1 Verbalizer = Level of Inner Aspect

Both Borer (2005b) and Alexiadou et al. (2010c) as well as Alexiadou (2020) cite Verkuyl (1993) to advocate the existence of the inner and outer Aspects. However, the two authors structure the layers differently. In this section, I will outline their perspectives, beginning with the inner aspectual level that encodes telicity.

Both Alexiadou et al. (2010c) and Borer (2005b) see telicity as a property associated with lexical Aspect/Aktionsart, that is an aspectual value composed within the *v*P domain. While Borer employs a separate functional projection for inner Aspect (Asp_Q), for Alexiadou it is the result of the *combination* of the *v* head and the root. The *v* head is a pure verbalizer and does not by itself correlate with any Aktionsart or transitivity properties. Nevertheless, the inner Aspect can be calculated within this projection on the basis of subclassification of roots and their point of merge.

Alexiadou et al. (2015) assume that roots fall into two main classes depending on their encyclopedic semantics: *manner* vs. *result*. These two types are integrated differently into syntactic structure which has semantic consequences. Atelic activities involve a manner root being merged as a modifier of *v*, as *hammer* in (194) on the right, while telic predicates involve a stative root/preposition or adjective being merged as the complement of *v*, as *flatten* in (194) on the left. In the former case we have mono-eventive structure, in the latter case bi-eventive, telic, structure as can be seen in (194).[42]

42 Embick (2004) claims that adjectival roots in verbs like *flatt-en* and resultative secondary predicates such as in *John hammered the metal flat* have different structures. While in the former *hammer* is the modifier of *v*, in the latter, *flat* is the complement of *v*.

(194) Telic structure (bi-eventive) Atelic structure (mono-eventive)

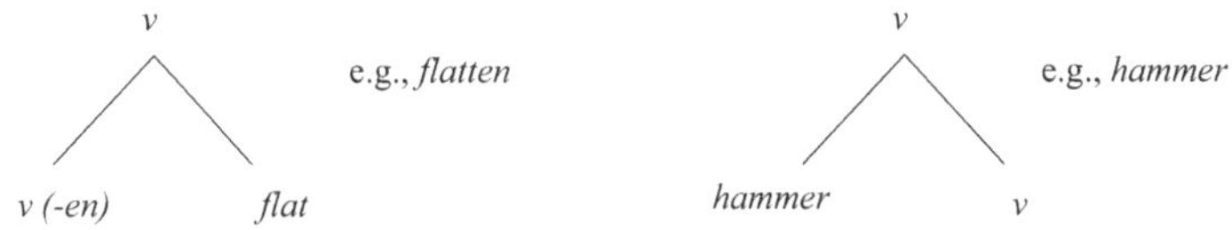

Whereas, in lexical resultatives such as *flatten*, the verb *flat* incorporates into *v* which is realized by affix *-en*, in case of compositional resultatives build on APs or PPs no incorporation is needed. I will return to this issue in section 4.4.2.1 when discussing the telicity of Czech verbs which is achieved by prefixes and show how this analysis can be incorporated into Czech language.

To identify telicity, specific tests are required. Alexiadou's research draws on Borik's (2002) study of Aspect as in *Theory of Aspect in Russian where the following* where the following three tests are employed:

1. **Adverbial modification:** Unlike atelic predicates, telic predicates can be modified by adverbials known as "frame" adverbials, such as *in an hour.*

(195)	a.	*Mary drove the car (for an hour)/(*in an hour).*
	b.	*Mary ran a mile (*for an hour)/(in an hour).*

2. **Conjunction:** When dealing with two telic predicates, such as in example (196b), the interpretation suggests the occurrence of two separate eventualities that happen independently within two temporal intervals indicated by Prepositional phrases (PPs). While this interpretation is possible, it is not the only one for sentence (196a), which contains an atelic predicate.

(196)	a.	*Mary drove her car on Monday and on Tuesday.*	ambiguous
	b.	*Mary ran a mile on Monday and on Tuesday.*	non-ambiguous

This combination of *v* with roots can specify the means through which the state is achieved. This distinction is similar to manner vs. result roots in Alexiadou (2010b).

3. **Progressive entailment:** When an atelic predicate is used in the progressive form, it implies the truth of a sentence with a verb in the simple past form, as shown in (197a). However, a sentence with a telic predicate does not exhibit the same entailment (197b).

(197) a. *Mary was driving the car.* → *Mary drove the car.*
b. *Mary was running a mile.* --/→ *Mary ran a mile.*

4.2.2 Voice P

Since Kratzer (1996), the Voice layer has been recognized as responsible for introducing external arguments. Alexiadou includes this layer into her verbal projection, as illustrated in (193). When we compare this projection with Borer's (2005) framework, we can observe that no Voice layer is utilized. The reason for this divergence lies in their respective assumptions about the nature of Voice. Specifically, Kratzer (1996) assumes that Voice is a functional head that denotes the relationship that holds between the external argument and the event described by the Verb. In contrast, Borer (2005b) separates the event from the verb, which is realized by the functional node Event Phrase. Subsequently, external arguments arise as entailments derived from this event structure and no Voice projection is needed.

Nevertheless, Agent roles or Originators, if not introduced elsewhere, originate in the Event Phrase, as was described in 4.1.4. Thus, the EP can be seen to some extent as analogous to a Voice projection.

As for the concept of Voice in Alexiadou, she presents her hypotheses in several studies: Alexiadou et al. (2006, 2015) and Alexiadou (2012, 2014b). In these works, she claims that there are two types of Voice heads in English: Active and Passive heads, and those two projections are designed to account for the following range of verbal forms in English:

(198)				
	a.	Transitive/Causative	Active Voice	*He murdered a woman.*
	b.	Unergative	Active Voice	*He runs.*

(198)				
	c.	Unaccusative/ Anticausative[43]	No Voice	*The tree fell.*
	d.	Passive	Passive Voice	*The window was opened.*
	e.	Reflexives, Dispositional Middles = Unergative	Active Voice[44]	*He washed himself/ This book sells well.*

Since nominalizations can potentially be constructed from all of these forms and thematic roles will influence our future argumentation, I will dedicate some time to discussing them in detail.

First of all, Alexiadou assumes two thematic roles introduced in Voice, *Causer* and *Agent*, illustrated below.[45]

(199)	a.	*He murdered a woman.*	Agent
	b.	*The storm broke the window.*	Causer

Causer DPs are predominantly found in causative constructions that convey a change of state. These Verbs are typically bi-eventive or resultative, as discussed in the previous section. They exhibit greater constraints compared to Agents, which can appear in both mono-eventive (e.g., unergative) and bi-eventive structures, as shown in the structures (200) below taken from Alexiadou (2014b p. 23).

43 Anticausatives refer to any intransitive use of a verb that also has a lexical causative use. The object of the causative variant is the grammatical subject of the anticausative variant, thus anticausative verbs are prototypical instances of unaccusative verbs.

44 In her earlier writings Alexiadou (2012) speculates that reflexives, unaccusatives as well as dispositional middles could contain Middle Voice, but this is refuted in Alexiadou (2014b) where reflexives and dispositional middles behave like unergative predicates in English. In Greek they are like unaccusative.

45 PP causers and DP causers do not have an identical distribution. PP causers as in the sentence *The window broke from the storm* are introduced in *v*P.

(200) a. Unergative structure b. Transitive/Causative structure

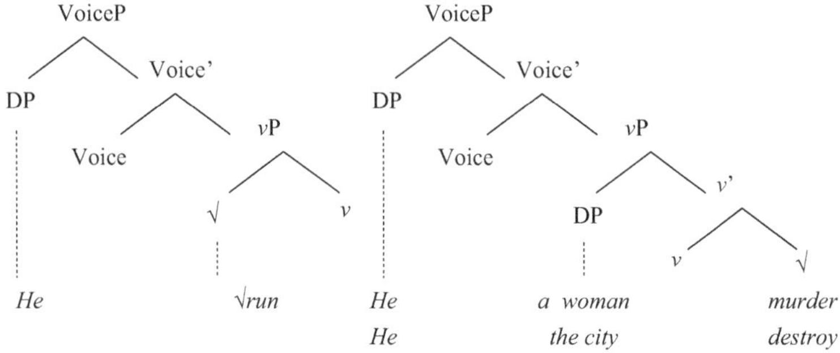

By contrast, unaccusatives as in (201) lack the Voice layer. Their decomposition is only into *v* with a change of state semantics:

(201) The unaccusative/anticausative structure, see Alexiadou et al. (2006, p. 196)

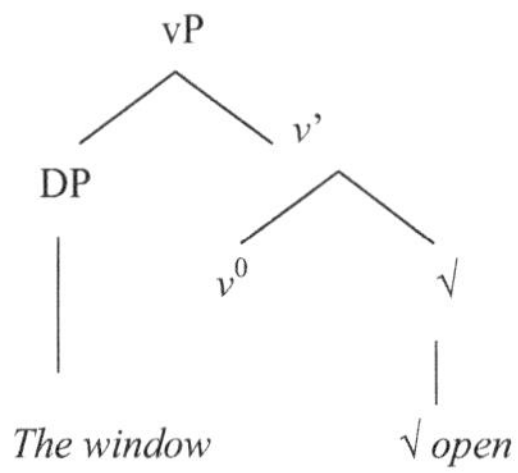

Furthermore, reflexives are of particular interest for us as the reflexive morphology is inherited in Czech nominalizations. According to Alexiadou's more recent view reflexives are categorized as unergatives with the structure in (200a).[46] Across languages, Alexiadou et al. (2015) distinguish between

46 See some tests in Alexiadou (2014b, p. 32). To name just one, resultative secondary predicates can only be predicated of internal arguments; in the absence of such an internal argument a (fake) reflexive has to be inserted. It is then possible to have resultative phrase over co-referentiality with subject Phrase. In this way, they pattern with unergative and not unaccusatives:

iv *The ice froze (*itself) solid.*
*John laughed *(himself) sick.*

semantically reflexive verbs (202) and reflexively marked anticausatives (203). One such language where these two types occur is German, see the examples below:

(202)	a.	*weil*	*eine*	*Frau*	*sich*	*anmeldete*	**Semantically reflexive verb**
		as	a_{NOM}	woman	SELF	registered	
		'because a woman registered'					
	b.	$[_{TP}$ T $[_{Voice\ P}$ DP Voice $[_{vP}$ v REFL]]]					
(203)	a.	*weil*	*sich*	*eine*	*Tür*	*öffnete*	**Reflexively marked anticausative**
		because	SELF	a_{NOM}	door	opened	
		'because a door opened'					
	b.	$[_{TP}$ T $[_{Voice\ P}$ REFL Voice $[_{vP}$ v DP]]]					

Alexiadou et al. (2015) assume that marked anticausatives involve non-thematic Voice projection—expletive Voice, where the reflexive element is merged but remain without any thematic interpretation. The other argument *eine Tür*/'a woman' is merged in *v*P. On the other hand, semantically reflexive verbs have two thematic roles, a nominative Agent *eine Frau*/'a woman' in Spec Voice and the reflexive marker in object position.

4.2.2.1 Passive in Broad Strokes

As the nominalization process is, according to Alexiadou (2017d) akin to passivization, we need to introduce this mechanism at least in broad strokes. For languages such as English, the passive construction is anticipated to merge at a higher level, positioned above the projection of Voice that has not yet projected its external argument, as illustrated in (204).[47]

47 Alexiadou often cites Bruening (2013) for a possible way of implementation.

(204) Passive structures

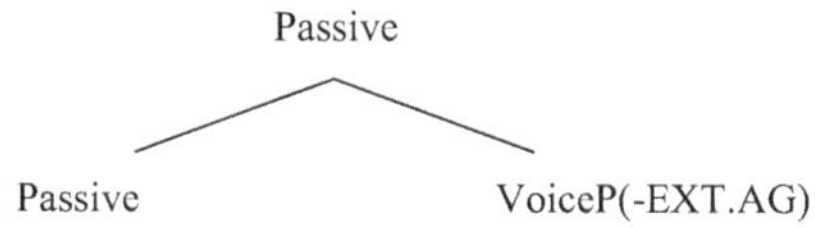

This means that passive is an operation on an active transitive verb phrase.[48] Additionally, *by*-phrases despite being adjuncts, strictly select for a projection of Voice.

Before concluding this section, I will clarify why derivations that contain a Voice projection are more economical compared to those that do not, such as in Borer's approach. Alexiadou et al. (2015) propose certain constraints associated with the Voice projection aimed at ruling out ungrammatical structures, as illustrated by the following examples:

(205) a. **The gardener wilted the flowers.*
b. **All the chickens killed.*

Alexiadou et al. (2015), divide verbs into following types which determine whether they can occur with the Voice P projection. This information is resolved at the level of the Encyclopedia.

(206) a. √Agentive (*murder*, *assassinate*)
b. √Internally caused (*blossom*, *wilt*)
c. √Externally caused (*destroy*, *kill*)
d. √Cause unspecified (*break*, *open*)

For instance, internally caused Verbs do not permit the Voice head and can only assign the Causer PP thematic role. Consequently, sentences like (205a) are considered ungrammatical. On the other hand, agentive predicates such as *murder* require Voice which is Agentive. It can only be formed on manner roots that do not express results. Hence, these structures do not exhibit

48 Passives in English cannot be equated with anticausatives because they do not reduce morphology. Anticausatives have active morphology which is not always the case cross-linguistically.

alternation with intransitive structures, commonly known as anticausatives, see the ungrammatical example in (205b).

The above-mentioned constraints help prevent the extensive overgeneration that may occur within Borer's framework, which struggles to effectively eliminate the ungrammatical examples in (205). Therefore, I will advocate for the inclusion of Voice into the verbal functional projection.

4.2.3 Outer Aspect

The grammatical, outer Aspect is located in AspectP projected above the VP level. Following the work by Verkuyl (1993) and Borik (2002), Alexiadou assumes that it hosts features that encode [+/-Perfective], [+/-Generic], [+/-Progressive].

For instance, in English, perfective Aspect[49] (as in (207a)) can indicate completed events in the past, while imperfective Aspect (as in (207b)) can express ongoing progressive actions.

(207)	a.	*John broke the glass.*	[+Perfective], [-Progressive].
	b.	*John was painting the wall.*	[-Perfective], [+Progressive].

The domain of outer Aspect is also sometimes called *viewpoint Aspect*, a term used by Borik (2002) and Smith (1997).[50] In their theory, viewpoint Aspect provides a temporal perspective on events. It locates events relative to a specific point of view known as the *Reference time*. A well-known metaphorical description of viewpoint Aspect effectively captures the distinctions between perfective and imperfective Aspects. It is given in terms of different points of view from which an eventuality or a situation is described:

- Perfective (looking at the event from the outside)
- Progressive (looking at the event from inside)

49 It should be noted that traditional English grammar does not call any synthetic verb forms in English "perfective" rather than "perfect."

50 Borik's (2006) notion of (im)perfectivity is not related to eventualities but it is defined in temporal terms. She claims that if the viewpoint is defined for the same entities as situation types, then it is hard to separate the two layers.

A typical diagnostic for an Outer Aspect is the Aspect shift, originally introduced by DeSwart (1988).[51] Alexiadou et al. (2010c) demonstrate this phenomenon using verbal gerund that can impose their own aspectual value irrespective of the inner Aspect of the main verb:

(208) a. *John wrote the letter (in three days)/(*for three days).*
b. *John's writing the letter for three days annoyed everybody.*

In the above example, the verbal construction *wrote the letter* in (208a) is telic which is signaled by the aspectual modifier *in three days*. Nevertheless, the verbal gerund imposes its own value and changes the interpretation to an unbounded one. Therefore, the modifier *for three days* is compatible with the construction in (208b).

Another indicator of the outer Aspect is its insensitivity to the inner aspect of the verb, allowing it to appear with both telic and atelic bases. This can be seen in (209) and (210) where the verbal gerund as well as progressive *-ing* coexist with telic and atelic bases:

(209)	a.	*Mary drew* ***circles*** *(for several hours).*	ATELIC
	b.	*Mary is drawing circles.*	
	c.	*Mary's drawing circles annoyed me*	
(210)	a.	*Mary drew* ***a circle*** *(in five minutes).*	TELIC
	b.	*Mary is drawing a circle.*	
	c.	*Mary's drawing a circle annoyed me.*	

In contrast, *nominal gerunds*, as illustrated in (211), are sensitive to inner Aspect of verbs and permits only nominals based on atelic bases. This is corroborated by examples (212b) and (213b) which are telic and consequently disallow nominalizations:

51 In DeSwart's (1988) progressive, perfect and duration adverbial *in* or *for X-time* are interpreted as operators which can modify eventuality. To illustrate this, *She climbed the mountain in three days* is grammatical but **She was climbing the mountains in three days* is not.

(211) *John's speaking of his father*

(212) a. *the train arrived in five minutes*
b. **the arriving of the train*

(213) a. *the balloon exploded in five minutes*
b. **the exploding of the balloon*

We can observe that the *-ing* morpheme can appear in various structures and form different types of nominals. This will be discussed in greater detail in Chapter 6, where I will explore how these aspectual phenomena relate to their ability to pluralize.

4.2.3.1 A Note on Perfectivity

The present perfect Tense in English should not be equated with the notion of perfectivity. In the studies comprised in Alexiadou et al. (2003), discussing the perfect constructions, the authors pose the question of whether the perfect is a viewpoint Aspect, as a kind of proposed in the preceding discussion. The authors argue that the perfective Aspect is, in fact, a relative Tense: "It relates the reference time to some other time in the past, say a second reference time" (Alexiadou et al. 2003, p. 14). This would mean that structurally Perfect phrase is located above Perfective phrase, akin to the configuration in our syntactic tree (214):

(214) Aspectual architecture

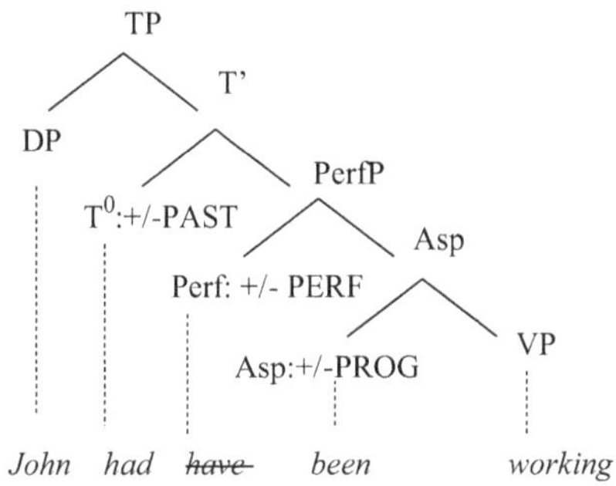

4.2.3.2 Boundedness

A fundamental concept in this study is Boundedness. Alexiadou et al. (2010c), in their article *Number/Aspect interaction in the syntax of nominalizations*, exploit this feature [+/-BOUND] (*Boundedness*), originally introduced by Jackendoff (1991), to draw parallels regarding Number and Aspect which has implications for the countability of nominals. These issues will be thoroughly explored in Chapter 6, but for now, let's provide a brief introduction to this notion.

Boundedness does not characterize only verbal domains, but it cuts across major categories and can be extended to nominal and adjectival domains as well. The upcoming discussion will, however, focus on nominal and verbal domains. For the applications of this feature to other domains, readers are referred to Alexiadou (2010a).

What is intended by boundedness is that unbounded entities are not located in space and time, as proposed by Jackendoff (1991, p. 19). This does not entail that these entities are absolutely without boundaries, it just simply suggests that such boundaries are not of concern. Take for example the countable Noun *apple* and uncountable Noun *water*. While the former has clear perceptible boundaries, the same cannot be said about the latter. Despite that, boundaries might be somehow present. When we utter the sentence: *There is a lot of water in this lake* we do not imply that the *water* is absolutely without boundaries, its boundaries are limited by the size of the lake. However, in this context, the precise boundaries of the water are not of primary interest or consideration.

In semantic literature, the mass/count distinction is frequently compared to aspectual specification in the verbal domain, as highlighted by works such as Bach (1986); Krifka (1989) and Jackendoff (1991). In the study by Alexiadou et al. (2010c), they propose that count Nouns are similar to telic and perfective events in being BOUNDED while mass Nouns to atelic and imperfective in being UNBOUNDED. To identify boundedness in the nominal domain, Alexiadou (2007) proposes the following criteria:

- Homogeneity (=Borer's divisibility)
- Cumulativity

In the verbal domain, Alexiadou (2007) claims that the relevant property related to boundedness is the concept of coming to an end-point. This can be tested by the progressive test, introduced in section 4.2.1, which shows whether the predicate contains any minimal parts. The activity running in (215a) does not impose any minimal parts. We can say as soon as Sue is running that she has run and refer to the running she has done. In contrast, the sentence in (215b) does not entail such inferences.

(215) a. *Sue is running.* →*Sue has run.*
b. *Sue is running a mile.* -/→ *Sue has run a mile.*

A word of caution is necessary. Although the notion of end-point, also known as *telos* or *goal* of a predicate, is often used to stablish its telic characteristics, Borik refrains from using it. For instance, even past activities can imply an end-point in atelic predicates, as exemplified by the sentence *Franz Kafka lived in Prague.* To address this limitation, Borik proposes the concept of homogeneity as a more comprehensive alternative, which can be assessed through various tests introduced in section 4.2.1.

4.3 Comparison of Borer and Alexiadou and Applicability for Czech Data

I have previously outlined differences in theoretical approaches between Borer and Alexiadou in earlier sections. Here, I will summarize the key points and say which theoretical assumptions appear to be more suitable for Czech data.

First, the table in (216) provides a comprehensive comparison of the labels used in each model, highlighting the contrasts between their respective approaches:

(216)		Alexiadou (2020)	Borer (2005a)
	v	CP	EP
	iv	TP	TP
	iii	AspectP	
	ii	VoiceP	-
	i	vP	Asp_Q
		root	root

At the lowest level of both models lies a root. In Borer's framework, the head related to Aspect immediately follows, whereas in Alexiadou there are two additional projections: the categorizing *v* and *Voice*.

Second, *inner Aspect* is for both authors related to telicity/atelicity, which can be compositionally derived from its lexical specification and its (non) quantized arguments. Alexiadou (2020) does not introduce any specific projection for this decomposition and telicity arises as a consequence of the way the root merges with *v*. I concur with Alexiadou's viewpoint on this matter as this mechanism can reduce the necessity of introducing a cumbersome semantically vacuous Shell F^SP projection in atelic contexts, which are needed in Borer's model.

The next level in Alexiadou (2020) is *Voice*, the main function of which is to introduce external arguments. On the other hand, in Borer's (2005) framework, all arguments emerge from the structure itself, making the inclusion of a projection specifically designed to introduce arguments unnecessary. However, it is worth noting that in Borer's model, Agent roles or Originators, if not introduced elsewhere, originate in EP (Event Phrase). This resemblance can be seen as analogous to a Voice projection.

In my study, I will adopt Alexiadou's perspective which allows for the inclusion or exclusion of the Voice projection in derivations, thereby making them more econominal. According to this view, unaccusative Verbs do not necessarily project this projection. The decision to project it depends on constraints dividing verbs into internally and externally caused etc. that are resolved at the level of the Encyclopedia. In contrast, in Borer's framework, the EP, which is analogous to Voice Projection, is required in all structures. Therefore, I believe that the more selective inclusion of Voice projection helps prevent the excessive overgeneration of structures, which results from Borer's framework, where any root can be embedded under any structure with no explicit constraint. This overgeneration of structures is a major drawback acknowledged by the author herself.

As for Outer Aspect, while both authors agree that certain phenomena can be subsumed under this category, Borer (2005b) does not deal with this issue in detail. The primary discrepancy between both authors lies in their treatment of perfectivity. While Alexiadou et al. (2010c) consider it as the level of outer Aspect that is universal across languages, Borer (2005b) views perfectivity as a morphological marker specific to Slavic languages and equates it with telicity. I will return to these issues in the next section 4.4.1.2 discussing Slavic data.

Finally, both authors recognize the role of the TP functional head in relation to Tense-related matters. As Tense is not expected to generally occur in nominalizations, it was not addressed in depth.

4.4 Verbal Functional Projection in Czech

Before introducing and discussing the verbal functional projection in Czech, it is essential to look more closely at the existing perfective/imperfective opposition, given the complexity of aspectual issues in Slavic languages. Additionally, I will devote a separate section to examining Alexiadou and Borer's perspectives on perfectivity and imperfectivity, particularly considering Borer's (2005b) analysis of Slavic data in her book, *The Normal Course of Events*.

Finally, I will evaluate their theoretical assumptions w.r.t. aspectual issues and examine how they apply to Czech data. Based on the findings from the analysis of Czech, I will propose potential modifications to their frameworks, taking into account the specific aspects observed in the language.

4.4.1 (Im)perfectivity in Slavic Languages

Most traditional Slavic grammarians have traditionally employed the term Aspect precisely for the (im)perfective aspectual contrast, see, for example, Kopečný (1962b). In other works, Perfectivity/Imperfectivity is sometimes envisaged on a par with telicity (Verkuyl 1998) and sometimes with outer Aspect (Smith 1997) in English. These concepts need to be scrutinized in order to find out what the confusion about the different types of Aspects and their equivalence stems from. Specifically, it is crucial to investigate whether the discrepancies in the treatment of perfective/imperfective Aspects are merely based on different terminologies or if there are indeed structural differences between these types of Aspects. As we analyze these concepts, we must be mindful of the distinction between language universals and language-specific characteristics, as outlined in section 3.3.

4.4.1.1 Czech (Im)perfective Morphology

Let us define first the notion of (im)perfectivity. Perfective Verbs in Czech are often derived from imperfective Verbs by adding a perfective prefix. An example illustrating this is below in (217b) with the bold prefix *na-*. (I mark the resulting perfectivity in the glosses.[52])

(217) a. *Honza psal knihu.*
John write$_{PAST.(IMPF)}$ book
'John wrote a book.'

b. *Honza* ***na****-psal knihu*
John on$_{PF}$.write$_{PAST}$ book
'John has written a book.'

An important characteristic of Czech perfective Verbs is their incompatibility with the analytic future auxiliary *bude*, as shown in the contrast between (218a) and (218b).

(218) a. *Honza* ***bude*** *psát knihu.*
John AUX$_{FUT}$ write$_{INF}$ book
'John will write a book.'

b. **Honza* ***bude na****-psat knihu*
John AUX$_{FUT}$ on$_{PF}$.write$_{INF}$ book
*'John will write a book.'

To get the future interpretation with a perfective Verb, Czech uses the form of the Verb which is identical with the present Tense of imperfectives. Compare the morphology of the Verbs in (219), where the unmarked agreement morpheme ***-e*** triggers a present interpretation, with an identical suffix in (b) where the presence of the perfective prefix *na-* results in the future interpretation. Notice that the imperfective prefix can have its own interpretation.[53]

(219) a. *Honza píš-****e*** *knihu*
John write$_{3.SG(IMPF)}$ book
'John writes/is writing a book.'

b. *Honza* ***na****-píš-****e*** */****pře****-píš-****e*** */****do*** *-píš-****e*** *knihu*
John on$_{PF}$.write$_{3.SG}$ / re$_{PF}$.write$_{3.SG}$ / in$_{PF}$.write$_{3.SG}$ book
'John will write/will rewrite /will finish writing a book.'

52 Recall that only features relevant for the discussion are marked in the glosses.

53 The interpretation of the perfective prefix is sometimes related to similar Preposition but often unpredictable and sometimes very minimal. The prefixes are idiosyncratically selected by the stem and none is fully productive.

As a result of the above paradigm, the Verbs in perfective aspectual forms are never able to receive an actual present interpretation.[54]

The incompatibility of the future AUX and perfective infinitives is similar to the incompatibility of perfective infinitives following temporal aspectual Verbs, for example, *začít* 'start', *přestat* 'finish'. The paradigm is illustrated below:

(220) a. *Honza* ***začal/přestal*** *psát* *knihu.*
John start$_{PRES}$ stop$_{PRES}$ write$_{INF}$ book
'John started/stopped writing a book.'

b. **Honza* ***začal/přestal na***-*psat* *knihu*
John start$_{PRES}$ stop$_{PRES}$ on$_{PF}$.write$_{INF}$ book
*'John started/stopped writing a book.'

No such restriction holds for the other Czech auxiliaries which combine with participles rather than infinitives. Here are examples illustrating their usage in past and conditional:

(221) a. *Já* ***jsem /bych*** *psal* *tu knihu.*
I AUX$_{PAST}$/ AUX$_{COND}$ write$_{PRT.(IMPF)}$ the book
'I was writing a book/I would write the book.'

b. *Já* ***jsem /bych pře***-*psal* *tu knihu*
John AUX$_{PAST}$/AUX$_{COND}$ re$_{PF.}$write$_{PRT}$ the book
'I wrote a book/I would rewrite the book. '

Besides unmarked imperfective forms in Czech, there are also marked forms of Verbs with the suffixes ***-ova, -va, -a, -ě/e,*** see for example Čechová (2000, p. 137–138). These are following the stem and preceding the Tense marker and agreement as illustrated in (222). These suffixes often combine with the perfective prefix and create the 'secondary/derived' imperfective. In (222) I

54 I will come back to the topic in section 4.4.2.5.

show that the prefix ***pře-*** (in bold) and the presence of the imperfective suffix ***-ova*** (in bold underlined) voids its perfective interpretation. The inflected form in (222) with the combination [PF] … [IMPF] is imperfective and therefore compatible with the future AUX.

(222) *Marie* ***pře****-pis-****ova****-l-a* *knihu.* --- *budu* ***pře****-pis-****ova****-t*
Mary re$_{\text{PF.}}$write$_{\textbf{IMPF}\cdot\text{PAST.AGR}}$ book --- I will re$_{\text{PF.}}$write$_{\textbf{IMPF}\cdot\text{INF}}$
'*Mary was rewriting a book.*' --- 'I will rewrite.'

The Czech (im)perfective morphemes allow multiplication. Adding another perfective morpheme (the so-called *superlexical* prefix) voids the imperfective suffix *-ova-* as we can see below. The combination [+PF][PF] … [IMPF] in (223) gets perfective reading and therefore cannot combine with the future AUX.

(223) *Marie* ***do*** *-* ***pře*** *-pis –* ***ova*** *-l-a knihu.* --- * *budu* ***do-pře****-pis-****ova****-t*
Mary finish$_{\text{PF}}$· book --- * I will finish$_{\text{PF.}}$
re$_{\text{PF.}}$write$_{\textbf{IMPF}\cdot\text{PAST.AGR}}$ re$_{\text{PF.}}$write$_{\textbf{IMPF}\cdot\text{INF}}$
'*Mary finished rewriting a book.* ' --- * 'I will be finishing rewrite'

As illustrated above, the Czech perfectivity seems to be highly systematic combinatorial phenomena, perhaps comparable with English perfect and progressive Aspects. However, as many traditional linguists notice, the combinations of possible prefixes and stems are restricted and unpredictable. No prefix is fully productive. The choice and interpretation of a prefix, as well as the resulting phonetic adaptations of the prefix + stem complexes, are rather idiosyncratic. I will get back to the more thorough structural analysis of the Czech aspectual morphology and its classification in section 4.4.2.3.

Prior to that, in the next section, I will outline how (Im)perfectivity is captured in the theory of Borer and Alexiadou. My main aim will be to find an answer for the following question: Can (im)perfectivity be equated with (a)telicity?

4.4.1.2 Borer's View of (Im)perfectivity and (A)telicity

Borer (2005b) devotes a large part of her second book *The Normal course of events* to aspectual issues in Slavic languages and she specifically uses Czech data to demonstrate these phenomena. She claims that the term Perfect is a morphosyntactic-semantic classification referring to the morphological realization of grammatical/outer Aspect.

As for the perfectives and primary imperfective—that is a bare unmarked stem in Slavic (as in (217a) above—those are morphological terms equated with telicity and atelicity, thus subsumed under inner Aspect.

On the other hand, the category of outer Aspect is attributed only to secondary imperfectives in Slavic as in (222) above characterized by the imperfectively marked stem. Besides stating that secondary imperfective in Czech and perfect as well as progressive in English are cases of outer Aspect, no further proposals or explanations for outer Aspect are extensively provided. Neither is the explanation for incompatibility of perfective forms with FUT AUX and temporal aspect Verbs offered. Her book is mainly devoted to the inner Aspect projection.

Let us describe telicity in Czech in structural terms. As outlined in section 4.1.1, telicity in English was defined as quantity instantiated by the presence or absence of inner Aspect -Asp$_{Q}$. Similarly for Czech, telicity is a quantity structure achieved by the use of perfective prefixes such as <*na*> in (224), as described in Borer (2005b):

(224) *Petr* [$_{TP}$ *napekl* [$_{AspQ}$ [$_{DP}$ <e>$_{d}$ [$_{\#P}$ <e^{na}>$_{\#}$ [*housky*]]] <na> *pekl* <e>$_{\#}$ [$_{VP}$ *pekl*]]]
Peter [$_{TP}$ *pref.bake* [$_{AspQ}$ [$_{DP}$ <e>$_{d}$ [$_{\#P}$ <e^{pref}>$_{\#}$ [buns]]] <pref> *bake* <e>$_{\#}$ [$_{VP}$ *bake*]]]

The perfective prefix is a head feature which assigns a range to Asp$_{Q}$ <e>$_{\#}$, resulting in the interpretation of a telic event. But it has an additional role, it triggers the projection of [DP <e>$_{\#}$] where the prefix assigns a range, leading to a quantity interpretation of the DP. Compare the quantificational nature of the DP in perfective and imperfective contexts:

(225)	a.	*Petr*	*snědl*	*housku.*	b.	*Petr*	*jedl*	*housku*
		Peter	$_{PF}$ate	roll		Peter	ate$_{PAST.(IMPF)}$	roll
		'Peter ate a roll.'				'Peter ate a roll.'		

While the perfective context in (225a) forces a specific interpretation where the whole roll was eaten, in imperfective (225b) such strong implication is not necessary, and the example does not necessarily imply that the whole roll was eaten.

Regarding the nature of perfective prefixes, being a head feature, the prefix merges directly with Asp_Q and triggers the incorporation of the verb. Alternatively, Borer proposes that it might be perceived as a Preposition-like element incorporating into verb in the L-domain before the verb moves to Asp_Q.

One of our main goals is to find out whether telicity and perfectivity can be considered equivalent. Traditionally, the problematic cases for equating telicity and perfectivity are the following ones which contain the so-called superlexical prefixes, whose structural description will be further explored in section 4.4.2.3.

(226)	*Petr*	*(**pro**)-spal*	*pět hodin/(*za pět hodin).*
	Peter	through$_{PF}$.sleep	five hours/in five hours
	'Peter slept five hours/(*in five hours).'		

The prefix *pro* 'through' is perfective but it describes an atelic event as indicated by *for X-time phrase*. Thus, unlike other Verbs such as (217b), this time a prefix does not seem to play a role in marking telicity. These examples pose a challenge within Borer's proposal where telicity and perfectivity are not distinguished.

Borer (2005b) does not find the presence of measure phrases indicating atelicity in cases such as (226) problematic. She explains that the *in-X-time* phrase cannot co-occur with these examples because they already have inherent measurement built into them. For example, *prospat* 'through$_{PF}$.sleep' could mean "sleep a lot." Subsequently, durative temporal expressions such as *for X-time* would be permissible because they could be licensed as modifiers on "a lot" and indicate the length, for example, five hours.

As a result, these predicates are cumulative, as 'sleep a lot' added to 'sleep a lot' is clearly 'sleep a lot'. However, they are not divisive. Subtracting 'sleep a lot from 'sleep a lot' need not give rise to 'sleep a lot'. This predicate is thus not homogeneous.

Atelicity, on the other hand, is the absence of any relationship between the imperfective marking and the direct object. This gives rise to structures such as (227a) and (227c) which are not restricted in the interpretation of their DPs. Conversely, quantity structures (227b) and (227d) manifest themselves in the interpretative meaning of DPs:

(227)

a.	*Pil*	*tři*	*kávy.*
	drink$_{\text{3.SG.PAST(IMPF)}}$	three	coffee$_{\text{PL.GEN}}$
	'He drank three portions of coffee.' (**Weak**)		
	'He drank those three portions of coffee.'(**Strong**)		
b.	*Vy-pil*	*tři*	*kávy.*
	out$_{\text{PF}}$.drink$_{\text{3SG.PAST}}$	three	coffee
	'He drank up three portions of coffee.' (**Weak**)		
	*'He drank up those three portions of coffee.' (**Strong**)		
c.	*Pil*	*kávu.*	
	drink$_{\text{3.SG.PAST.(IMPF)}}$	coffee $_{\text{SG}^{\cdot}\text{.GEN}}$	
	'He drank coffee.' (**Generic**)		
	'He drank the coffee.' (**Strong**)		
d.	*Vy-pil*	*kávu.*	
	out$_{\text{PF}}$.drink$_{\text{3.SG.PAST}}$	coffee $_{\text{SG}^{\cdot}\text{.GEN}}$	
	*'He drank coffee.' (**Generic**)		
	'He drank the coffee.' (**Strong**)		

This has already been explained in section 3.5.4 where it was shown that strong Quantifiers are impossible in perfective contexts. Similarly, cardinality expressions may not receive a strong interpretation (227b). Bare NPs, on the other, hand must be strong (227d) and cannot get generic interpretation.

4.4.1.3 Alexiadou's View of (Im)perfectivity and (A)telicity

As previously mentioned, Alexiadou's approach is influenced by Borik's (2006) distinction between two aspectual levels. Although Borik's *Theory of Aspect in*

Russian primarily focuses on the Russian language, the following paragraphs will consider Borik's arguments and evaluate them with examples from Czech.

For Borik (2006), the two aspectual levels are: *telicity* and *Perspective Aspect/ outer Aspect*. While the former represents the property of a predicate, the latter is an outer Aspect captured in two temporal notions: *Speech time* and *Reference time*. The opposition between perfective and imperfective in Russian is thus analyzed in terms of Perspective Aspect/outer Aspect. This concept of perfectivity is distinct from Borer (2005b) for whom perfectivity in Slavic is the same as telicity.

According to Borik (2006), *telicity* is neither a sufficient, nor a necessary condition for perfectivity. If this were true then two implications would have to hold: perfective-> telic and telic->perfective.

Let's begin with the first implication by examining the example, previously discussed in (226), which poses a challenge to this equation. Recall that Borer classifies it as quantity. In this example we have a perfective verb *pro-spal* 'through$_{PF}$sleep' as indicated by its incompatibility with the FUT auxiliary or a temporal phase verb:[55]

(228)	*Petr*	**bude/začne*	*(****pro****)-spat*
	Peter	AUX$_{FUT}$/starts	(through$_{PF}$).sleep
	*'Peter will/start sleep.'		

According to the telicity tests proposed by Borik (2006) and described in section 4.2.1, this predicate is not considered telic: consider the use of adverbial modification *in X-time/for X-time* in example (229) which fails to prove telicity:

(229)	*Petr*	*(****pro****)-spal*	*čtyři hodiny (*za pět hodin).*
	Peter	through$_{PF.}$sleep	four hours/in five hours
	'Peter slept four hours/(*in five hours).'		

Another test utilized by Borik is the divisibility test which yields the same conclusion as the previous one and does not indicate that the predicate is

55 Borik actually uses the same complementation test of phase Verbs to distinguish perfectivity from imperfectivity, both of which fall under the category of outer Aspect.

telic either. Should the predicate be divisive, it should actually hold for any of its subintervals. In our case if *Peter* slept four hours, he must have slept even two hours or one hour. Obviously, the predicate *prospat* 'through$_{PF}$sleep' is divisive and thus homogeneous and atelic.

Finally, consider the application of a conjunction test in (230) which predicts that if the predicate is atelic, the sentence should result in ambiguity and have two interpretations:

(230)	*Petr*	*(pro)-spal*	*čtyři hodiny*	*v pondělí a v úterý.*
	Peter	through$_{PF.}$sleep	four hours	on Monday and on Tuesday.

'Peter slept four hours on Monday and on Tuesday.'

Indeed, the atelic nature of the predicate in (230) can be interpreted in two ways. The first interpretation suggests that Peter slept four hours on both Monday and Tuesday. The second interpretation implies that Peter slept a total of eight hours, with four hours of sleep on Monday and an additional four hours on Tuesday.

To sum up, the implication perfectivity > telicity does not hold. This is in contrast with Borer's framework where both notions are equated. The explanation lies in the different treatment of predicates such as *prospat* 'through$_{PF.}$sleep'. In Borer's framework, these predicates inherently include some kind of measurement, making the *for-X-phrase* merely a modifier. In contrast, Borik does not embed any measure phrase into predicates and *for-X-time phrases* are their integral parts.

Now, we can proceed to the other relation between telicity and perfectivity. In the above, we have seen that perfective is not always telic. According to Borik (2006), neither is the other implication valid: telic-> perfective. This is corroborated by the next example:

(231)	*Nepůjdu*	*do kavárny.*	*Už*	*jsem jedla.*
	not to$_{PF.}$go	to a café	already	AUX$_{PAST}$ eat$_{(IMPF).PAST}$

'I will not go to a café, I have already eaten.'

The Verb *jíst* 'eat' is clearly imperfective because the combination with a phase verb *začala jíst* 'start eat' is grammatical. Despite being imperfective, this construction still conveys a sense of completion, which is evident in the translation. Borik (2006) acknowledges this and points out that this is a typical characteristic of imperfective verb forms with *už* 'already'. The divisibility test to diagnose the telicity is hard to apply because the frame adverbial is not permissible:

(232)	*Nepůjdu*	*do kavárny.*	*Už*	*jsem jedla*	*(*od 2.00*	*do 5.00).*
	not to$_{\text{PF.}}$go	to a café	already	AUX$_{\text{PAST}}$ eat$_{\text{(IMPF.PAST)}}$	from 2.00	to 5.00

'I will not go to a café, I have already eaten (* from 2.00 to 5.00).'

While Borik does not explicitly mention these cases, in Czech, we can easily test imperfective forms with telic interpretation with *in-x-time* adverbials:

(233)	*Už*	*jsem*	*jednou*	*běžela*	*do obchodu*	*za deset minut.*
	already	AUX$_{\text{PAST}}$	once	run$_{\text{(IMPF.PAST)}}$	to the store	in ten minutes

'I have already run to the store in ten minutes.'

Again, the verb in (233) is imperfective as the grammaticality of *začala běžet* 'start run' indicates and also telic. As a result, the implication telicity > perfectivity cannot be confirmed either.

To sum up, we have shown that the (a)telicity and (im)perfectivity are not equivalent in Borik (2006) system because two implications: telicity-> perfectivity and perfectivity-> telicity do not hold.[56] Alexiadou et al. (2010c) follow

56 The Perfective/Imperfective contrast in Borik (2006) is built on Reichenbach's decomposition into event time E, reference time R and speech time S, which are taken as intervals. E is included in R by default. The S-E relation is responsible for the temporal interpretation, for example, E >S would indicate past. The S-R determines the grammatical viewpoint Aspect. Consequently, Perfective and Imperfective are defined for Russian in the following way:

Borik (2006) and consequently reach different conclusions from Borer (2005b) where telicity/atelicity is equated with perfectivity and primary imperfectivity. Obviously, perfectivity as well as primary and secondary imperfectivity in Czech have now the same status as progressive in English. All are cases of outer Aspect in Alexiadou et al. (2010c).

4.4.1.4 Comparison of Both Frameworks wrt. Aspectual Issues

After exploring the viewpoints of both theorists on aspectual phenomena in English and Czech, we can present a brief summary and a comparative table to illustrate the key differences between their approaches:

(234) Aspectual distinction in Borer (2005b) and Alexiadou et al. (2010c)

	Czech		**English**	
	Inner Aspect	**Outer Aspect**	**Inner Aspect**	**Outer Aspect**
Borer (2005b)	(A)telicity= Quantity Perfectivity Primary imperfectivity	Secondary imperfectives	(A)telicity= Quantity	Perfect= Perfectivity Progressive
Alexiadou et al. (2010c)	(A)telicity	Perfectivity Primary imperfectivity Secondary imperfectivity	(A)telicity	Perfect (im)perfectivity Progressive

---

PF: $S \cap R = \varnothing \ \& \ E \subseteq R$

IPF: $\neg (S \cap R = \varnothing \ \& \ E \subseteq R)$, namely, $S \cap R \neq \varnothing \vee E \nsubseteq R$

As E-R relation is fixed, the perfectives are distinguished by the fact that they impose a non-overlapping relation between the speech time and the reference time. This is able to capture the fact that perfective is incompatible with the present Tense. No such condition is required in the case of imperfectives.

Obviously, this is a rather different architecture from other authors working in the Reichenbachian system where the reference time serves as an intermediary between the event and the speech time. In Ramchand (2004), this sequence is observed, and Reference time mediates between E and S, as we will see in section 4.4.2.1. In addition, no satisfactory explanation for the incompatibility of FUT aux and perfective Verbs is offered. Borik (2006) speculates that it could be the residual perfective semantics of the verb *to be*.

Once again, it is evident from table (234) that both authors approach aspectual issues in both English and Czech by considering *two levels*. However, the specific arrangement of each level varies between the two authors. The key distinction lies in Borer's equating of perfectivity and telicity in Czech, whereas the concept of perfectivity does not extend to the realm of outer aspect in English. In contrast, Alexiadou et al. (2010c) incorporate the concept of perfectivity as an outer Aspect in both languages.

For the purposes of this thesis, and given the discussion in the preceding sections, I will follow Alexiadou et al. (2010c). I am going to assume that in Czech, perfective Verbs that are often marked with perfective prefixes should not be equated with telicity. I conclude that telicity and perfectivity represent two different concepts in Czech. I will further show that Czech utilizes two types of perfective prefixes, the prefixes that mark the verb as telic or bounded and prefixes that do not necessarily influence the verb's interpretation. I will present some arguments developed by Caha and Ziková (2022) in the domain of Czech prefixes that confirm these claims.

Furthermore, I will agree with Borer (2005b) and diverge from Alexiadou et al. (2010c) that primary and secondary imperfectives are different notions, with the latter generated higher in the syntactic structure. This last argument will be motivated by the behavior of Czech *-ní/tí* nominals and will be the subject of Chapter 5.

Having thoroughly examined the proposals of both authors for the verbal domain and their perspectives on aspectual issues in Czech, we can now proceed to apply this knowledge to analyze Czech data in the next section.

4.4.2 Layers in the Czech Verbal Functional Projection

For Czech, I introduce the following functional projection in (235). It starts with the root combining with *v*P which includes the inner Aspect of Verbs. Moving upwards, we find the Outer Aspect, which is divided into two projections: AspectP associated with perfective and primary imperfective Verbs, and ProgP associated with secondary imperfectives. The head VoiceP is responsible for introducing external arguments and is also the locus of Tense in Czech. IP, on the other hand, is the projection for Mood in both English and Czech with features [+/-REALIS], as described and justified at length by Veselovská and Emonds (2015). The top CP serves as the landing site for interrogative phrases or focused constituents.[57]

(235) Czech verbal functional projection

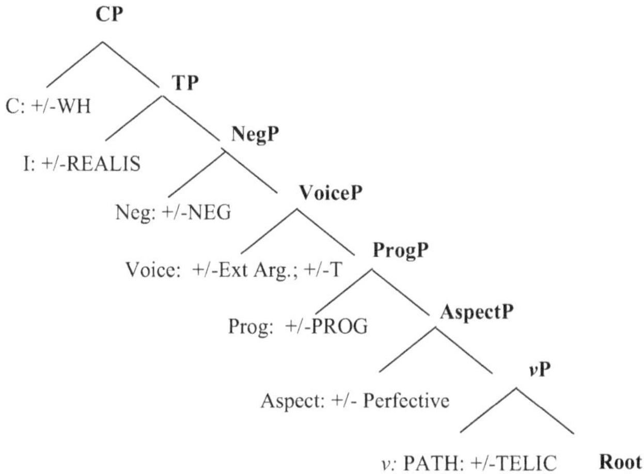

I will provide a thorough explanation of these layers in the subsequent section, where they will be scrutinized in more detail.

4.4.2.1 Inner Aspect Decomposed

As demonstrated above, the main point of disagreement between Borer (2005b) and Alexiadou et al. (2010c) revolves around whether telicity and perfectivity can be equated. I advocate for maintaining a distinction between these two levels. My primary argument stems from the analysis of Czech data by Caha and Ziková (2022) who present compelling reasons for separating these two aspects. After the discussion of aspectual issues, I will outline the role of the *v* node in the Czech verbal structure.

57 For the feature content of IP and CP, see Veselovská and Emonds (2015) and Veselovská (2011). I will not take a stand here w.r.t. the more structured CP level used plausibly for the integration of information structure.

Caha and Ziková (2022) work with Ramchand's decompositional model for Verbs and therefore a brief introduction into this model is necessary. Similar to Borik (2002), Ramchand (2008) operates within the Reichenbachean system, which defines Aspect in terms of E (Event time), S (Speech Time), and R (Reference time). However, Ramchand diverges from Borik by treating E, R, and S as points rather than intervals.

Second, in contrast to Borik's system, which does not require the Reference time to interact with the Speech time, Ramchand's framework involves the mediation of R (Reference time) between E (Event time) and S (Speech time). The specific mechanism of this mediation can be described as follows: there exists an inner aspectual head, referred to as the AspP head which binds the event variable introduced by the VP (known as the First phase: predicate over events) and introduces a Reference time denoted as "t" (predicate over times). Subsequently, the Tense node serves to anchor the Reference time to the Speech time.

In this section, I will describe the first phase which is the non-temporal lexical level. In the next subsection, I will proceed to the aspectual level.

The first phase of decomposing can be described as follows: Each verb may have three sub-components: *Initiation*, *Process* and *Result*. Take for example the sentence *Alex gave Mary a book. Alex* is an initiator of the process, and *the book* is changing location. This leads to the change of state with the result that *Mary* has a *book*.

Caha and Ziková (2022) argue that this model is able to account for Czech perfective prefixes which are located below Result (ResP) and can move upwards to the ResP to provide a result to the whole event, thereby making the verb telic. In this model, prefixes and particles minimally lexicalize Path components and the projection of Result. This characteristic distinguishes them from Prepositional Phrases (PPs), which solely lexicalize Paths. The process is depicted in (236) which demonstrates the derivation of English particles and Czech perfective prefixes[58]

58 The scheme (235) does not address the final morphological realization of the Czech bound prefix and the examples assume later nominalization. As the description of the first step of the derivation, however, they provide a good example of the concept of decomposition.

(236) Ramchand's (2008) model adapted by Caha and Zikova (2022) for Czech

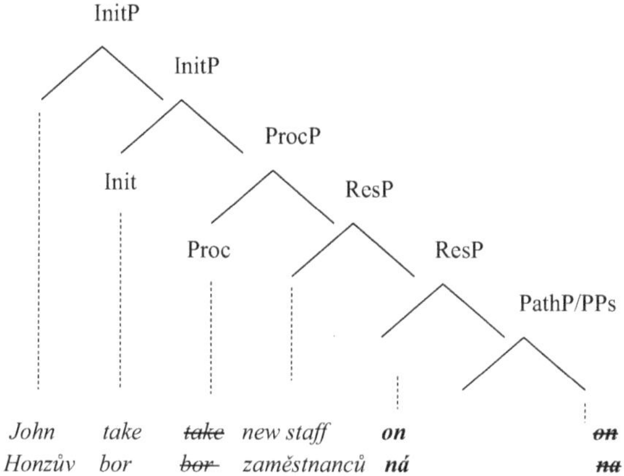

Let us elaborate on the process that leads to the above analysis. First, the fact that English particles are intransitive Prepositions goes originally back to Emonds (1976), contrast the examples below:

(237) a. *The police will fire tear gas* ***in*** *the window.*
b. *The police will fire tear gas* ***in****.*

In (237a) the Preposition *in* requires its complements to express the specific end-point of the path.[59] However, unlike the Preposition *in*, the particle *in* (237b) does not require the complement since it already incorporates the necessary information within itself and it can be inferred from the context.

Looking at the Czech data, we can find out that there are the so-called improper Prepositions in Czech as in (238) which are not followed by any complement (in traditional framework they would be categorized as a kind of Adverbs):

59 Depending on the Preposition, it can express end-point (*to*), starting point (*from*) or route (*via*).

(238)	a.	*Marie*	*šla*	***kolem*.**
		Mary	$go_{(IMPF)}$	around
		'Mary went around.'		
	b.	*Marie*	*(****kolem**-)*	*šla.*
		Mary	around	$go_{(IMPF)}$
		'Mary (*around)-went.'		

The Czech intransitive Prepositions do not undergo transformation into prefixes. However, the absence of a complement alone cannot be the sole distinguishing factor between Prepositions and prefixes. Caha and Zikova (2022) argue that prefixes also contribute to the result or outcome of an event. This is supported by their example adopted here as (239). Notice that the prefix *-ob* alters the aspectual value of (239a) containing the (here transitive) Preposition *kolem* 'around', without affecting its meaning.

(239)	a.	*Marie*	*motala*	*provaz*	***kolem** stromu*	*(*za den)/(celý den).*
		Mary	$wrapped_{(IMPF)}$	rope	around tree	in a day/the whole day
		'Mary was wrapping the rope around the tree (*in a day)/ (the whole day).'				
	b.	*Mary*	***ob**-motala*	*provaz*	***kolem** stromu*	*(za hodinu)/(*celý den).*
		Mary	$round_{PF.}$wrapped	rope	around tree	in an hour/the whole day
		'Mary wrapped the rope around the tree (in a day)/(*the whole day).'				

This decompositional idea about bringing a *result* to *events* is fully compatible with Alexiadou's eventive *v* which introduces events and takes stative roots as their complements. Recall that when *v* merges as a modifier of root, then we have Verbs with resultative semantics. Conversely, when a root is the complement of *v*, we have atelic structure.

The main idea can be preserved in Czech, but it needs to be adjusted for prefixes. In Czech, prefixes rather than stative roots are often the components that make the verb telic, thus when they are complements of *v*, the resultative structure is born as in example (240b). Otherwise, when the root is just a modifier of *v*, the structure will be atelic as in (240a). I will also assume the option proposed by Borer that a prefix might be viewed as a Preposition-like element incorporating into a Verb as described in section 2.2.2. Furthermore, if the prefix raises to AspectP, it will become Perfective.

(240) a. Atelic

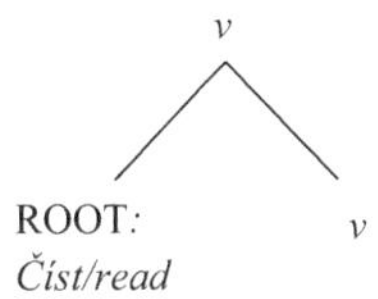

b. Telic structure

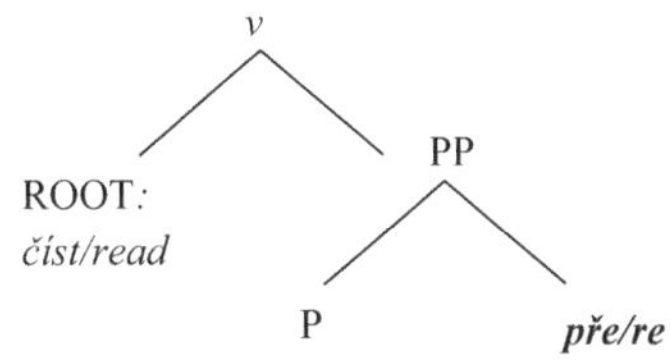

In my model I include the projection *v*. However, I do not suppose that its main function is to verbalize roots as in DM, but instead, it contributes to resultativity checking the feature [+/-TELIC] which it inherits from the incorporated prefix.

Furthermore, if I argue that the verbalizing function is redundant and adopt a binary approach to features, this would imply that *v* is not projected in atelic contexts. We might consider as an alternative Borer's shell $F^{s}P$, in contexts where direct arguments are projected. Nevertheless, this mechanism is cumbersome and at least in nominalizations this *v* projection is necessary in early stages of derivations to license certain modifiers, see section 5.4.2.1. Therefore, I propose that inner aspect is characterized by a Path feature that is consistently valued as either +Telic or -Telic.

4.4.2.2 Outer Aspect

Besides describing paths alongside which the event proceeds, prefixes also fulfill an aspectual function. Caha and Ziková (2022) demonstrate that the Czech prefixes can alternate between these two structural positions,[60] which

60 Caha and Ziková (2022) follow Borik (2006) and use tests envisaged for distinction between two aspectual levels.

has an effect on their length. In the lower resultative position, the prefix is interpreted as non-aspectual with features [Path], [Bound] and [Res]. Upon moving to a higher aspectual position, it acquires aspectual features like [Path] and [Bound].]. This process is represented in picture (241) which outlines the initial step in the derivation of deverbal nominals containing these prefixes. Since this initial stage is not visible in Czech Verbs, the demonstration of these processes needs to be illustrated using nominalizations, which start their derivation as Verbs.

(241) Caha and Ziková (2021) Deverbal nominalizations and prefixes

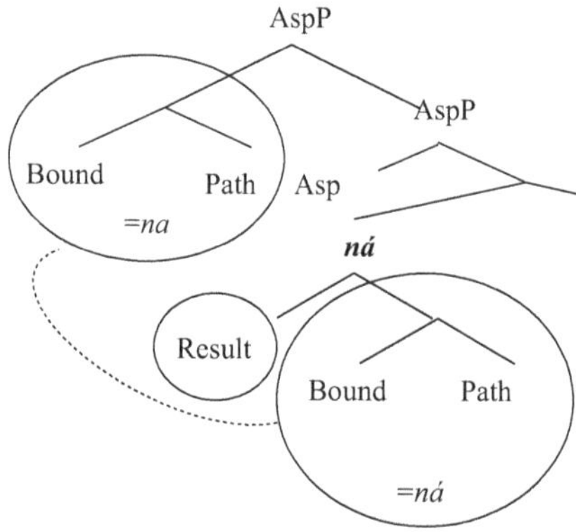

The process of prefix shortening is depicted in the table in (242), with examples provided by Caha and Ziková (2022, p. 11):

(242)	Verb	Zero-derived Noun	*-ní/tí* nominal	Preposition	Meaning
	na-stoupit	*ná-stup*	*na-stoupení*	*na*	'Get on'
	u-stoupit	*ú-stup*	*u-stoupení*	*u*	'Get out'
	pro-lézt	*prů-lez*	*pro-lezení*	*pro*	'Crawl through'

This table includes nominals, the classification of which will be detailed in Chapter 5. Currently, we can say that *-N/T* nominals and verbal prefixes pattern together in having a short prefix. Zero-derived Nouns, on the other hand, are less verbal and have a non-aspectual prefix which is long.[61]

4.4.2.2.1 Boundedness

Various authors have proposed different criteria for Boundedness. I have already outlined Alexiadou's perspective in section 4.2.3.2. In this section, we will review these criteria and discuss the contributions of other authors to this topic before determining which criteria will be adopted for the Czech model.

In the model proposed by Caha and Ziková (2021), prefixes and Prepositions share the feature Path which can often lead to the fact that delimited trajectories of paths lead to delimited events. Their criteria for boundedness are listed below:

- Non-cumulativity
- Having an end-point
- Clear transition between boundaries

Hence, the prepositional phrase *cesta do školy* 'a way to school' exhibits non-cumulativity, as adding the same predicate would imply multiple ways to school. In contrast, *cesta kolem řeky* 'a way around the river' demonstrates cumulativity, as the addition of the same predicate would still result in the way around the river.

The resemblance between these criteria and those proposed by Alexiadou (2007) is striking. In Alexiadou's framework, boundedness in the verbal domain is determined by the presence of a decisive end-point. Nevertheless, Alexiadou does not clearly specify the difference between telicity and perfectivity regarding the end-point.

For the purposes of this work, I will assume that telicity is non-temporal and involves predicates with a bounded path (usually detected by the *in-X time* phrase). Conversely, perfectivity is temporal, indicating whether a situation has reached its temporal boundary. The examples given in (243a-b)

61 This type of alternation is found with a subset of prefixes. There are other types of changes. Nevertheless, all are explained by movement from a lower aspectual position to a higher one. Additionally, Caha and Zikova explain the alternations in the roots.

illustrate the latter point. The imperfective verb, being unmarked, allows for the description of a situation as either finished or ongoing. On the other hand, the perfective verb must be terminated and cannot be continued by a sentence stating that it hasn't been finished yet (243c):

(243)	a.	*Petr četl tu knihu minulý týden,* Peter read$_{\text{(IMPF)}}$ the book last weak	*ale ještě ji nemá dočtenou.* but he hasn't finished it yet.
	b.	*Petr četl tu knihu minulý týden* Peter read$_{\text{(IMPF)}}$ the book last weak	*a dočetl ji.* and finished it.
	c.	*Petr* ***pře****-četl tu knihu minulý týden,* Peter re$_{\text{PF.}}$read the book last weak	*# ale ještě ji nedočetl.* # but he hasn't finished it yet.

The best way to capture the boundedness of perfective events formally is to assume the existence of a definite event time within a higher aspectual phrase, as opposed to an indefinite as proposed by Ramchand (2004). In her proposal, the AsP introduces a time variable t and binds an event variable e. Those two variables are related formally by a temporal trace function τ(e) which maps an event to the 'time line'

The default denotation of AsP is that t picks some arbitrary moment with the time trace of the event giving rise to unboundedness. In case of perfectivity, however, there is a presupposed salient time moment in τ(e), resulting in bounded predicates.

Moreover, superlexical prefixes, which can be perfective but embed atelic events as described in section 4.4.1.2, have the ability to grammaticalize over time and assert definite time directly. Therefore, they are not dependent on any resultant state being present. These prefixes will be the subject of the next section where their function in syntactic structures will be described.

What must also be addressed before concluding this section, are special cases where imperfective predicates exhibit boundedness, such as in examples (244)-(245).

(244)	*Už*	*jsem*	*jednou*	*běžela*	*do obchodu*	*za deset minut.*
	already	AUX$_{\text{PAST}}$	once	run$_{\text{(IMPF).PAST}}$	to the store	in ten minutes

'I have already run to the store in ten minutes.'

(245)	*Když Petr studoval rychločtení, tak*	***četl***	*vojnu a mír*	*za dvě hodiny.*
	When Petr studied fast-reading, then	read$_{(IMPF)}$	war and peace	in two hours

'When Petr took a course in fast-reading, he was reading War and Peace in two hours.'

These examples will qualify as bounded by the fact that they have a feature +TELIC and result in the plurality of the event. For further exploration of this topic, I can refer to Dočekal and Kučerová (2009), who discuss this phenomenon in their paper on *the Bound Reading of Imperfective Verbs.*

In summary, I suppose that both telicity and Perfectivity exhibit boundedness. Telicity is associated with delimitation at the *v*P level, whereas perfectivity operates at the AspP level. Telicity is characterized as non-temporal, whereas perfectivity is temporal in nature.

4.4.2.3 Other Outer Aspectual Heads

I have already distinguished two aspectual levels: inner Aspect and AspectP, which check features PATH: [+/-Telic]; [+/-Perfective] respectively. However, it appears that Czech exhibits additional aspectual heads, as supported by Karlík (2007b).

Another higher level of Aspect is the *ProgP* which is the locus of secondary imperfectives realizing the feature [+Prog]. The positioning of ProgP is above AspectP in the hierarchy because (as we have seen already in section 4.4.1.1) the perfective Aspect needs to be derived first before the secondary imperfective Verbs can be formed using the suffix *-ova*. In the grammatical examples in (246a) the Verbs contain both the perfective prefix *vy-* and the imperfective *-ova* suffix, while the contrasting example in (246b) has no prefix and the imperfective suffix is not acceptable.[62]

62 In Ramchand (2004), secondary imperfective is at the same level as perfective but it has to cancel its value. She also proposes that it might be the case that there is a separate functional head for secondary imperfectives.

(246)	a.	*psát -> vy-psat -> vy-pisovat*		b.	**pisovat*
		write$_{(IMPF)}$->pref-write$_{PF}$-> pref-write$_{IMPF}$			*write$_{IMPF}$

Furthermore, secondary imperfectives can be perfectivized by superlexical prefixes (e.g., *po*). I have already exemplified this with the example (223) in section 4.4.1.1. This step must follow the formation of secondary imperfectives because attempting to perfectivize them directly (as shown in (247b)) results in ungrammatical sequences:

(247)	a.	*po-vy -pis-ova-t*	b.	**po-vy-psat*
		pref-pref-write$_{IMPF}$		*pref-pref-write$_{IMPF}$

Superlexical prefixes in Czech are homonymous with lexical prefixes but both groups display different characteristics. As outlined in Sveonius (2004), the diagnostics for *superlexical prefixes* typically involve their external localization, notably their stacking outside lexical prefixes (as shown in (247a)). They are also oblivious to Argument structure of Verbs and cannot change it, see (249). In contrast, lexical prefixes, as illustrated in (248), can have an effect on the Argument structure:

(248)	a.	***vy**-řezat*	*díru*	*ve dveřích*
		out$_{PF}$.cut	hole$_{ACC}$	in the door
	b.	**řezat*	*díru*	*ve dveřích*
		*cut$_{(IMPF)}$	hole$_{ACC}$	in the door
(249)	a.	*zpívat*	*(píseň)*	
		sing$_{(IMPF)}$	Song	
	b.	***za**-zpívat*	*(píseň)*	
		pref$_{PF}$.sing	song	

Sveonius (2004) also notes that superlexical prefixes are not ordinarily included in nominalizations. In Czech, N/T nominals are compatible with superlexical prefixes (SP), while type II nominals are not. This prediction is supported by the following examples (250), where only N/T nominals can undergo double prefixation with both lexical prefixes (e.g., *vy, za*) and superlexical prefixes (e.g., *po*). In contrast, type II nominals do not allow for double prefixation:

(250) a. vy_{PF}*-taž-*e_{TH}*-n-í* po_{SP}-vy_{PF}*-taž-*e_{TH}*-n-í* vs. *vý-tah* **po-vý-tah*

b. za_{PF}*-vír-*$á_{TH}$*-n-í* po_{SP}-za_{PF}*-vír-*$á_{TH}$*-n-í* vs. *zá-věr* **po-zá-věr*

In her study, Zikova (2012) argues that this distinction is the result of the presence or absence of a *theme vowel* required by the superlexical prefixes. According to her analysis, N/T nominals have a theme vowel, enabling them to be compatible with superlexical prefixes. On the other hand, type II nominals lack a theme vowel, which restricts the use of superlexical prefixes, as is evident in the examples (250).

For all these reasons, superlexical prefixes are located higher in the structure. In Ramchand, they occur directly in the AspP or possibly some higher functional projection. This stands in a stark contrast to lexical prefixes which are generated lower in the structure.

The last phenomena in Czech which should be subsumed under outer Aspect is *iterativity* which is formed by means of *-va* suffix, as, for example, *hrá-l-> hrá-va-l->hrá-vá-va-l* 'played', *chodí-> chodí-vá/*'walk$_{3RD}$'. Iterative constructions typically cannot express present time only non-actual present time. Ramchand (2004) proposes that there is an iterative aspectual head, higher up than superlexical prefixes. Kopečný (1962a) has labeled it "the third Aspect."

The effect of iterativity is very much comparable to [+/-Plural] as discussed by Jackendoff (1991) and Veselovská and Karlík (2004). Both features [+Plural] and [+ITER] lead to unboundedness. To illustrate this, consider our tests for boundedness in the nominal domain first: *jablko*'apple' is not cumulative but plural *jablka* 'apples' is. Similarly, in the verbal domain in Czech the feature [+ITER] can be adjoined to imperfective Verbs and turn them it into sequence of bounded events which eventually results in unbounded. To be more specific, consider the pair of Verbs *chodil* 'walk' *->chodí-va-l*, where the iterative form is clearly cumulative, we can even express it morphologically with further *-va* suffix: *chodí-vá-val*.

The range of plausible candidates for aspectual heads is summarized in (251):

(251)	IterP	Superlexical	ProgP	AspP	*v*
	[+/-ITER]	[+/-PERF]	[+/-PROG]	[+/-PERF]	[+/-TELIC]

Although the hierarchy in Czech might look as in (251), no concrete proposal regarding this hierarchy will be offered besides stating that the dividing line seems to be the AspectP. Above this level nominalizations do not tolerate pluralization as exemplified below. These structural arrangements will be crucial in the discussion about the countability of nominals in Chapter 6.

(252)

a. *dvě stavby*
Two constructions

b. **dvě pře-stav-ová-ní*
*Two $re_{PF.}$ $building_{IMPF.NT}$

c. **dvě malová-vá-ní*
*Two $paintings_{ITER.NT}$

d. *dvě pře-malová-ní*
Two re_{PF}-$paintings_{NT}$

e. **dvě do-pře-stav-ová-ní*
*Two $pref_{PF}$-$re_{PF.}$ $buildings_{IMPF.NT}$

To conclude this section: for the purposes of my work, to demonstrate aspectual phenomena, I use the following three functional heads: *v*, AspectP and ProgP. I will leave the precise ordering of remaining aspectual heads within this domain for further research.

4.4.2.4 Voice Projection

The Voice projection serves two functions in Czech. Firstly, it functions as the locus of Tense, and secondly, it introduces external arguments. Let's begin with the first function. Discussing the specific characteristics of the multifunctional Czech Verb *být* 'be', Veselovská (2008) introduces several tests to distinguish the Czech AUXs. She argues that only two Czech AUXs occupy the high functional T position, while other Czech AUXs and Verbs are situated somewhat lower in the structure. One of the tests she employs is negation, which clearly reveals that the preterite and conditional AUXs as in (253) and (254) are generated above the negation while the passive AUX in (255) is generated below. The examples below are from Veselovská and Karlík (2004, p. 174):

(253) a. *Já jsem ne-chválil.* b. **Já ne-jsem chválil.*
I AUX_{IS} not-praised I not AUX_{IS} praised
'I did not praise.'

(254) a. *Já bych ne-pracoval.* b. **Já ne-bych pracoval.*
I AUX_{BYS} not-worked I notAUX_{BYS} worked
'I would not work.'

(255) *Já ne-jsem chválen.*
I not AUX_{IS} praised
'I am not praised.'

Assuming that negation is situated below T, the passive AUX (255) must be below T. In my model I assume it is in the VoiceP head.

Subsequently, the Czech past tense as in (253) is expressed by a combination of the auxiliary *jsem* 'AUX_{IS}' which signals only mood in TP and the L-participle (*pracoval* 'worked') that is canonically realized on the Voice projection.

Veselovská and Emonds (2015) and Karlík (2007b) situate AspectP below VP. In the literature the highest VP has been replaced by VoiceP. Therefore, in my narrative AspectP should be located below VoiceP. Veselovská and Emonds (2015) claim that +/- PERF is an inherent feature of some Verbs and should be situated lower in syntactic trees. I suppose that independent evidence can be derived from the structures such as (256), where the passive AUX is situated presumably in VoiceP and the secondary imperfective prefix is attached to V. If Aspect were positioned higher than Voice, we would expect the secondary imperfective prefix to appear on the auxiliary instead.

(256) *Já ne-budu přestavovat dům.*
I not AUX_{FUT} re_{PF}-$build_{IMPF}$ house
'I will not rebuild the house.'

Now we can address the issue of introducing external arguments and various verbal forms. Recall that in Borer (2005b) external arguments are rather a result of an event structure, that is EP and Asp_QP. I have dispensed with the Asp_Q and replaced it with the *v*P level. I have also argued for the Voice projection as it can avoid massive overgeneration of structures. Consequently, I will assume a separate VoiceP to introduce external arguments as in Alexiadou's framework:

(257) English verbal forms

a.	**Transitive**	**Active Voice**	*Petr zabil Roberta.* $Petr_{NOM}$ $kill_{PAST}$ $Robert_{ACC}$ 'Peter killed Robert.'
b.	**Unergative**	**Active Voice**	*Petr běží.* $Peter_{NOM}$ run_{PRES} 'Peter is running.'
c.	**Unaccusative/ Anticausative**	**No Voice**	*Strom spadl.* $tree_{NOM}$ $fall_{PAST}$ 'The tree fell.'
d.	**Passive**	**Passive Voice**	*Petr byl představen.* $Peter_{NOM}$ AUX_{IS} introduced. 'Peter was introduced.'
e.*[63]	**Reflexives =Unergative**	**Active Voice**	*Petr se umyl.* $Peter_{NOM}$ self $wash_{PAST}$ 'Peter washed himself.'

63 As far as reflexive passives, Hudousková (Volencová 2009) argues that the reflexive particle *se/si* in impersonal passives correlates with Agents, and similarly Medová and Taraldsen (2007) propose that reflexives are actually generated as Possessors in the position of external arguments.

Dispositional Middles =Unergative		*Kniby se prodávají dobře.* books self sell$_{PRES}$ well. 'The books sell well.'	

In English as well as Czech, active Voice, reflexives and dispositional middles/mediopassives[64] share the same morphology, whereas the passive is morphologically (and syntactically) marked. Interestingly, Haspelmath (1990) observed that no language marks the active and passive in the same way. On the other hand, mediopassives are not consistently demarcated cross-linguistically. Some languages treat them as active forms, while others classify them as non-active and may either share morphology with the passive or have their own distinct form.

Regarding passive Voice, many unresolved issues remain about the precise application of this process. Since I will frequently refer to it within the domain of nominalizations, I will briefly outline some main points here and compare Borer and Alexiadou's proposals with that of Veselovská and Karlík (2004) for Czech.

According to Veselovská and Karlík, the passivization process in Czech results from the characteristics of the Czech passive AUX *být* 'be', and its *structural* position. The authors use different labels for verbal functional projections but translating them into my model the passive AUX is inserted into our VoiceP. The position of the AUX in the head which is normally (in actives) occupied by a Verb, leads to deagentivization (*be* does not assign the Agent thematic role). It also blocks Accusative Case assignment and forces the PF adjectival morphology of the following participles.

Thus, when comparing these descriptions of passivization with the ones provided by Borer and Alexiadou in sections 4.1.4.1 and 4.2.2.1, respectively, we find that the common denominator is deagentivization. All these authors agree that although external arguments are demoted, they remain

64 In Czech tradition, dispositional middles are called mediopassives while for Alexiadou (2012) this term covers totally undetermined forms for passives/anticausative which is not found in English.

implicitly present and can be expressed as *by*-phrases (in Czech, Agent PPs are realized using the instrumental case). Since *by*-phrases can be preserved in nominalizations and influence their argument-taking status, I will return to this issue in Chapter 5.

4.4.2.5 Mood

The functional layer IP in Czech is the locus of Mood. The position of the features related to Mood in English and in Czech are discussed in detail in Veselovská and Emonds (2015, p. 281). Based on the arguments derived from the feature analysis of the analytic verbal forms in both languages the authors propose that temporal interpretation are combinations of Tense and Mood.

As for Tense, located in the verbal head below negation, they propose two fundamental binary features:

- [-T] (unmarked): **Generalized Present.** An event or state that either holds now, or is destined to hold at some future time that becomes now.
- [+T] (marked): **Generalized Non-present.** An event or state that is unrelated to what holds now, either because it is in the past, is counter to present reality, or is hypothetical and hence unrelated to present facts.

As for the other feature—Mood, located in the functional domain above negation, they propose that Mood is characterized by two features:

- [-M] (unmarked): **Realis.** An event or state that is part of perceived reality, that is, it holds in the present or it is held in the real past.
- [+M] (marked): **Irrealis.** An event or state that is not specified as part of reality, that is, it is not claimed to hold either in the present or in the real past.

They argue that the Mood features are able to distinguish two forms: the past Tense auxiliary in (253) and conditional auxiliary (254) which are defined as [-M] and [+M] respectively and which are clearly located above negation.

In their article, these authors also attempt to explain the incompatibility of the feature +PERF with future auxiliary Verbs as we have seen in (218). They propose that the basic syntactic feature of PERF:

(258) **Definition and locus of +PERF:** The canonical feature +PERF on a lexical V reports that a verbal event/State holds "at a point of time" different from the deictic now.

Subsequently, they claim that the only restriction for perfect is that its point of time cannot be now. The definition (258) holds the key to why Czech perfective Verbs with present Tense agreement morphology ([-M] and [-T]) refer to future. If a clause Tense is [-T], it can be only present or future. As our conditions excludes Now (present), then perfect can only refer to future. This is the case in (259a). The interpretation of past perfect as illustrated in (259b) is equally natural in this system, since it is defined as [+T], [-M], it satisfies the condition that it does not hold now. By virtue of being Perfect, Veselovská and Emonds (2015) state that the event is perceived as completed because it cannot continue beyond the verb's past.

(259) a.

Marie	*postaví*	*dům.*	[-M]	[-T]
Mary	pref$_{PF.}$build	house	~~Present/Past~~	~~Present~~/Future
'Mary will rebuild the house.'				

b.

Marie	*postavila*	dům.	[-M]	[+T]
Mary	pref$_{PF.}$build.$_{PAST}$	house	~~Present~~/Past	Past/~~Future~~
'Mary rebuilt the house.'				

I agree with this analysis, but I do not take it as complete. The feature +BOUND for perfective which has the effect of completion of events is not superfluous, as we will see in Chapter 5. I will demonstrate that nominalizations in Czech do not include Tense, but they can still reflect the distinction between complete and incomplete actions as suggested here by the use of aspectual adverbials in examples (260):

(260) a. *měnění* *pneumatik* *dvě hodiny/(??za dvě hodiny)*
changing$_{NT}$ tires two hours/in two hours
'changing of tires for two hours/(??in two hours)'

b. *vyměnění* *pneumatik* *(*dvě hodiny)/za dvě hodiny*
out$_{PF.}$changing$_{NT}$ tires in two hours/for two hours
're-changing of tires (*for two hours)/in two hours'

Moreover, as was illustrated above, Perf does not combine with temporal Aspect Verbs. Veselovská and Emonds (2015) do not discuss temporal Verbs in their analysis, but the sentence below (261) is defined as [-M], [+T] and still Perfective nominalization is not possible:

(261)	*Marie*	*začala*	*s měněním/ (??vyměněním)*	pneumatik	[-M]	[+T]
	Mary	$\text{start}_{\text{(IMPF).PAST}}$	$\text{with changing}_{\text{NT}}$/ $\text{out}_{\text{PF.}}\text{changing}_{\text{NT}}$	~~tires~~	~~Present~~/ Past	Past/ Future
	'Mary started with changing/(??re-changing) tires.'					

I am not able to offer a better analysis beyond saying that the feature +BOUND is not mutually exclusive with features [+/-M], [+/-T]. I am also not going to discuss features related to higher functional projections as they are not usually contained in nominalizations.

4.5 Chapter Summary

In the preceding chapters I have compared Alexiadou and Borer's verbal nominal projection and used it for implications in the Czech verbal nominal projection. I proposed the verbal projection in (235) for Czech repeated here for convenience as (262).

(262) Czech verbal functional projection

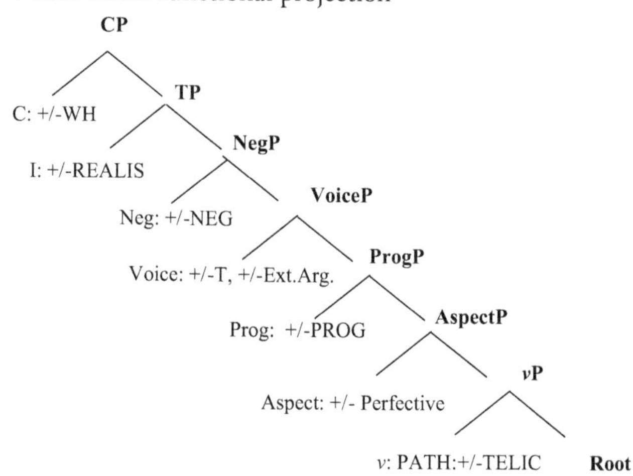

The labels employed in the Czech model are depicted in table (263) together with their assumed equivalents in the studies discussed in the preceding sections for the Borer's and Alexiadou's models, namely with the structures used in (172) and (193).

(263)

Alexiadou (2020)	Borer (2005a)	Czech Model
CP	EP	CP
TP	TP	TP
-		VoiceP
AspectP		ProgP
VoiceP	-	AspectP
vP	AspQ	vP

While some labels in the table above may look similar, their functions are distinct. The most important functional heads for the issue of nominalizations are the ones that are concerned with the introduction of external arguments and Aspect. These were discussed with a primary focus.

In my model, the *v*P does not primarily serve the function of verbalizing as in Alexiadou's work. Instead, it is mainly seen as responsible for inner Aspect, and the verbalization of the root is a secondary effect.

As far as Aspect is concerned, I concur with Borer (2005b) that it is essential to separate functional head for secondary imperfectives from perfectivity. At the same time, I agree with Alexiadou et al. (2010c) and diverge from Borer (2005b) in considering telicity and perfectivity as distinct heads. The arguments for separating telicity from perfectivity in Czech was based on the length alternation of Czech prefixes developed by Caha and Ziková (2022) which would be unexplainable without these two domains. Therefore, in the Czech structure Aspect is decomposed into three aspectual levels: inner Aspect, which deals with encoding (a)telicity, AspectP for (im)perfectivity, and ProgP, which is the locus of secondary imperfectives in Czech. There might be some more aspectual heads, but no specific hierarchy of ordering will be provided here.

I assume that both perfective and telic Verbs are bounded, and I will follow Caha and Ziková (2022) in supposing that boundedness at the lower level in *v* is related to boundedness at AspectP. This can be syntactically represented by raising a complex head with an incorporated prefix. To provide a comprehensive overview, Verbs with imperfective morphology can also exhibit boundedness, achieved at the telicity level. Conversely, Verbs with perfective morphology that are atelic such as *(pro)spal* 'through$_{PF}$.sleep' contain superlexical prefixes in the sense of Sveonius (2004) that are attached higher in the structure and can also lead to boundedness.

I have argued for the inclusion of the Voice projection employed in Alexiadou's framework rather than the analogical EP layer in Borer's theory. If combined with constraints on roots, the Voice projections can help us avoid the massive overgeneration of structures. Also, I locate VoiceP above AspectP unlike Alexiadou (2020) where the order is reversed.

The last distinction between my approach and that of both linguists lies in the treatment of Tense-related concept. I will follow Veselovská and Emonds (2015) who argue that Tense is not canonically realized in IP but lower in the structure in both English and Czech. I will locate it in the VoiceP projection. For these authors the IP level is not associated primarily with Tense but with the features of Mood.

These conclusions about syntactic mechanisms and layers in verbal domains, along with the arguments derived in the preceding chapter regarding nominal layers, provide a solid foundation for the analysis of nominalizations in the next chapter.

Functional Layers in Nominalization

The primary objective of this chapter is to evaluate the processes of nominalization in Czech. Given that nominalizations are hybrid in nature, comprising both nominal and verbal layers, this chapter will build on the findings from the previous two chapters, which focused on the nominal and verbal functional layers. Nevertheless, it will extend these arguments by providing a more in-depth analysis of the structure of nominalizations and exploring the interactions between these layers.

Both linguists A. Alexiadou and H. Borer have extensively addressed these issues in their work on nominalizations. Before providing a detailed explanation of their proposals, I will briefly introduce books and articles where they deal with these topics. Hagit Borer devotes to this issue her third book of the three-volume set *Taking Form* (2013). This book further develops her Exo-skeletal model focusing on a contrastive analysis of Hebrew derived nominals and English nominalizations. Artemis Alexiadou, on the other hand, deals with nominalizations in many articles but her main arguments are summarized in her book *Functional structure of Nominals* (2001). Since then, many aspects of nominalizations have been revised in her later articles, for example, Alexiadou (2009); Alexiadou (2017d). Aspect and Number related problems are analyzed in Alexiadou et al. (2010c). The cross-linguistic comparison of nominalization and an overview of the role of functional projection in nominalizations can be found in Alexiadou (2020).

In this chapter, I will summarize the primary conclusions drawn from these works. Following this theoretical discussion, I will consider the appropriateness of these proposals for Czech data, while also incorporating empirical analyses of Czech linguists, some of which were already introduced in section 1.4. The main emphasis will be given to the features of Number and Aspect, supplemented by some corpus data.

5.1 Borer (2013)—The Structure of Nominalizations

In her large third volume of the Exo-skeletal trilogy—*Taking Form*—Borer (2013) examines the process of nominalization in detail. She argues that Grimshaw's complex event nominals (CENs) come in two varieties: (i) the Long Argument structure nominalizations (LASNs) and (ii) Short Argument structure nominalizations (SASNs). This section will focus on describing these structures.

Both of these structures can have a quantity and non-quantity construal as (264) and (265) illustrate. The distinction between LASNs and SASNs is based on the position of the external argument: in LASNs, the external argument occurs pre-nominally and is marked as genitive as in (264a) and (264b) below. The short variety, in contrast, has two flavors: one where the external argument is expressed as a *by*-phrase and the other in where it remains overtly unmarked, as in (265a-c):

(264)	LASN	quantity	a.	*Kim's formation/forming of the team*
		non-quantity	b.	*Kim's pushing of the cart.*
(265)	SASN	quantity	a.	*the formation/forming of the team (by Kim)*
		quantity	b.	*the team's formation (by Kim)*
		non-quantity	c.	*the smelling of the stew (by Robin)*

In her study, Borer (2013) provides evidence that LASNs are derived from *active* structures while SASNs embed a piece of *passive* structure. To demonstrate her proposal, I will start with the derivation of LASNs and then proceed to explain SASNs.

The structure for Long AS nominalizations are schematically represented in (266) providing examples (a) with quantity and (b) non-quantity predicates.

(266) Derivation of LASNs (quantity + non-quantity)
 a. *Kim's **formation** of the team.*
 b. *Kim's **pushing** of cart*

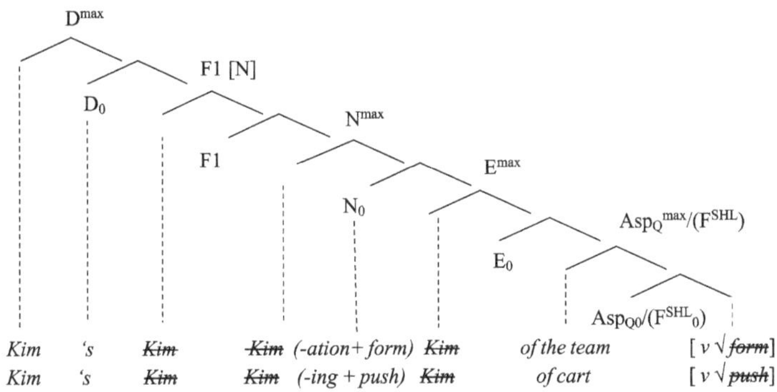

The quantity predicate contains the Asp_Q projection while the non-quantity predicate incorporates an F^{SHL} projection. This option is demonstrated in the graph provided above.

We can further observe that event layers are embedded under N which contains the suffix *-ation*. Borer (2013) terms these derivational suffixes as C-functors, a concept explored in section 2.2.1.

The event layers in nominalizations proposed by Borer and outlined in the scheme (266) can be compared to the ones which she suggests for the verbal functional domain, as described in section 4.1 and repeated here for convenience in (267):

(267) $[_{EP} <e>_E [_T [_{AspQ}{}^{max} <e>_{\#} [_{VP}]]]]$

Compared with the verbal domains in (267), in the nominalizations (266) the layer Tense is missing. This layer is responsible for subject-verb agreement, Tense and Nominative Case, all absent in AS-Nominals.[65]

Also, the Event Phrase (EP) can merge both above T and above grammatical Aspect (G-ASP), leading to a non-incremental functional architecture in

65 Most linguists assume that T is not present within AS nominals, but van Hout and Roeper (1998) argue for its presence.

AS-Nominals. This means that we cannot expect that the verbal structure can be pruned off at certain point, retaining the lower layers for nominalizations while omitting the higher levels as the Cartographic approach would have it (Cinque 2002).

Consequently, in the absence of Tense in nominalizations, the root's categorization is achieved minimally through the EP serving as a necessary prerequisite for defining an event that must be present in AS-Nominals.

Furthermore, the V-head present in both (267) and (266) merges in nominalizations with the suffix *-ation* (a functor $C_{N[V]}$) whose complement must be verbal. The derivation is thus dependent on the matching identity between the complement of the C-functor and the complement of the extended verbal projection.

Regarding the nominal layers in Borer (2005a), they were discussed in section 3.1 (theoretical framework in section 2.2) and summarized in (93) which I repeat below for convenience in (268):

(268) $[_{DP} \langle e \rangle_{d} [_{\#P} \langle e \rangle_{\#(DIV)} [_{CL}{}^{max} \langle e \rangle_{DIV(\#)} [_{NP}]]]]$

All these layers can be included in nominalizations. For the sake of space, I have only included F1 [N] and D as representatives of some nominal components of a structure.

Having explained the nominal and verbal layers in LASNs, our next task is to explain how arguments are licensed within these structures in (266). This is related to Case marking, where Borer suggests that the English *prenominal genitive 's* is the spell out of Case realization in SpecD or Spec#. In order to be case marked in this node, the external argument *Kim*, introduced in SpecE, needs to raise. In contrast, the internal argument *of the team* does not have to move and stays put in $SpecAsp_{Q}$. Also, in active sentence where the nodes G-ASP or T are missing, Borer expects *of* to be a spell out of the objective Case. This makes the morpheme *of* ambiguous between genitive and accusative which is not a standard treatment in other frameworks, see the comment in the footnote.[66]

66 In other words, *of* for Borer is objective marking which is dependent on T or G-ASP in some languages. While in Hebrew such marking is optional, in English it is obligatory

The second type of Borer's nominals are Short Argument Structure Nominals (SASNs). These are derived from passive structures and can be further divided into two sub-types: one for quantity predicates and another for non-quantity predicates. Let us begin by focusing on quantity SASNs as outlined in (269). We are also already familiar with the structural representation of passives as presented in Borer (2005b) in section 4.1.4.1. The derivation of SASNs is then quite straightforward: they are achieved by embedding the passive structure π under a nominalizer (Borer's C-functor).

(269) Derivation of SASNs (quantity structure)
 a. *the **formation/forming** of the team (by Kim)*
 b. *the team's **formation** (by Kim)*

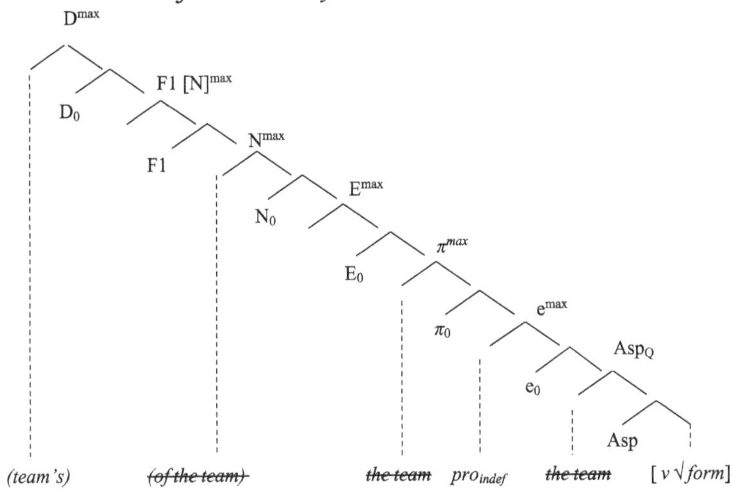

The primary difference from verbal passives lies in the fact that in the verbal domain, verb movement is blocked due to the impossibility of e to T

in the absence of T or G-ASP. This also means that *of* is for Borer ambiguous between objective and genitive marking, which contrasts with how other linguists treat this issue, for example, Emonds (2000) or Alexiadou (2020). These frameworks typically treat *of* as a nominal property and exclude it in the presence of a verb (V) in accordance with economy principles.

movement. However, in the nominal domain, there is no T element and consequently there is no obstruction to its movement to a higher position (in English not as high as in Hebrew to D).

In contrast, the following examples are cases of SASNs which are non-quantities:

(270) a. *the **forming** of complex molecular structures (by the scientists)*
b. *the **smelling** of the stew (by Robin)*

For these, the direct object merges directly in π. There is, however, an addition complication. π itself does not assign a theta role and it can only acquire the role of an event Participants if it stays put. Furthermore, in order to be *of*-marked, it would need to move to some nominal domain and cross E(vent) where it inevitably be assigned the role of an Originator which is not licit. Thus, Borer proposes a somewhat stipulative analysis where Case assignment for DP1 is achieved through Agree, in parallel fashion with the nominal domain where Nominative Case is assigned through Agree with T. As a result, DP1 gets the role of an event Participant. The whole process is demonstrated in (271):

(271) $[_{D}[_{F2\text{-}N}[_{F1\text{-}N}\,\textit{of}\,[_{N}\,[_{E}\,\text{V-C}_{N[V]}\,[_{\pi}\,[\,\textit{of}\,\text{DP1}]\ \text{V̶}\ [\text{e DP2 V̶}\,[_{C=V}\ \text{V̶}\,(\text{PP})]]]]]]$

The independent evidence for the passive analysis of SASNs Borer (2013) finds particularly in Hebrew. In this language, LASNs receive objective marking *et* as in (272a) whereas SASNs exemplified in (272b) have *šel* which is the equivalent of *of*-phrases. Compare the constructions below and see Borer (2013) for more examples:

(272)

a.	*ha.hokaxa*	*šel*	*ha.matematiqa'it*	*(*'**et** ha.ṭeʔana)*	*be-xodšayim*
	the.proof	of	the. mathematician	OM the.theorem	in two months

'the mathematician's proof *(of the theorem) in two months'

b.	*ha.hokaxa*	**(**šel** ha.ṭeana)*	*(ʔal yedey ha.matematiqa'it)*
	the.proof	of the theorem	by the.mathematician
	'the proof *(of the theorem) (? by the mathematician)'		

The example (272b) is for Borer (2013) clearly an AS-Nominal as in Hebrew *by*-phrases cannot be licensed in authorship contexts such as *a picture by van Gogh.*

5.1.1 Argument Structure Nominals and Referential Nominals

Armed with the concept of C-functors from section 2.2.1, we can now elucidate the differences between Argument Structure (AS) nominals as described above and Referential (R) nominals.

First, recall that the structural description between AS-Nominals and simple events remained unaccounted for in Grimshaw (1990). It was not explained why both constructions illustrated in (273) can be eventive although only the (273a) takes arguments obligatorily.

(273)	a.	*The frequent **examination** (*) of students took place in the principal's office.*	AS
	b.	*The frequent **examinations** took place in the principal's office.*	**Simple event**

Borer (2013) proposes that the conundrum can be resolved if we assume that R-Nominals and AS-Nominals have the structures outlined in (274). Her analysis depends on the assumption that Verbs or roots in themselves do not inherently select arguments. Subsequently, when R-Nominals are directly embedded within a nominal structure, no event structure is expected. What renders R-Nominals eventive is the C-functor which can take the V as its complement. The other way round—that is, that V would select a higher C-functor—is not allowed.

AS-Nominals, on the other hand, are associated with verbal layers F1 [V], F2 [V] which allow the head to re-merge and re-project, eventually incorporating into the stem. Thus, all event-related information, including arguments of AS-Nominals can properly come from the verbal functional structure.

(274) (a) R-Nominals

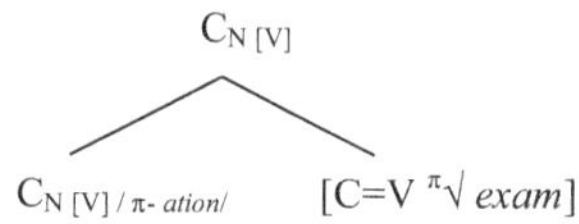

(b) AS-Nominals

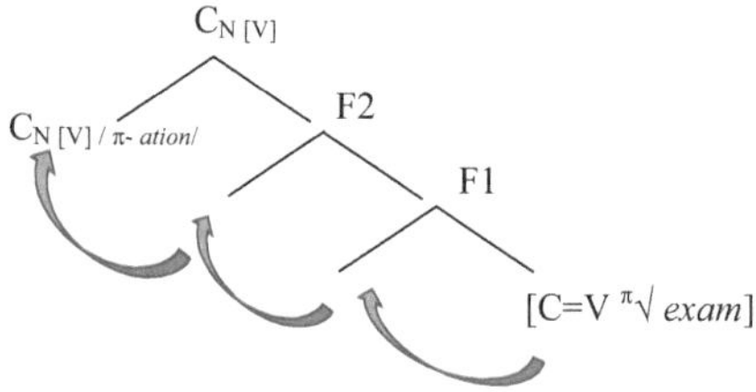

As mentioned earlier, Borer's derivation is heavily dependent on the matching between the complement of the C-functor and the complement of the extended verbal projection. If the C-functor were defined as $C_{N\,[A]}$ and the extended projection were verbal, the derivation would collapse. This assertion carries significant implications. First, it becomes evident that the responsibility of assigning an event argument cannot be attributed solely to C-functors. Second, it also implies that Nouns can never serve as the source of event structure. They are rather vehicles for passing event properties.[67]

Instead, the primary origin of the event functional projection arises from the Event phrase, as explained in section 4.1.3. Therefore, in AS-Nominals minimally the EP needs to be present. Alongside this, modifiers such as ASP_Q (Aspect Phrase) can modify events and be included into AS-Nominals. It is also worth emphasizing that the event-related functional projection does not primarily introduce arguments, as explained in section 4.1. Rather, arguments acquire specific interpretations such as an Originator or a Subject-of-Quantity, if they are present in this projection

67 It is worth noting that this claim does not pertain to the arguments of Nouns that do not represent events, such as relational Nouns (e.g., *a story about Mary*). Since all arguments originate from the structure, there is an expectation of a nominal extended projection present between the C-functor and the root.

5.1.2 Grimshaw's Criteria Revisited

Since Grimshaw (1990), there have been several tests for the identification of AS-Nominals. These criteria, however, have been challenged in many aspects. Borer (2013) is no exception, taking these criteria as a starting point and proposing her modifications. Some of these revisions are discussed in relation to the de-adjectival nominals illustrated below in (275) and (276):[68]

(275) a. *the court's (*deliberate)* ***awareness*** *of the problem (for many years)*
b. *Pat's* **consciousness** *of my presence (for several minutes)*

(276) a. ***awareness*** *of the problem (*by the authorities)*
b. ***consciousness*** *of my presence (*by my cats)*
c. *****awareness*** *of the problem in order to solve the situation*

Some of the Grimshaw's diagnostics are clearly not met by de-adjectival nominals, in particular Agent modification, Agent control and *by*-phrases. Given that de-adjectival nominals are not eventive but rather stative these findings are not unexpected because the hallmark of non-quantity nominals is the inability to pluralize, which de-adjectival nominals being statives certainly are.

For this reason, Borer (2013) notes that among the criteria stipulated by Grimshaw (1990) and summarized in section 1.3.3, only the following three remain relevant for stative nominalizations. Notice the tight connections of arguments with Aspect:

(277) a. obligatory arguments
b. subjects are arguments
c. allow some aspectual modification

Consequently, AS-Nominals do not necessarily have to be eventive but can also be stative. According to Borer's proposal, de-adjectival nominals contain a stative event that is embedded within their structure. I will use the criterion

68 Examples with Determiners such as **the awareness of the problem (by the authorities)* are ungrammatical because of the competition between PRO and the definite article *the* for the position SpecDP. It will be the subject of the next section.

of *by*-phrases to assess the AS capacity of Czech nominalizations, and this divergence between eventivity and stativity needs to be taking into account when evaluating the data.

5.1.3 PRO—Evidence for Passive Voice in SASNs

Many linguists suppose that prenominal possessors in AS-Nominals are never true event arguments—this viewpoint has been adopted by Chomsky (1970), Grimshaw (1990), Marantz (1997), Alexiadou (2001; 2017a). Consequently, Agent prenominal DPs must be Possessors with agentive interpretation. Borer (2013), on the other hand, provides a plausible argument by means of the phonetically null PRO for the opposite.[69]

This argument is related to the whole architecture of nominalization, namely whether nominalizations are built from active or passive sentences and whether the process of passivization can apply within them. We will see that answers to these questions are not unified in the linguistic literature and I will assess these questions thoroughly in section 5.4 when considering Czech data.

Borer's (2013) main claim in this respect is that the SEAs of SASNs are quite similar to the characteristics of the SEA in short clausal passives and quite distinct from the properties PRO in gerunds and infinitives. This supports her claim that SASNs emerge from the nominalization of verbal syntactic passive structure.

Borer's (2020) argument in favor of the above assertion is based on the study by Lebeaux (1984). Lebeaux argues that in target cases when silent subjects do not c-command each other nor is there any obvious antecedent that could control both of them, they tend to have universal/generic interpretation. Hence, these subjects need to refer to the same antecedent as formalized in the so-called Lebeaux effect given in (278):[70]

69 PRO is a base generated phonetically null DP, and it is not a residue of movement like NP-traces. Chomsky and Lasnik (1993) propose that it is the only element which can bear a special null case.

70 Generic interpretations can range over pluralities, most typically human groups or possibly kinds (i.e., *all those who are sick, all who are poor*, etc.). Existential expressions assert existence. More examples were discussed in relation to the DP layers in section 3.1.2.

(278) **The Lebeaux effect** (Lebeaux 1984)
Within an appropriately defined local domain, all occurrences of uncontrolled silent subject need to have a universal interpretation (=PRO-arb), and hence are identified.

Consider now the possibilities of subject construal in Infinitives, Gerunds and SASNs provided by Borer (2020):

(279) **✗ (Distinct Subject construal excluded)**
a. [PRO *to unionize the labor force*] *entails/is* [PRO *to fire workers*]
b. [PRO *to unionize the labor force*] *entails/means* [PRO *firing workers*]

(280) **✗ (Distinct Subject construal excluded)**
a. [PRO *unionizing the labor force*] *entails/means* [PRO *firing workers*]
b. [PRO *destroying the work environment*] *entailed/meant* [PRO *reorganizing the labor force*]

(281) **✓ (Distinct Subject construal possible)**
a. [*The unionizing of the labor force*] *entails* [*the raising of salaries*]
b. [*The destruction of the work environment*] *entailed* [*the reorganization of the labor force*]

Although Borer (2020) specifically selected the examples to favor a distinct subject construal, such construal is not licit in gerunds (280) and infinitives (279). The only reading available for, for example, (280b) is that the individuals who caused damage to the work environment are the same ones that reorganized the labor force. In contrast, in SASNs in (281), distinct subject construal is possible.

The last point testifies in favor of a passive analysis for SASNs because their SEAs tally with the SEAs of passives. Borer (2020) envisages for passives and SASNs a null indefinite pronominal pro_{indef} which can have two readings: existential and generic as illustrated in (282):

(282) a. *Committee work was successfully avoided. (→ by some)*
b. *In the Middle Ages, it was believed that if you travel West you would get to India (→ by all)*

Whereas in their existential reading the option of the same subject construal is dis-preferred, in their generic reading the same subject reading becomes possible. The examples given in (283) confirm that a disjoint interpretation is available:

(283)

	✓ **DS (Distinct Subject construal possible)**
a.	*Mail was collected before tea was prepared.*
b.	*The workers had to be organized before salaries could be raised.*

The range of interpretations available for PRO in gerunds and Infinitives is a subset of interpretation available for $\text{pro}_{\text{indef.}}$ in passives and SASNs. Structurally, PRO can also occur in LASNs nominals and then these two have different positions in AS-Nominals. PRO is located in SpecD while $\text{pro}_{\text{indef}}$ can occupy a position below the final realization site of N.

(284) a. $[_{D} \ldots\ldots\ldots N \ldots [_{\pi} \pi [_{e}\ \text{pro}_{\text{indef}} \ldots\ldots [_{C=V} V]]]]]$
b. $[_{D}\ \text{PRO N} [_{E} \ldots\ldots [_{C=V} V]]]]]$

Evidence for the existence of PRO in AS-Nominals can be found in de-adjectival nominals, henceforth Adjectival Argument Structure Nominals (AASNs). We have already shown that they cannot passivize. Thus, they do not have recourse to $\text{pro}_{\text{indef.}}$ Yet, the ungrammaticality of (285) when contrasted with grammatical cases in (276) where the definite article is missing signals that PRO must be present. If the definite article is in complementary distribution with PRO in SpecD, the examples below cannot license an external argument and ungrammaticality arises.

(285) a. **The **awareness** of the constitutional problem*
b. **The **consciousness** of my presence (*by my cats)*
c. **The **readiness** to leave (*by Robin)*

This is a welcome result because external arguments are no less optional in AS-Nominals than they are in clausal structures. It now emerges that sentences such as (286) will, in principle, be ambiguous between structure (284a) and (284b).

(286) *ongoing* ***deprivation*** *of entire population*

It might be a case of nominalized passive or active structure with silent SEA-PRO in SpecD.

This section has demonstrated that SASNs emerge from the nominalization of verbal syntactic passive structure. I will return to the consequences of this claim when discussing Czech data.

5.1.4 By-phrases

As mentioned earlier, *by*-phrases can testify in favor of argument status of nominals. Therefore, we need to elaborate their derivation process in more detail. In Borer's architecture, they are generally treated on a par with other PPs. Subsequently, they are classified based on their complements either as nominal or prepositional, whether they are followed by a Noun (287a) or another Preposition (287b) respectively:

(287) a. *I broke the glasses* ***to*** *three beautiful pieces.*
b. *She emerged* ***from*** *under the house.*

Let's explore the derivational process and the formation of Prepositional Phrases (PPs). In principle, any item from the conceptual array (288a) can merge with a Preposition (P) that categorizes it, assigns it an interpretation, and provides its Case. This resulting PP can then merge with an L-head (as shown in (288b)) or alternatively combine with an additional PP:

(288) a. *<emerge, house>*
b. < *emerge* [$_{P}$*from* [$_{DP}$ *the* [$_{N}$*house*]]] >
c. < [$_{V}$ *emerge* [$_{P}$*from* [$_{DP}$ *the* [$_{N}$*house*]]] >

For Borer, *by*-phrases can identify the AS status of nominals and thus be generated VP internally under two conditions. First, they have to express *agentive* meaning. Second, the languages should not have the option of *authorship by*. To illustrate this, in languages like English, where authorship *by* is possible, as in *the book by Chomsky*, the *by*-phrase becomes ambiguous. However, in Hebrew, which does not allow for authorship *by* constructions, *by*-phrases remain unambiguous and serve as a sign of verbal projection in the language. This diagnostic will be applied in the domain of Czech nominalizations in section 5.4.2.

5.1.5 Rigidity of AS-Nominals vs. Flexibility of R-Nominals

According to Borer (2013), there is a clear asymmetry in word order constrains on AS-Nominals and R-Nominals. This asymmetry arises from structural factors but differs from the explanation provided by Alexiadou, as we will see in section 5.4.3. I will elaborate on Borer's mechanism in the upcoming part to determine later which approach better explains processes within nominalizations.

Borer (2013) demonstrates these discrepancies between AS and R-Nominals with Hebrew examples, but analogous constraints can be found in other languages. For example, the phenomenon is discussed for Romance languages in Zubizarreta (1979); Cinque (1980) and Giorgi and Longobardi (1991), and Polish data are given in Rozwadowska (1997).

Consider first the free word order of R-Nominals in Hebrew which allows for multiple cases of the Genitive Preposition *šel*:

(289)	a.	*ha.tmuna*	***šel***	*van Gox*	***šel***	*ha muzeon*
		the picture	of	van Gogh	of	the museum'
		'Van Gogh's picture of the museum'				
	b.	*ha.tmuna*	***šel***	*ha muzeon*	***šel***	*van Gox*
		the picture	*of*	*the museum*	*of*	*van Gogh*
		'Van Gogh's picture of the museum'				

No such freedom is allowed in AS-Nominals in Hebrew. The word order obj>subj in (290b) as well as subj>obj in (290a) is not permissible when both arguments are marked with genitive *šel*:

(290)	a.	* *ha.'isup*	***šel** Lyn*	***šel** ha.pitriyot*
		the collection	of Lyn	of the mushrooms
		*'the collection of Lyn of the mushrooms'		
	b.	* *ha.'isup*	***šel** ha.pitriyot*	***šel** Lyn*
		the proof	of the mushrooms	of Lyn
		*'the collection of the mushrooms of Lyn'		

From the previous example, one might speculate that there is a restriction on postnominal subjects in AS-Nominals. However, this is not the case, as demonstrated by the examples in (291). The generalization is that in AS-Nominals, postnominal subjects are permissible when there is no object present (291b) or when the indirect object is present but marked differently than with *of* (291a).

(291)	a.	*ha.hištabcut*	***šel***	*Rina*	*be-šuk*	*ha.ʕaboda*	*(b-a.šana ha.'axrona)*
		the integration	of	Rina	in labor	the market	during the past year
		'Rina's integration into the market (during the past year)'					
	b.	*ha.rica*	***šel***	*ha-yeladim*			
		the running	of	the children			
		'the running of the children'					

We can now compare the situation with English. In English, both AS-Nominals (292c) and R-Nominals (292a) allow for two types of genitives. One is the prenominal genitive realized with *-s*, and the other is the postnominal genitive realized with an *of* phrase. Two postnominal genitives are not permissible, neither with R-Nominals (292b), nor with AS-Nominals

(292d). Moreover, postnominal subjects are grammatical in exactly the same cases as in Hebrew as (292e) and (292f) show:[71]

(292) a. *John's* ***picture*** *of the sunflower*
b. **picture* *of the sunflower of John/** ***picture*** *of John of the sunflower*
c. *John's* ***destruction*** *of the city*
d. **the* ***destruction*** *of the city of John/*the* ***destruction*** *of John of the city*
e. *The constant* ***laughter*** *of children*
f. *? the constant* ***thinking*** *of CEOs of their profit*

For the sake of space, I will not repeat the examples from other above-mentioned languages. I will only summarize the facts mentioned in Borer (2013) about the possibilities of prenominal and postnominal genitives in R and AS-Nominals. Table (293) below provides an overview of the maximum number of allowed prenominal and postnominal genitives in these languages:

(293)	R-Nominals		AS-Nominals	
	Prenominal	Postnominal	Prenominal	Postnominal
English	**1**	**1**	**1**	**1**
Hebrew	-	**3**	-	**1**
Romance, Polish	**- (only pronouns)**	**3**	**- (only pronouns)**	**1**

On the basis of the data in table (293) and preceding examples, there are two key points that require clarification. Firstly, we need to explain why English R-Nominals do not permit multiple occurrences of *of*-phrases. Secondly, we need to understand the reason for the contrast in word order rigidity between AS-Nominals and the optionality within R-Nominals cross-linguistically.

71 Borer (2013) sets aside the nature of 's in cases such as *a car/picture of John's* as these are prohibited in AS nominals: **the destruction of the city of John's.*

As for the ban on the iteration of *of-phrases* in English, Borer (2013) supposes that it resembles a phonological restriction reminiscent of similar concatenation of *-ing* which she calls the "*Double-of Filter.*" The ungrammaticality of R-Nominals (292b) with the ungrammatical structure in (294) in English can be attributed to the *Double -of Filter.* This mechanism covers also cases of AS-Nominals in (292d) with two postnominal genitives.

In contrast, the rigidity of word order in AS-Nominals with prenominal genitives (295) stems from *structural* reasons. The need to license two arguments forces the higher one to raise and be case marked with 's in DP. As for the internal argument *the city* in (295) cannot move to any nominal functional specifier because *John* has left a copy in all of them. Instead, it can be case marked in $\text{SpecAsp}_{\text{Q}}$ where it functions as the spell out of the objective Case in English in the absence of T.[72]

(294) a. *$[_{\text{D}}$ $[_{\text{F3-N}}$*picture* $[_{\text{F2-N}}$***of** John* $[_{\text{F1-N}}$ ***of** the sunflower* $[_{\text{N}}$ ~~*picture*~~]]]]]
b. $[_{\text{D}}$***John's*** $[_{\text{F3-N}}$*picture* $[_{\text{F2-N}}$ $[_{\text{F1-N}}$ ***of** the sunflower* $[_{\text{N}}$ ~~*picture*~~]]]]]

(295) a. *$[_{\text{D}}$ $[_{\text{F2-N}}$*destruction* $[_{\text{F1-N}}$*of* ***John*** $[_{\text{N}}$ ~~*destruction*~~ $[_{\text{E}}$~~***John***~~ $[_{\text{AspQ}}$*of the city*]]]]]
b. $[_{\text{D}}$***John's*** $[_{\text{F2-N}}$*destruction* $[_{\text{F1-N}}$~~***John***~~ $[_{\text{N}}$ ~~*destruction*~~ $[_{\text{E}}$~~***John***~~ $[_{\text{AspQ}}$ *of the city*]]]]]]

Now, consider the Hebrew R-Nominal from example (289a) and AS-Nominals from (290a). The structure for the R-Nominal is in (296a) and it shows that in contrast to English, the Double-*of* Filter is not operative in Hebrew (nor in Polish and Romance), thus nothing prevents Hebrew R-Nominals from appearing with two genitives.[73]

However, in Hebrew AS-Nominals (296b), a similar limitation as in English arises, only one DP can move, the other is blocked by a trace and has to stay put. Moreover, objects marked with *šel* in Hebrew must undergo Case marking within a nominal domain, which renders them illicit. This situation is analogous to what happens in Polish and other languages.

72 Rightward movement and adjunction are excluded.

73 This reveals the ad hoc nature of Borer's empty Double *-of* filter.

(296) a. $[_{\text{D}}$ *tmuna* $[_{\text{F2-N}}$ ***šel*** *van Gox* $[_{\text{F1-N}}$ ***šel*** *ha muzeon* $[_{\text{N}}$ ~~*tmuna*~~]]]]]
$[_{\text{D}}$ *picture* $[_{\text{F2-N}}$ *of Van Gogh* $[_{\text{F1-N}}$ *of the museum* $[_{\text{N}}$ ~~*picture*~~]]]]]

b. *$[_{\text{D}}$ *ha.'isup* $[_{\text{F2-N}}$ *šel Lyn* $[_{\text{F1-N}}$ *šel ha.pitriyot* $[_{\text{N}}$ ~~*ha.kaxa*~~ $[_{\text{E}}$ ~~*Lyn*~~ $[_{\text{AspQ}}$ ~~*ha.pitriyot*~~]]]]
*$[_{\text{D}}$ *collection* $[_{\text{F2-N}}$ *of Lyn* $[_{\text{F1-N}}$ of *the mushrooms* $[_{\text{N}}$ ~~*collection*~~ $[_{\text{E}}$ ~~*Lyn*~~ $[_{\text{AspQ}}$ ~~*the mushroom*~~]]]]]

In contrast, Hebrew AS-Nominals with object marking *et* are the realizations of objective marking which can be licensed in Asp_{Q} in the absence of T. Therefore, Long AS-Nominals as shown in (297) are possible.

(297) $[_{\text{D}}$ *ktiba* $[_{\text{F1-N}}$ *šel Ran* $[_{\text{N}}$ ~~*ktiba*~~ $[_{\text{E}}$ ~~*Ran*~~ $[_{\text{AspQ}}$ *(et) miktab*]]]]]
$[_{\text{D}}$ *writing* $[_{\text{F1I}}$ *an* $[_{\text{N}}$ ~~*writting*~~ $[_{\text{E}}$ *Ran* $[_{\text{AspQ}}$ *the letter*]]]]]

We have not touched so far on the fact that both orders NSO as well as NOS are possible in R-Nominals as in (289a) and (289b) respectively. Borer (2013) puts forward that only the complex NO or VO could move. She excludes the possibility that the N-head and the complement are subject to separate fronting. Consequently, the word order in the result nominals is achieved by movement SNONOS as demonstrated in (298) below.

(298) $[_{\text{F4-N}}$ $[_{\text{F3-N}}$ Possessor/Author $[_{\text{F2-N}}$ *picture* $[_{\text{F1-N}}$ Depicted $[_{\text{N}}$ ~~*picture*~~]]]]]

Conversely, VO is unable to move to some specifier because the incorporation of V to N would be blocked, and the derivation would crash.

This distinction between AS-Nominals and R-Nominals would be unexplainable under Grimshaw's framework who postulates the separation of the external argument in nominalizations. In turn, this external argument would have to merge with some projection of N and then (in English) possibly re-merge with D. Consequently, nothing would block the movement of the internal argument in AS-Nominals.

The rigidity of AS-Nominals as opposed to R-Nominals stems from the Case-licensing mechanism. As I will explain later, in Alexiadou the rigidity of AS-Nominals is also related to Case licensing but stems from ergative patterns in nominalizations. I will assess these issues in section 5.4.3 when analyzing Czech data. The objective will be to determine which theory is more appropriate and able to explain a complete range of nominalizations with as little appeal to ad hoc devices as possible.

As part of this, I will also examine ditransitive, unaccusative, and unergative structures, which are briefly introduced in the subsequent sections.

5.1.6 Ditransitives

The system for Case licensing outlined above accounts for the fact that ditransitives cannot occur in English nominals as in (299b):

(299) a. *Carly's generous **giving of** candy to the children*
b. **Carly's generous **giving** (**of**) the children (**of**) candy*

The third argument cannot be licensed in any nominal functional projection as all merger sites have been pre-empted by moving of the logical subject *Carly* to SpecD. Nor can it receive an objective marking *of* due to the extension of the Double -*of* Filter. What can of, course converge is the derivation, where the goal argument *to the children* in (299a) is otherwise licensed.

5.1.7 Unaccusatives and Unergatives

Unaccusatives (300) and Unergatives (301) belong to the category of intransitive AS-Nominals, making them examples of Long active AS-Nominals rather than Short passive AS-Nominals:

(300) a. *the **arrival** of the train*
b. *the **sinking** of the ship*

(301) a. *the **moving** of the train*
b. *the **dancing** of children*

While in certain languages, for example, German, unergatives occasionally form passives (302), it is a well-known fact that unergatives do not cross-linguistically passivize.

(302) *Es wurde den ganzen Abend gentantz/gelacht/ gesprochen.*
it AUX$_{PAST}$ the$_{ACC}$ whole$_{ACC}$ evening$_{ACC}$ dance/laugh/speak$_{PAST.PRT}$
'People were dancing/laughing/speaking the whole evening.'

Such cases in (302) are analyzed as impersonal passives (Roeper 2020), which are not commonly found in English. They do not give rise to passive nominalizations (303) either:

(303) **Die Getanzheit/Gesprochenheit/Gelachheit des Abends*
the dancing/speaking/laughing evening$_{GEN}$
*'Dancing/Speaking/Laughing of the evening. '

As far as unaccusatives are concerned, Borer (2013) claims that unaccusative do not take *by*-phrases and do not allow implicit argument control as their clausal counterparts, see below:

(304) a. *The **arrival** of the train (*by the conductor).*
b. *The **sinking** of the ship (*by the navy)*
c. *the **accumulation** of dust (*in order to grow tomatoes)*
d. *the **separation** of the cream (*in order to make the cake)*

In the derivation of both unaccusatives and unergatives, the argument might be Case marked in situ or alternatively in some nominal projection. Their V incorporates into N and raises to some higher nominal functional layer, but not to D. The only difference lies in unaccusatives having the functional layer Asp$_{Q}$ present, causing the argument to originate lower in the structure. On the other hand, unergatives lack this Asp$_{Q}$ layer, resulting in the argument starting from a higher position, as depicted below:

(305) a. [$_{D}$ [$_{F2\text{-}N}$ V-C$_{N[V]}$ [$_{F1\text{-}N}$ ***of*** DP1 ~~V-C~~$_{N[V]}$ [$_{N}$ ~~DP1~~ ~~V-C~~$_{N[V]}$ [$_{E}$ ~~DP1~~ ~~V~~ [$_{C=V}$ ~~V~~]]]]]
b. [$_{D}$ [$_{F2\text{-}N}$ V-C$_{N[V]}$ [$_{F1\text{-}N}$ ***of*** DP1 ~~V-C~~$_{N[V]}$ [$_{N}$ ~~DP1~~ ~~V-C~~$_{N[V]}$ [$_{E}$ ~~DP1~~ ~~V~~ [$_{ASPQ}$ ~~DP1~~ ~~V~~ [$_{C=V}$ ~~V~~]]]]]

5.1.8 Zero-Derived Nominals

Borer (2013) supports the idea that there is no zero realization for $C_{N[V]}$, meaning there is no zero-nominal suffix. This contrasts with the Distributed Morphology, where such an option is possible. This distinction will impact the lower part of the nominalization and therefore requiring further discussion of this topic.

In Borer's theory, the relationship between the pair *a walk/to walk* is captured by the same root which gets categorized by corresponding nominal or verbal projection D, T:

(306) a. [D [$_{C=N}$ √WALK]]
b. [T [$_{C=V}$ √WALK]]

She discusses several characteristics of the zero-derived nominals (ZNs) which lead her to this proposal. First and foremost, the property of zero-derived nominals is their inability to form AS-Nominals. This can be illustrated by comparing the examples below:

(307) a. *the **walking**/(***walk**) of the dog for three hours*
b. *the **importation**/(* **import**) of goods from China in order to bypass ecological regulations*

Second, zero-derived nominals may exhibit stress shifts when compared with their verbal correlates. In the Exo-skeletal model, these phonological changes testify in favor of a root analysis.

(308) a. *permít*$_V$ → *pérmit*$_N$
b. *progréss*$_V$ → *prógress*$_N$
c. *ekspórt*$_V$ → *éksport*$_N$

Third point suggests if zero-nominal suffix were able to incorporate verbal structure, it should be compatible with verbalizing suffixes such as *-ize* and *-ify*, just like some overt suffixes are. However, this is not observed as (309) indicates:

(309) a.	*crystal-ize*	**the crystal-ize-* $Ø_N$	*the crystalization*
b.	*acid-ify*	**the acid-ify-* $Ø_N$	*the acidification*

Borer also quotes some exceptions as in (310) that could potentially form AS-Nominals. She does not extensively explore these exceptions in her discussion. In a footnote, she remarks that all these forms are of Latinate origin and do not exhibit stress shifts. As a result, it is speculated that in these instances, a suffix may be postulated that is phonologically robust enough to block stress shift.

(310) *change, release, use, murder, discharge, endeavor, consent, resolve, descent, decline, collapse, rape*

During the analysis of Czech data in section 5.4.2.1, I will evaluate whether zero-derived nominals possess a nominal suffix or if they are devoid of such a suffix.

5.1.9 Adverbs

According to Cinque (1999) and other authors, Adverbs have the ability to indicate the existence of certain functional projections. Moreover, they often share meaning with their adjectival variants, suggesting an interplay between these two-word groups.[74]

In particular, Borer proposes that specific types of Adverbs are licensed in particular projections. Very schematically, this proposal is outlined below:

(311)
- $[_{C/T}$ (proposition) **evidential** adv (V)
- $[_{E}$ **“agentive”** adv (V)
- $[_{T}[_{G\text{-}ASP}$ **g-asp** adv (V) [**manner** adv V]]]]]

The scheme above predicts that the occurrence of agentive and manner Adverbs *frequent* and *cruelly* in examples such as (312) signals the eventive

74 This observation is not unexpected since Adjectives and Adverbs are often argued to be part of a unified A-category (see, e.g., Emonds 2000 for extensive argument). I am not going to question categorial taxonomies here, assuming simply parallelism of both meaning and form.

characteristics of AS-Nominals in Hebrew. Borer (2013) also points out that in Hebrew, Adverbs can appear together with Adjectives in AS-Nominals, which rules out the possibility that Hebrew AS-Nominals are sometimes gerunds and sometimes being more nominal.

(312) *Ha.**dikkuy** ha.**takup** šel ha.caba **be'akzariyut** 'et ha.'oklosiya*
the oppression the frequent of the army cruelly OM the population
gorem le-harbe sin'a.
cause to-much hatred
'The army's frequent cruel/intentional oppression of the population gave rise to much hatred.'

Not all Adverbs can, however, occur in AS-Nominals. Evidential and aspectual Adverbs, in particular, are not licit which can be explained by the absence of G-ASP, which bars aspectual Adverbs:

(313) *ha **biššul** *(**tamid**) šel Dan *(**tamid**) et ha.cli*
the cooking always of Dab always OM the roast
'the cooking (*always) of Dan (*always) the roast'

The distribution of Adverbs in English further corroborates this analysis. English gerunds lack T but possess G-ASP, which explains why evidential Adverbs are not prohibited, while aspectual Adverbs are acceptable.

(314) a. *Mary ('s) **eating** pasta **often**.*
b. *Bill **always talking** to his neighbor.*

(315) a. **Mary('s) **presumably eating** pasta.*
b. **Bill **evidently talking** to his neighbor.*
c. **(Mary's) (**fortunately**) **discovering** this evidence (**fortunately**) shed light on the interpretation*

Furthermore, Borer (2013) sees the relative grammaticality of manner and agent-oriented Adverb in AS-Nominals (316) compared to their complete ungrammaticality in R-Nominals (317) as evidence for the assertion that R-Nominals do not include verbal functional structure:

(316) a. *?Even though it was expected, I was nonetheless shocked by Jane's* ***resignation*** *from the bank so* ***quickly****.*
b. *?The* ***disassembling*** *of this antique furniture* ***successfully*** *will require many hours of work, but its potential renovation is dependent on it.*

(317) a. **the* ***race*** *to the mountains* ***deliberately***
b. **Sarah's* ***wedding*** *to Tom* ***happily***

Importantly, there is an interaction between Adverbs and adjectives in the syntactic structure. The actual content of Adverbs can, in fact, be expressed by adjectives both in AS-Nominals (318) as well as in simple events (319). It can even include the content of Adverbs which is barred in gerunds. Compare the modifier *presumably* in gerund (315a) with the one in the AS-Nominal (318b):

(318) a. *The* ***fortunate discovery*** *of this commentary may shed light on the interpretation.*
b. *The court presupposed the* ***presumed destruction*** *of the evidence.*

(319) a. *John's* ***fortunate trip*** *to the mountains*
b. *her* ***presumed lecture*** *on biology*

The above explanation can help us roughly describe distributional characteristics of English and Hebrew AS-Nominals. I will apply this diagnostic to Czech nominals and identify the existence of individual functional projections.

5.1.10 Compositionality of Nominals

Derived nominals can be characterized also with respect to their *compositionality*. By 'compositional' we refer to the fact that the Content of the whole can be directly computed from the Content of its parts. If so, then AS-Nominals are always compositional while no such restriction holds for R-Nominals, which can be either compositional or non-compositional.

Recalling the construction of Content as a component of meaning from section 2.2.3, we can now elaborate on the Content in more detail. First of all, Borer assumes that Content matching is not only cyclical but also optional.[75]

Interestingly, R-Nominals and AS-Nominals are *morpho-phonologically identical* which means that the very same morpho-phonological derivative is ambiguous between the two. For example, the word *transformation* can be an AS-Nominal or R-Nominal. Therefore, the differences in the content between the two cannot be accounted to surface forms. Rather, the culprit is the presence or absence of the argument structure within these constructions. According to Borer, the Content beyond the merger of extended functional projections[76] must be compositional.

Let us explain this with some concrete examples. While in R-Nominals in (320) the content can be matched either in phase I or phase II, in AS-Nominal in (321), the only option is assigning the content to *transform*. This limitation arises due to the presence of functional projection layers which delimit the Content domain and gives rise to compositionality.

(320)	Phase I	***transform***	→ TRANSFORM	Compositional
			→φ	Non-compositional
	Phase II	$[_N$ **[*transform*] *ation*]]**	→TRANSFORM + $C_{N[V]}$	Compositional
			→TRANSFORMATION	Non-Compositional

(321) $[_N\ [_{ExP}\ [_{ExP}$ [*transform*]] *ation*] →TRANSFORM + $C_{N[V]}$

75 Borer (2013) illustrates her viewpoint using examples from the poem Jabberwocky by L. Carroll, where items like *slithy* or *mimsy* lack explicit content. Additionally, she points to instances like *bloody* where no content is attributed to *blood*, but the content is instead matched with the entire derivative as a whole.

76 Borer calls this an Exp-segment. This means segments of Extended Projections (e.g., for a verbal Extended Projection T, G-ASP and so on).

After discussing Borer's (2013) framework for nominalizations and its significant aspects, we can now proceed to examine Alexiadou's approach to nominalizations and draw a comparison between their perspectives to motivate the choice of the model I will use for my analysis of Czech data in the following sections.

5.2 Alexiadou (2020)—The Structure of Nominalizations

In her article *D vs. n nominalizations within and across languages* (Alexiadou 2020), the author proposes a unified structure for all types of nominalizations as in (324). Let us compare her scheme with the structure she used with Nouns (as in (119) in section 3.2) repeated here for convenience in (322):

(322) Nominal Functional Projection
[DP [#P (quantity) [DivP plural marking [*n*P Gender [Root]]]]]

And with the verbal domains (as in (193) in section 4.2) repeated below in (323):

(323) Verbal Functional Projection
[CP --- [TP --- [AspectP --- [VoiceP *external arg* [*v*P *internal arg* [Root]]]]]

For nominalizations (339) Alexiadou proposes that the verbal layers are embedded under nominal layers and can be nominalized either by *n* or D.

(324) Structural representation of nominalizations in Alexiadou (2020)

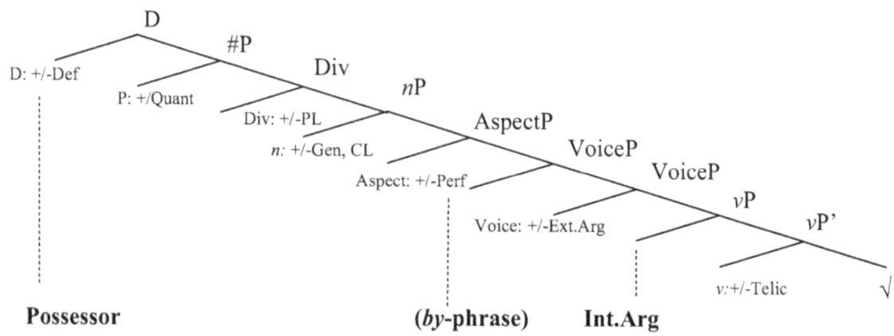

For English, Alexiadou (2020) does not expect higher verbal layers such as T, CP and therefore these are not included in our structure.[77] Unlike Borer (2013), however, Alexiadou (2020) does not posit different structures for AS-Nominals and R-Nominals. Instead, she argues that various nominalizations arise due to the different height attachments of the nominalizer, as will be explained later. All the functional projections in the structure depicted above have been demonstrated in the previous two chapters. Their roles in nominalizations will be illustrated in the following section through various examples.

5.2.1 n-based and D-based Nominalizations

In Alexiadou's (2020) model, various types of nominalizations across languages can be formed based on the cut-off points within the structure where *n* or D can attach. This leads to the establishment of two nominalization strategies described in (325): (a) the n-nominalizations and (b) the D-nominalizations.

(325) a. [CP [TP **n** [AspectP **n** [VoiceP **n** [vP]]]]]
b. [**D** [CP **D** [TP **D** [AspectP [VoiceP [vP]]]]]

A key distinction between these two types is the level of the verbal structure they can comprise. Alexiadou assumes that while the verbal extended projection can be interrupted at any point, *n* cannot nominalize TP and CP. These two layers can only be nominalized by D. I will summarize other distinct characteristics of these two nominalization types in the following section referring to English examples and the structure in (324).

Let us start with *n*-based nominalizations. When the nominalizer *n* attaches directly to the root, no verbal characteristics are expected and various non-eventive nominals are derived as illustrated below:

(326) a. *a cat/a table/a dog (*for/in three hours)*
b. [D [#P [DivP [nP [√]]]]]

The first functional layer above the root in the verbal projection, as shown in (324), is *v*P. After the attachment of *n* to this functional projection, *result*

77 These structures are possible in Turkish or Japanese; see Alexiadou (2020).

(328d) and *simple event nominals* (328a-c) are generated with the structure in (327). The verbal (*v*) level in these Nouns can be detected by the presence of adjectives like *rapid* and *rough* which modify the event of delivering, estimating and measuring in (328). Although the *v* layer is present and can license internal arguments, as we will discuss later, SENs and RNs do not require their internal arguments obligatorily:

(327) [D [#P [DivP [nP[*v*P[√]]]]

(328)	a.	*the rapid* ***delivery***	**SEN**
	b.	*the rough* ***estimation***	
	c.	*the* ***examination*** *lasted for hours*	
	d.	*the* ***examination*** *was on the table*	**RN**
	e.	*The* ***examination*** *(*) of students took a long time.*	**Derived nominals**

The next functional head in the verbal projection in (324) is the layer of Voice which introduces external arguments. The diagnostics for the presence of Voice is a self-action interpretation. Compare the sentences in (329):

(329)	**Voice diagnostics**	
a.	*The children were being registered.* i. *Th=Ag: *The children registered themselves.* ii. Th ≠ Ag: *The children were registered by someone.*	**Passive**
b.	*The reported mentioned the painfully slow* ***registering*** *of children.* i. *Th=Ag ii. Th ≠ Ag	**Nominal Gerund**
c.	*The report mentioned the painfully slow* ***registration*** *of the children.* i. Th=Ag ii. Th ≠ Ag	**Derived nominals**

Nominal gerunds (329b) and verbal passives (329a) pattern together in that they do not allow a *self*-action interpretation. The exclusion of self-action interpretation is a standard diagnostic for passives in Kratzer (1996). English nominal gerunds thus arguably contain passive-like Voice, which does not project genuine external arguments.

By contrast, the derived nominals in (329c) are compatible with *self*-action signaling a lack of Voice. For these reasons, Alexiadou proposes that these derived nominals have an intransitive base, resembling unaccusatives, and their external arguments are expressed as Possessors. These prenominal possessives are generated in SpecDP directly and can be thematically interpreted as an Agent/Causer because in English Spec(DP) is considered as an A-position (since Abney 1987) (Alexiadou 2001).

Also, missing the Voice layer, derived nominals in (329c) have the same structure as Result nominals and SENs in (327). It means that the height attachment of the nominalizer cannot be the whole story. More needs to be said about licensing of arguments and this issue will be addressed at a later point in our discussion.

An additional support for intransitivity in nominals, Alexiadou (2001) finds in examples such as (330) where Agent cannot normally appear in prenominal position:

(330) a. **John's* ***growth*** *of tomatoes*
b. *the* ***growth*** *of tomatoes*
c. *John* ***grows*** *tomatoes*

If nominals were normally transitive, these restrictions would not occur. This asymmetry has already been noticed by Chomsky (1970) who took it as an argument of lexicalist treatment of derived nominals.

As far as the level of AspectP is concerned, it is evidenced by an Aspect shift (see section 4.2.3) and aspectual adverbials. While they are not permitted in nominal gerunds, verbal gerunds allow them:

(331)		[D [#P [DivP [nP[$\text{Voice}_{\text{INTRANS}}$ P[vP[√]]]]	**Nominal Gerund**
	a.	*John's (*constantly)* ***omitting*** *of details (*constantly).*	
	b.	*Bill's (*always)* ***talking*** *of his neighbor (*always).*	

(332)	[D [Aspect P[Voice$_{TRANS}$ P[vP[√]]]]	
a.	*Mary's constantly **writing** a letter to John*	**Verbal Gerund**
b.	**Mary's constantly **writings** a letter to John*	
c.	*Bill always **talking** to his neighbor.*	
d.	**Bill always **talkings** to his neighbor*	

Also, notice that verbal gerunds need to be nominalized by D. As a result, they cannot pluralize (332b) and (332d)—pluralization is a nominal feature situated in DivP. Once *n* is projected, the whole nominal structure would have to be present. Both *n*-based and D-based nominalizations identified by Alexiadou (2020) have syntactic correlates which can be seen below:

(333)	n-based	D-based
Gender	✓	✗
DivP	✓	✗
All types of Determiners	✓	✗
Internal argument with GEN	✓	✗
External argument with NOM	✗	✓

5.2.2 Argument Structure of Nominals

As for the licensing of the AS, in her earlier work Alexiadou (2001) assumes that internal arguments could be introduced by roots. This option was revised later on in Alexiadou (2014c)[78] and in the present-day model the responsibility for the introduction of internal arguments lies with the *v* layer. This move remains controversial because the *v* layer is also present in simple and result nominals. If simply the attachment of a nominalizer played a role, the distinction between Grimshaw's (1990) notion of a complement (an expression that corresponds to a position in the lexical conceptual structure of the head) and an argument, which is reserved for AS-Nominals, were blurred.

To solve this, Alexiadou (2009) suggests that *v* cannot be a prerequisite for licensing AS, that is, she divorces the verbalizers from argument licensers.

78 Particles, PPs and small clauses can also introduce internal arguments in Alexiadou's framework.

Subsequently, arguments are introduced in other designated layers, for example, external arguments (*by*-phrases) are licensed by Voice or as Possessors in SpecDP. Internal argument can be introduced by *v* but relying solely on the height of nominalizing attachment fails to account for the distinctions between SENs and CENs nominals as suggested above. Therefore, Alexiadou (2009) explains that there is an interplay between obligatoriness of arguments, aspectual issues and countability. All nominals licensing AS need to bind their internal arguments with some aspectual operator as argued in Alexiadou and Schäfer (2010).

Aspectual issues of derived nominals are represented with two aspectual levels (telicity/perfectivity) which has implications for nominals that exhibit both levels, or just one aspectual level. Notably, verbal gerunds possess presumably both of these aspectual levels, and the higher level is in the complementary distribution with the Number layer. This accounts for the divergence of verbal gerunds from prototypical derived nominals, as they cannot be modified by adjectives and do not exhibit pluralization, see Alexiadou's (2017d) example below:

(334) **He could not stand her **criticizings** me.*

On the other hand, certain types of AS-Nominals lack (+/-Perfectivity) and have only the inner Aspect (+/- Telicity). Interestingly, a subtype of them has the ability to pluralize, which is associated with their inner Aspect, see the examples in (335) quoted in Alexiadou (2009). Telic nominals can undergo pluralization while preserving their aspectual structure, whereas atelic nominals cannot.

(335) a. *He caused <u>three</u> **murders** of witnesses that was supposed to testify at trial.*
b. *There was at least <u>one</u> **pushing** of the cart to New York by John.*

To conclude the current discussion, we can state that when the internal argument is bound by some inner Aspect operator, *v* is an Argument licenser whereas when the argument is not bound, it will be just a verbalizer.

Notice that Borer's (2013) assumption that the functional event structure correlates with AS licensing no longer holds in Alexiadou's framework due to the presence of *v*. Also, in Borer's framework, AS-Nominals will always contain at least the event phrase (EP) node. In contrast, in Alexiadou's model, the structural correlate of Borer's EP node—Voice—can be absent. Consequently, the predictions about the source of AS differ: in Alexiadou's framework, the source seems to be aspectual, whereas in Borer's framework, it is spatial, as the EP is existentially bound by a spatial operator, as described in section 4.1.3.

I will get back to this topic in section 5.4.5 where I will provide more comprehensive examination of Argument licensing within Czech nominals and resolve these issues regarding the sources of AS.

5.2.3 Rigidity of AS-Nominals vs. Flexibility of R-Nominals

Alexiadou (2017b) argues that the rigidity of AS-Nominals is closely linked to the ergative patterns observed in nominalizations across different languages. This view contrasts with Borer's predictions, outlined in section 5.1.5, where the asymmetry between AS and R-Nominals is attributed to different factors, without expecting ergativity to play a role. These matters will be further detailed in the upcoming subsection.

The ergative patterns in nominalizations are linked to a particular type of nominal structure that contains an *n* head. This *n* head selects for a structure that does not project an external argument which renders the whole construction passive-like. Thus, it can embed either a structure with a deficient VoiceP, as in nominal gerunds observed in example (331), or an unaccusative structure (336).

As a reminder, unaccusative Verbs do not undergo passivization, and their corresponding nominals in (336) do not permit *by*-phrases. This was previously illustrated in section 5.1.7. In Alexiadou's framework, these structures will lack Voice in their functional projection, and their arguments will be projected in Spec *v*P, as discussed in section 4.2.2 related to Voice in the verbal domain.

(336) *The arrival of the train (*by the conductor).*
[D [#P [DivP [nP[vP[√]]]]

In literature, it has been claimed, in fact, that ergative languages are reflexes of a passive/unaccusative system, for example, Nash (1996). These languages have a deficient Voice head, and there is only one structural argument checking structural case. The other argument, in the case of transitives, surfaces with ergative Case. Ergative is then seen in as a prepositional or a possessive Case.

Alexiadou (2017d) argues that this phenomenon is precisely observed in nominalization, which explains why two genitives cannot co-occur with AS-Nominals. Before embarking on the consequences of ergativity in nominalizations, let me deal with ergative languages more in detail.

The term ergative is used to describe a grammatical pattern in which the subject of an intransitive clause is treated in the same way as the object of a transitive clause. Examples from the ergative language Tonga are quoted in Alexiadou (2001) to exemplify this concept.

(337)	a.	*Na'e*	*tamate'i*	*'a-Kollaiate*	*'e Tevita*
		AUX_{PAST}	kill	$_{ABS}$Goliathh	$_{ERG}$David
		'David killed Goliath.'			
	b.	*Na'e*	*alu*	*'a-Tevia*	*ki Fisi*
		AUX_{PAST}	go	$_{ABS}$David	to Fiji
		'David went to Fiji.'			

More specifically, in ergative languages the Agent is referred to as the A-argument and is marked with ergative Case, the Patient is called the P-argument and is marked with absolutive Case as seen in (337a), the sole argument of intransitives named the S-argument receives absolutive Case (337b). This state of affairs resembles nominalizations where the theme *the city* in (338a) and the intransitive subject *John* in (338b) have the same Case-Genitive. The external argument/Causer in (338a) is introduced by PP.

(338) a. *The destruction of the city by Caesar*
b. *The arrival of John*

The similarities between the patterns in nominalizations and ergative languages described above are summarized in (339). This table also visualizes patterns in Nominative-Accusative languages:

(339)	N/A system	E/A system	Nominalizations
A-argument	NOM	ERG	PP
S-argument	NOM	ABS	GEN
P-argument	ACC	ABS	GEN

Having analyzed ergative patterns, we can now consider their implications in nominalizations, specifically regarding Case assignment. According to Alexiadou (2017d), Case assignment is seen as a property of a particular domain. In the verbal domain, the relevant domain is CP while in the nominal domain the candidates are *n*Ps and DPs.

Specifically in the cases of nominal gerunds or derived nominals, the domain is *n*P. As discussed above, *n*P has properties similar to passives, and its task is to turn a transitive verb into a passive construction. More importantly, there is only one head for one argument to agree (presumably AspectP). Alexiadou claims that the argument that receives structural Case is the one which surfaces with a genitive form. For the other argument, in the case of transitive verb, the only option is to surface as a *by*-phrase adjoined to $\text{Voice}_{\text{PASSIVE}}$ or escape *n*P and merge higher in SpecDP. This latter situation is visible in example (340):

(340) *Caesar's* ***destruction*** *of the city*

Ergative patterns of nominalizations thus arise in a similar way as in ergative languages with a deficient Voice head and only one structural argument checking structural Case. The question of ergativity within nominalizations leads to different consequences than those that were established in Borer (2013). Therefore, in section 5.4, I will employ a range of diagnostics to ascertain whether Czech nominalizations align with this pattern.

5.2.4 Passivization Process in Nominals

Alexiadou (2001) argues that the nominals of the type (341a) are not derived through a process of passivization as it developed in Borer (2013). Consequently, there can be no object movement, for example, *the city* into prenominal position giving (341a). This is because all nominals are inherently passive-like/unaccusative from the outset, and passivization is not required for their formation.

(341) a. *city's* ***destruction*** *(in two days)*
b. ***destruction*** *of the city (in two days)*

Note that Grimshaw has also advanced the argument that Nouns are intransitive, but in her theory, intransitivity pertains to the notion that Nouns function as defective theta-markers. From this, a number of facts follows, the most significant of which is that passive complex event nominals do not exist. Therefore, they need to be classified as result Nouns. Alexiadou (2001) casts doubt on Grimshaw's analysis and argues that passive nominals are eventive. In support of her claims, she provides examples like (341), demonstrating that passive nominals can even be modified by aspectual modifiers.

These nominals are derived by directly merging the theme DP at SpecDP. Given that SpecDP is not restricted to a single thematic role, such a direct merging is possible without necessarily assigning an agent interpretation to the DP. On this view, passive nominals differ from non-passive ones in the base position of their theme arguments.

Additionally, the nominals of types (341a) and (341b) in Alexiadou's framework are already similar to passives/unaccusatives. Borer (2013), on the other hand, views (341b) as ambiguous between active and passive, and (341a) as derived through object preposing. This topic affects the internal structure of nominalizations and will be examined thoroughly using Czech data.

5.2.4.1 By-phrases

A related issue to the previous topic is the use of *by*-phrases. Alexiadou (2001) explains that *by*-phrases in verbal passives must be distinguished from those in nominalization. The reasoning for this, partly described above in relations to Case assignment, is as follows: in verbal passives the theta role is transmitted to the *by*-phrase whereas this transfer does not occur in nominalizations, where the *by*-phrase is rather dependent on the affected internal theme. This concept is captured by William's (1987) generalization (p. 365):

(342) The Agent is assigned to a *by*-phrase if there is an internal theme.

A supportive argument can be found elsewhere in the literature. Notably, *by*-phrases in verbal passives can bear any thematic role while *by*-phrases found in nominals are thematically limited. In derived nominals *by*-phrases can only be interpreted as Agents, Instruments or Creators, as illustrated in examples cited by Alexiadou et al. (2009):

(343)	a.	*the **imprisonment** of refugees <u>by the government</u>*	***Agent***
	b.	*the **destruction** of the city <u>by lightning</u>*	***Causer***
	c.	*the **fear** of Harry (*<u>by John</u>)*	****Experiencer***
	d.	*the **receipt** of the package (*<u>by John</u>)*	****Recipient***
(344)	a.	*Harry was **feared** <u>by John</u>.*	***Experiencer***
	b.	*The package was **received** <u>by John</u>*	***Recipient***

These findings further support the claim that nominalizations exhibit ergative patterns because theta roles are assigned differently to *by*-phrases in nominalizations compared to the verbal domain.

A point of clarification is necessary. It has been shown above that Derived nominals as in (345) have an intransitive base and resemble unaccusatives in excluding self-action. However, it is important to note that *by*-phrases are still possible in these constructions:

(345) a. *The **destruction** of the city <u>by Caesar</u>*
b. *the **translation** of the book <u>by Peter</u>*

More specifically, according to Alexiadou (2020), the claim is not that *-ation* nominals always lack passive voice, but rather that they can lack it.

5.2.5 Adverbs

Alexiadou (2001) reaches similar conclusions as Borer (2013) with respect to Adverbs in nominalizations. Different types of Adverbs are linked to particular functional projections. There is, however, a slight discrepancy between their perspectives, regarding manner Adverbs. Alexiadou views manner Adverbs as a crucial test for the presence of the Voice projection while for Borer (2013) they testify only in favor of some lower verbal projection.

I will not cite any data because the other conclusions are the same as in Borer. What is important to emphasize is that if any types of adverbs are present in nominalizations, the eventivity of nominalizations can be confirmed.

I will apply these diagnostics to Czech data to assess the individual functional projections in nominalizations.

5.2.6 Zero-Derived Nominals

In contrast to Borer's perspective, which excludes the possibility of zero derivation, Alexiadou (2009) asserts that zero derivation is indeed possible. Without the option of zero derivation affixes, it could become challenging to account for cases that appear to function as argument-taking Nouns. Several examples demonstrating this phenomenon can be found in Newmeyer (2009):

(346) a. *the frequent* ***release*** *of the prisoners by the governor*
b. *the frequent* ***use*** *of sharp tools by underage children*
c. *an officer's too frequent* ***discharge*** *of a firearm*

Consider also the cases reported by Iordăchioaia (2020) in her corpus study of zero-derived nominals:

(347) a. *a complete* ***crash*** *of the US economy*
b. *investigated the deliberate* ***crash*** *of a Germanwings passenger jet into a mountain side*
c. *Tokyo allowed the continued* ***import*** *of South African coal*

Although Iordăchioaia (2020) haven't identified examples in her corpus with aspectual modifiers that would indicate their AS status, there appears to be some eventivity included in these cases, for example, they realize *of*-PPs in eventive contexts. Compare now the structure (348a) with (348b) which would be assigned to these nominals in Borer's and Alexiadou's frameworks respectively:

(348) a. [D … [$_{C=N}$ √*import*]]]]
b. [D … [*n*P[*v*P[√*import*]]]]

Obviously, Borer's (2013) structure lacks an explanation for why these constructions are eventive. I will further support my view in section 5.4.1 when dealing with Czech zero-derived nominals.

5.3 Comparison of Borer's and Alexiadou's Frameworks in Nominalizations

I mentioned some theoretical distinctions between the two relevant models on nominalizations already in the preceding sections. Here, I will briefly summarize the common basic assumptions and indicate the main points of contrast which will be further examined in the next section using Czech data.

Alexiadou, in her studies, as well as Borer suppose that deverbal AS-Nominals contain verbal layers which distinguish them from standard Nouns (including R-Nominals). With the nominals derived from Verbs, they both assume that the verbal part of the structure is subsequently nominalized by the merge of some nominal functional heads.

For Borer, argument structure and eventuality can emerge only in the presence of relevant verbal layers. She also postulates an Event Phrase that must be always present in AS-Nominals and is linked with a spatial dimension. The emergence of external arguments and internal arguments is orthogonal to the presence of functional nodes.

Alexiadou, in contrast, suggests that the *v*P level must minimally exist in AS-Nominals. This head is present even in simple event nominals and can introduce optional complements. Nevertheless, for a nominal to project argument structure, the event in *v* must be bound by aspectual operator in AspectP, which prioritizes the role of Aspect in licensing AS in nominals.

In this chapter, I will use Czech data to support the mechanism similar to the one employed in Alexiadou's theory, advocating for the existence of a *v*P layer. As demonstrated earlier in section 4.4.2.1, the phenomenon of prefix lengthening in Czech deverbal Nouns can be effectively accounted for by assuming the presence of the *v*P projection encoding telicity even in non-argument-taking Nouns. I will revisit this topic in section 5.4.1.

My next argument for the *v*P layer will be based on zero-derived nominals. As Borer (2013) does not postulate any zero nominalizer, the eventivity of zero-derived nominals is hard to capture. They arise in the context of nominalizers (C-functors) which require V complements. The drawback of this analysis is that there is no morphosyntactic difference between lexical Nouns such as a *cat* and zero-derived nominals (ZNs) such as *Beijing's continuing export* *of coal.* In my analysis of Czech nominals, I will assume that zero-derived nominals have at least the *v*P level encoding telicity.

Furthermore, while Alexiadou assumes that all nominalizations are intransitive, either passive or unaccusative, Borer (2013) takes a different stance. Borer distinguishes between Long Argument Structure Nominals (LASNs) in (349a-b) which are active and Short Argument Structure Nouns (SASNs) in (349c-d) which are passive. Consequently, the structure in (349d) is associated with object preposing. Alexiadou (2001) refutes this passivization process in nominals and proposes instead merging of arguments directly in SpecD.

(349)	a.	*Kim's* ***formation/forming*** *of the team*	**LASNs**
	b.	*Kim's* ***pushing*** *of the cart.*	**LASNs**
	c.	*the* ***formation/forming*** *of the team (by Kim)*	**SASNs**
	d.	*the team's* ***formation*** *(by Kim)*	**SASNs**

Also, Borer (2013) presumes incorporation of V to N and subsequent movement of N to D. For instance, in Hebrew N can raise up to D, while in English only partial movement is expected. Alexiadou (2001) follows Cinque's (1980) conclusion about ordering of adjectives and does not assume N-to D movement. There is only V-to N movement. These differing approaches have consequences for explaining the derivation of various syntactic structures and case marking of arguments within them.

In Borer (2013), for example, movement in conjunction with a Double *-of* Filter in English explains why double genitives are banned in AS-Nominals. This forces the higher argument to raise and receive Case marking with *'s* in DP, leaving behind a copy that hinders the lower argument from raising and necessitates it being Case marked in situ.

Alexiadou (2017d), on the other hand, proposes that case marking in *n*-nominalizations results from a deficient *v* and a single position for checking structural case. Remaining arguments either surface as PPs under VoiceP or escape *n*P domain and merge in SpecDP. A similar process is observed in ergative languages where similar case marking of objects and subjects is detectable, as seen in the context of nominalizations across languages.

I will demonstrate that both proposed mechanisms encounter specific challenges in Czech; nevertheless, they remain applicable. Nonetheless, I will illustrate using diagnostics involving binding phenomena, PRO interpretation, characteristic morphology, and Case patterns that Czech nominalizations exhibit more passive-like/unaccusative characteristics and exhibit ergative patterns.

5.4 Considering Czech Data

As discussed in section 1.4, providing some previous analyses of Czech of nominals, in Czech there exist minimally two types of deverbal nominals. These are divided on the basis of classification tests presented by Veselovská (2018b) and Karlík (2019):

- **Type I** are syntactically derived nominals which behave as complex event nominal and can become result nominals while
- **Type II** nominals behave as simple event nominals and can become result nominals in the sense of Grimshaw (1990).

In this study, I will call Type I nominals as **N/T nominals** while Type II will be referred to as **B/K nominals**[79] and provide further refinement of these generalizations.

5.4.1 The Structures for the Czech N/T and B/K Nominals

In the forthcoming section, I will present my proposal for the structural representations of both types of Czech nominalizations mentioned above, which I will justify in the remaining parts of this chapter. These two types of Czech nominalizations are depicted in schemes (352) and (353) below. To adequately capture them, I will employ nominal and verbal layers described in earlier chapters.

79 The labels are formed based on the two typical suffixes used in those nominalizations: with B/K, they are *-ba/-ka* (as in ***stavba*** 'building' and *procházka* 'walk') and with N/T, *-ní/-tí* (as in *stavění* 'building' *and písknutí* 'whistling'). According to Borer's terminology, B/K nominals can be categorized as AS-Nominals with the potential to transform into R-Nominals. In contrast, B/K nominals correspond to R-Nominals.

Regarding the verbal domain, the proposed nodes and feature content were outlined in section 4.4.2, originally presented as (235), repeated here in (350):

(350) [CP -- [IP-- [NegP -- [VoiceP-- [ProgP-- [Aspect P -- [*v*P-- [Root]]]]]

As for nominal projection, the layers were illustrated in (165), repeated here in (351):

(351) [DP-- [QP-- [DivP -- [GenderP-- [Root]]]]]

Let us start with N/T nominals in (352) which are the Czech CENs variety. We can see that they can contain large part of the verbal projection, as depicted in (350).

- ***v*** layer is associated with the feature PATH and its values +/-TELIC.
- **AspectP** is the locus of perfectivity and imperfectivity.
- **Prog P** is the place for secondary imperfectives and
- **VoiceP** is a deficient layer: It is passive and does not project external arguments, it can only serve as a locus of external arguments marked by Instrumental.

Above the VoiceP, the projections include TP and CP. I will argue that no Mood and Tense are projected in Czech nominalizations.

(352) The syntactic representation of Czech derived nominals—N/T nominal

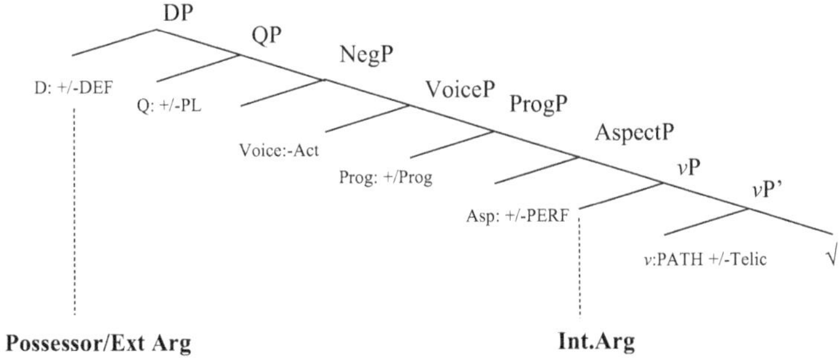

In contrast, nominal layers in N/T nominals as described in (352) are impoverished. Let's compare them with the feature content of the Czech nominal projection in (351) that might potentially be included in nominalizations:

- **GenderP**—with the features [+/-Human], [+/- FEM].
- **DivP**—with the features [+/- COUNT] realized in Czech by affixes.
- **QP**—with the features [+/-PL] providing position for, for example, Numerals.
- **DP**—with the features [+/-DEF] and hosting, for example, Articles.

In N/T nominals in (352), the neuter Gender is assigned by default and no GenP is projected. Neither is DivP present. Thus, only two nominal projections remain: QP and DP. The QP plays a role in countability. The precise mechanism will be described in Chapter 6. The DP functional projection is responsible for definiteness. Moreover, external arguments are introduced in SpecDP while Internal argument emerge in Spec *v*.

The proposed projection of the B/K nominals is in (353). They are interpreted as single event nominals, that is, they are less verbal and more nominal than the N/T nominals illustrated above. Comparing them with the standard verbal and nominal projections, they have only one verbal layer, *v*P, which is related to telicity. On the other hand, these nominals have a full array of nominal layers. At their lowest level is GenP which assigns Gender. Once this layer projects, other (higher) nominal layers can be expected, namely the nominal layers which can carry the features of countability and definiteness, that is, DivP, QP and DP.

(353) The syntactic representation of B/K nominals

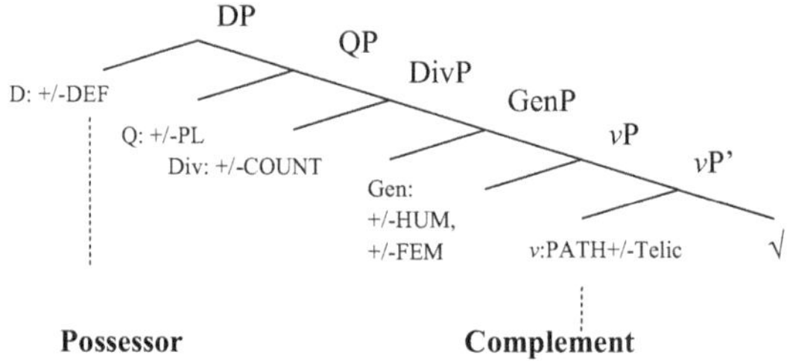

In the following sections, I am going to provide arguments which will show that the proposed structures are able to explain and predict the Czech data.

5.4.2 Structural Classification of Nominals in Czech

To justify the functional projections for the two types of nominalizations mentioned earlier, I will use the classification tests presented by Veselovská (2018b) and Karlík (2019) from section 1.4 as a starting point and subject them to a detailed examination based on the criteria proposed by Borer and Alexiadou.

According to Karlík (2019), a notable observation is that his syntactically derived nominals (here N/T nominals) can also function as result nominals. On the other hand, his lexically derived nominals (here B/K nominals) exhibit characteristics similar to simple event nominals and have the ability to transform into result nominals. Specifically, Karlík (2019) asserts that the B/K nominals:

i. never co-occur with negation,
ii. cannot be reflexivized using the particle *se*,
iii. do not include superlexical Aspect morpheme,
iv. cannot combine with iterativity,
v. do not have Aspect, and
vi. have no obligatory arguments.

I will not repeat all his examples as most of them were already demonstrated in section 1.4.2. Below I provide only examples illustrating the properties related to the lack of reflexivity and negation not explicitly illustrated yet.

First, we can see in (354) that nominals like *učení* 'learning' can be reflexive as CEN but not as RN. The SEN nominal *stavba* 'building' has no CEN counterpart.

(354)

a.	*Petrovo$_i$*	***uč-e-n-í***	***se$_i$***	*trvalo dlouho.*	CEN
	Peter$_{POSS}$	learning$_{NT.(IMPF)}$	self	took a long time	
	'Peter's self-learning took a long time.'				

b.	*Petrovo*	***uč-e-n-í***	*(*__se__)*	*leželo na stole/ (*trvalo dlouho).*	RN
	Peter$_{\text{POSS}}$	learning$_{\text{NT. (IMPF)}}$	self	was on the table/ took a long time	
	'Peter's learning material (*self) was on the table/(*took a long time)'				
c.	*Petrova*	***stav-ba***$_{\text{F.SG}}$	*(*__se__)*	*trvala dlouho.*	SEN
	Peter$_{\text{POSS}}$	painting	self	took a long time	
	'Peter's building (*self) took a long time.'				
d.	*Petrova*	*papírová*	***stav-ba*** *(*__se__)*	*ležela na stole/ (*trvala dlouho).*	RN
	Peter	paper-made	painting$_{\text{F.SG}}$ self	was on the table/ took a long time	
	'Peter's paper-made construction (*self) was on the table/ (*took a long time).'				

In (355) the variants of the nominals are presented with a negative prefix *ne-* (in bold). We can observe that only the nominal analyzed as CENs can be negated. The other, more nominal and less verbal nominals do not have the negative prefix.

(355)

a.	*Krm-e-n-í/**ne**-krm-e-n-í*	*ptáků*	*se mu vymstí.*	CEN
	feeding/non-feeding$_{\text{NT. (IMPF)}}$	bird$_{\text{GEN}}$	will cause him troubles	
	'Feeding/non-feeding birds will cause him troubles.'			
b.	*Krm-e-n-í/(*__ne__-krm-e-n-í)*	*pro ptáky*	*bylo na stole/ (*trvalo dlouho).*	RN
	food/*non-food$_{\text{NT. (IMPF)}}$	for birds	was on the table/took a long time	
	'Food/(*non-food) for animals was on the table/ (*took a long time).'			

c.	*Kres-ba/ (*ne-kres-ba)*	*portrétů*	*trvala dlouho.*	SEN
	reading/non-reading$_{F.SG}$	potrait$_{GEN.PL}$	took a long time	
	'Painting/(*non-painting) of the portraits took a long time.'			
d.	*Černobílá kres-ba/(*ne-kres-ba)*		*ležela na stole/ (*trvala dlouho).*	R-N
	black and white	painting/non-painting$_{F.SG}$	was on the table/took a long time	
	'The black and white painting/(*non-painting) was on the table/(*took a long time).'			

What these examples demonstrate is that although both Types of Czech nominals can have characteristics of result nominals, only some of them can be complex event nominals. Only when they can be analyzed as N/T nominals, they will exhibit a higher degree of verbal characteristics.

Compare the reflexivity and negation tests demonstrated above with English examples in (356) and (357). We can see that these properties are not just a specificity of Czech deverbal AS-nominalizations:

(356)	a.	*John's$_i$*	***description***	*of himself$_i$*
	b.	*Mary's$_i$*	***showing***	*of herself$_i$*
	c.	**John's$_i$*	***car***	*of himself$_i$*

(357)	a.	*Despite her **not knowing** most of the answers, Pauline passed the test.*	**Verbal Gerund**
	b.	**The **not processing** of the election results created a scandal.*	**Nominal Gerund**
	c.	**The **not exam** shocked everybody.*	**Result nominal**

In order to scrutinize the verbal layers in nominalizations in more detail in the forthcoming sections, I will refer repeatedly to the diagnostics in table

(358) which compares the indicators for verbal layers in nominalizations proposed by Borer and Alexiadou. These tests were initially introduced in earlier parts of this chapter when presenting the theories of nominalizations proposed by both linguists.

(358)

Alexiadou (2020)		Borer (2005a)	
---		**EP**	Agentive Adverbs
TP	Subject-verb agreement, Tense, Nominative Case	**TP**	Subject-verb agreement, Tense, Nominative Case
AspectP	Evidential, Aspectual Adverbials	**G-ASP**	Evidential, Aspectual Adverbials
VoiceP$_{\text{ACT/PASS}}$	ACC, Manner adverbs, Agentive Adverbs, *by*-phrases	π	*by*-phrases
vP	Eventive adjective modifiers	**Asp**$_{\text{Q}}$	Manner Adverbs

5.4.2.1 B/K Nominals

We will begin our discussion by focusing on the least verbal structures, namely on the B/K nominals that include zero-derived nominals. I will assume that B/K nominals project at least to *v*P, even in the case of zero-derived nominals. Recall that Borer does not utilize a zero-derived affix. Consequently, nominals with suffixes like *-ba* or *-ka* can be assigned the structure depicted in (359b) while zero-derived nominals must be represented with the structure in (359a). In contrast, Alexiadou does include *v*P as the layer above the root in both cases, as shown in (359c).

(359) a. [D … [$_{\text{C=N}}$ √*lov*/hunt]] Borer's framework (zero affix)
b. [D … [C$_{\text{N [V]}}$ √*zkouška*/exam]]Borer's framework
c. [D … [nP[vP[√*lov*/hunt]]]] Alexiadou's framework

The empirical evidence supporting the inclusion of the *v*P projection in Czech is provided by the study of Caha and Ziková (2022), as explained in section 4.4.2.1. The authors present thorough analysis of Czech prefixes that exhibit alternation between two structural positions overtly signaled by differences in prefix length and interpreted aspectual status. Their complex research reveals that Czech zero-derived nominals, which fall under the category of B/K nominals, possess at least inner Aspect feature in contrast to N/T nominals, which exhibit outer Aspect. Their illustrative example (242) is repeated below in (360) for convenience. Notice the possible Preposition *na*, 'on' when prefixed to the stem in the form of *na-/ná-*, acquires length when it forms the zero-derived Noun. Without the inner Aspect projection in zero-derived nominals, these changes would be inexplicable.

(360)	Preposition	Verb	Zero-derived Noun	*-ní/tí* nominal
	na	***na**-stoupit*	→ ***ná**-stup*	→ ***na**-stoupení*
	'on'	'get on'	'getting on'	'getting on'

Assigning the inner Aspect *v* projection to zero-derived nominals also better captures the Czech data because these nominals can express some limited eventivity (361a), duration (361b) and take optional complements (361a) like their verbal counterparts (361c), see below:

(361)	a.	*rychlá*	***vý-měna***	*(pneumatik)*	*zabrala pět minut*
		quick	out.change$_{F.SG}$	tires$_{GEN}$	took five minutes
		'a quick change (of tires) took five minutes'			
	b.	*rychlé*	***vy-měn-ě-n-í***	**(pneumatik)*	*zabralo pět minut*
		quick	out$_{PF.}$*change*$_{NT}$	tires$_{GEN}$	took five minutes
		'a quick changing *(of tires) took five minutes'			
	c.	*Petr*	*rychle*	***vy-měnil***	**(pneumatiky).*
		Peter$_{3.SG}$	quickly	out$_{PF.}$change$_{PAST.3.SG}$	tires$_{GEN}$
		'Peter quickly out-changed *(the tires).'			

However, it is important to note that zero-derived nominals do not exhibit sensitivity to perfective Aspect. By applying the temporal phase verb test introduced by Borik (2006), it becomes evident that zero-derived nominals are unaffected by perfectivity, as demonstrated in example (362a). Conversely, N/T nominals, as exemplified in (362b), align with the behavior of perfective prefixes in clauses, as depicted in (362c):

(362)	a.	*začal*	*s* ***vý-měnou***$_{F}$	*(pneumatik)*	
		start	with out.change	tires$_{GEN}$	
		'He started with the out-change (of tires)'			
	b.	*??začal*	*s* ***vy-měn-ě-n-ím***	**(pneumatik)*	
		start	with out$_{PF.}$ changing$_{NT}$	tires$_{GEN}$	
		??'He started with out-changing *(of tires)'			
	c.	*Petr*	*začal*	***měnit/*vy-měnit***	**(pneumatiky).*
		Peter	start	change/out$_{PF}$. change	tires$_{ACC}$
		'Peter started change/(*out-change) *(tires).'			

The previously mentioned characteristics, such as length alternation, eventivity flavor, durativity, and optional complementation, cannot be properly accounted for if zero-derived nominals are assigned the structure as in (359a).

Thus, I will concur with Alexiadou's framework, which includes a functional projection *v* (359c) for simple events. Although I do not attribute verbalizing function to this projection, I put forward that it can account for telicity as proposed in 4.4.2.1. Therefore, I will tentatively assign B/K nominals that behave as simple event nominals the following structure in (363a) where GenP attaches above the *v*P layer. If they behave as result Nouns and refer to tangible objects as in (354d), they exhibit the structure in (363a):

(363) **Czech B/K nominals**

a. [D … [GenP[*v*P[√]]]] Czech Simple event nominals

b. [D … [GenP[[√]]]] Czech Result nominals

It is worth noting that the inclusion of the GenP level is empirically justified, given that Type II nominals can express Gender freely, unlike N/T nominals which are neuter by default.

(364)	a.	*stav-ba*	*construction*$_F$
	b.	*jás-ot*	*cheering*$_M$
	c.	*stav-ě-n-í/mluv-e-n-í*	*construction*$_{NT}$/*speaking*$_{NT}$

The further nominal layers within these projections will be discussed in the next Chapter in more detail.

5.4.2.2 N/T Nominals

Moving forward with the analysis of the structure of N/T nominals, these are predicted to be able to possess a higher degree of verbal characteristics compared to B/K nominals.

The highest verbal projections are **CP/IP projections** with the feature of Mood or Tense.[80] However, N/T nominals do not have these features. Both Borer and Alexiadou propose several diagnostics to verify this, including subject-verb agreement, Tense, and Nominative Case, all of which are absent in Czech nominalizations.

The Aspect Phrase

In terms of the aspectual projection, we can observe that N/T nominals demonstrate sensitivity to perfectivity, as shown in (362b), that is, using the perfective prefixes.[81] Additionally, it is important to highlight that N/T nominals possess the capacity to form secondary imperfectives (365a) by incorporating the suffix *-ová*. This distinction sets them apart from B/K nominals (365b):

---

80 I will not commit myself to any claim concerning the CP which may be multilayered, to express the features related to information structure. CP can also furnish a structural escape hatch for long distance movements as Czech does allow many kinds of extractions from the nominal domain. This requires some structural analysis though not specific to nominalizations. For the purpose of this work, therefore, I cannot see any reason to introduce CP domains in my analysis.

81 Czech aspectual prefixes and suffixes are illustrated in previous sections, above all, 4.4.1.1.

(365)	a.	*vy-měň-ová-n-í*	*pneumatik*
		$out_{PF.}changing_{IMPF.NT}$	$tires_{GEN}$
	b.	**vý-měn-ova*	*pneumatik*
		$out.change_{IMPF}$	$tires_{GEN}$

The secondary imperfective verbal suffix *-ová* associated with N/T nominals in Czech exhibits a similar interpretation to the progressive Aspect found in English. However, unlike the English progressive, the interpretation of the secondary imperfective Aspect in N/T nominals is not as limited, as it encompasses a broader range of meanings beyond ongoing action. These additional interpretations can include habitual and iterative denotations.

According to Alexiadou et al. (2010c), both perfectivity and secondary imperfectivity would fall under the projection of AspectP. In contrast, Borer (2005b) categorizes telicity and perfectivity under Asp_Q, while secondary imperfectivity is regarded as an instance of outer Aspect G-Asp. To better understand the interplay between aspectual issues and countability, I assume that it is beneficial to distinguish these distinct layers: telicity, perfectivity, and secondary imperfectivity. Their functional projections will be labeled as *v*, AspP, and ProgP in this work as in the illustrative tree in (352) above.

The Voice Phrase

The VoiceP layer in the literature is associated with special properties, namely introduction of external argument, assignment of Accusative Case, licensing of particular set of Adverbs and agentive PPs. Extensive analysis of these aspects has been conducted in previous chapters; so we can now focus on summarizing the main implications of VoiceP for nominal structures.

Alexiadou argues that *n*-nominalizations cross-linguistically do not typically contain active Voice and have rather a deficient/passive Voice or are unaccusative. As a result, external arguments are not present in nominalizations. For Borer, some nominals are built on active while some are built on passive structures. Moreover, as table (358) depicts, Borer does not use the Voice projection and the closest functional projection is the EP node, which is in AS-Nominals by default. However, functional projections (EP, Asp_Q) in Borer need not introduce arguments in their specifiers. Instead, the interpretation of arguments within events is an entailment from event structure. Subsequently, the role Originator which is introduced in EP spans not only traditional Agents and Causers but also, importantly, subjects of activities, including those occurring with so-called variable behavior Verbs in their unergative instantiation.

I have argued in section 4.4.2.4 for including the VoiceP projection in verbal domains, which might or might not be projected, rather than Borer's EP projection, which must always be present in verbal domains. Consequently, the massive overgeneration of structures can be avoided. Despite these discrepancies, we can explore whether there are any tests that could detect any equivalent of this projection in nominalizations.

Both linguists, Alexiadou (2001) and Borer (2013), employ Adverb modification as a diagnostic tool for examining the presence or absence of the Voice/EP projection. Borer (2013) proposes a scheme for the licensing of Adverbs within specific projections described in section 5.1.9 and outlined below:

(366) [C/T (**proposition**) **evidential** adv (V) [E **agentive** adv (V) [T [G-ASP **g-asp adv** (V) [**manner adv** V]]]]]

There is, however, a slight discrepancy between their perspectives, particularly regarding manner Adverbs. Alexiadou (2001) views manner Adverbs as a crucial test for the presence of the Voice projection while for Borer they testify only in favor of some lower verbal projection. In Czech, aspectual adverbials (367a-b) or evidential Adverbs are not grammatical, but manner Adverbs are not entirely excluded. The one in (367c) even has an agentive flavor. Although, adjectives expressing the same content are usually preferred (367e):

(367) a. ***Do-d-á-n-í*** *zboží* *(zdarma)/(*obvykle)* *je možné.*
to$_{PF.}$delivery$_{NT}$ goods$_{GEN}$ freely$_{ADV}$/usually$_{ADV}$ is possible
'Delivery of goods (for free)/(*usually) is possible.'

b. ***Skládá-á-n-í*** *testu* *(nanečisto)/(*pravděpodobně)* *je možné.*
passing$_{NT. (IMPF)}$ test$_{GEN}$ mock$_{ADV}$/probably$_{ADV}$ is possible
'Passing of the (mock) test (*probably) is possible.'

c. ***Na-kresl-e-n-í*** *obrázku* *(? opravdu precizně)*
on$_{PF.}$drawing$_{NT}$ picture$_{GEN}$ really precisely$_{ADV}$
'drawing of the picture (? really carefully)'

d. ***Plac-e-n-í*** *daně* *(hotově)* *je možné.*
paying$_{NT.(IMPF)}$ tax$_{GEN}$ in cash$_{ADV}$ is possible
'Paying taxes (in cash) is possible.'

e. *(rychlé)* ***čtení*** *detektivky* *(? rychle)*
quick$_{A}$ reading$_{NT. (IMPF)}$ detective story$_{GEN}$ quickly$_{ADV}$
'(quick) reading of the detective story (?quickly)'

The substitution of Adverbs by Adjectives might be related to the fact that Adverbs in (367a-b) do not have adjective correlates while the Adverb in (367e) has this possibility. Thus, in some cases speakers are forced to use Adverbs. In other cases, they will opt for adjectives. In any case, in Alexiadou's framework these examples testify in favor of the Voice being present in Czech N/T nominals.

The next property associated with the active Voice is the assignment of Accusative Case. However, neither English nor Czech have the ability to generate the complements of nominalizations with Accusative Case. In Czech, these complements are typically marked with Genitive Case which is an equivalent construction of the English *of*-phrase.

Voice and by*-phrases*

Another characteristic related to the Voice projection is the inclusion of agentive *by*-phrases. Both Alexiadou (2017d) and Borer (2013) view agentive *by*-phrases as indicative of a passive Voice, although there are significant differences between their proposals. Borer suggests that in languages where authorship contexts are distinguished from agentive readings, for example, in Czech examples (368), the presence of *by*-phrases signals the passive nature of nominals, akin to the verbal domain. Notice that the Czech equivalents of the *by*-phrases are either the PP with Preposition *od* followed by Genitive, as in (a) or prepositionless Instrumentals as in (b).

(368) a. ***kniba*** *od Chomského/ *Chomským*
book by Chomsky/ Chomsky_{INS}
'a book by Chomsky'

b. ***chválení*** *našeho syna paní ředitelkou*
$\text{praising}_{(IMPF).NT}$ our son_{GEN} a headmaster_{INS}
'praising our son by a headmaster'

On the other hand, Alexiadou et al. (2009) do not anticipate that *by*-phrases in nominalizations will resemble verbal passives. The main supportive evidence is that cross—linguistically they can assign a limited set of theta roles.[82]

As far as the modification of nominalizations by Czech *by*-phrases is concerned, there is a higher restriction on agentive Ps with B/K nominals. While N/T nominals occur with them freely (369a; 370a), in B/K nominals they are felt as too heavy (369b; 370b); see also the discussion in Kolářová (2010).

(369)	a.	***na-malov-á-n-í***	**(krajiny)*	*významným malířem*
		$\text{on}_{PF.}\text{painting}_{NT}$	landscape_{GEN}	renowned painter_{INS}
		'painting *(of landscape) by a renowned painter'		
	b.	***mal-ba***	*(krajiny)*	*(* významným malířem)*
		$\text{painting}_{F.SG}$	landscape_{GEN}	renowned painter_{INS}
		'painting (of landscape) (*by a renowned painter)'		

(370)	a.	***ob-jev-e-n-í***	**(Ameriky)*	*Kryštofem Kolumbem*
		$\text{pref}_{PF.}\text{discovering}_{NT}$	America_{GEN}	Christopher Columbus_{INS}
		'Discovering *(of America) by Christopher Columbus'		

82 In the literature, Alexiadou et al.'s (2009) claim regarding the behavior of *by*-phrases has been refuted by Bruening (2013). He argues that the recipient as well as experiencer theta role can be assigned to nominals. See below some of his examples:

vi. *The receipt of at least three of those letters by their intended recipients is a matter of historical record.* RECIPIENT
The perception of his inadequacies by his wife. EXPERIENCER

b.	***ob-hajo-ba***	*(diplomových prací)*	*(?? našimi studenty)*
	$_{PREF}$-defense$_{F.SG}$	diploma theses$_{GEN}$	our students$_{INS}$
	'The defense (of theses) (?? by our students)'		

The examples with adverbs and *by*-phrases provided above evidence for the hypothesis that Czech N/T nominals involve passive Voice. The question at hand is whether N/T nominals are uniformly passive-like/unaccusative, as Alexiadou (2001, 2017d) proposes, or if some of them are constructed with active Voice and true external arguments, as Borer (2013) suggests. The related question is whether the process of passivization applies within nominals. These specific issues will be explored in the next sections.

Finally, let us consider the productive use of the negative particle-*ne*. In finite verbal forms (371b), it signals sentential (verbal) negation and can interact with the negative polarity items such as *žádný* 'any'. We can see the same interaction in example (371a) with N/T nominals but not with the B/K nominals in (371c) which do not tolerate the negative particle.

(371)	a.	***ne****-čt-e-n-í*		***žádných***	*novin*
		non-reading$_{NT.\ (IMPF)}$		any$_{GEN}$	newspaper$_{GEN}$
		'not reading any newspaper'			
	b.	***ne****-četl*		***žádné***	*noviny*
		not-read		any$_{ACC}$	newspaper$_{ACC}$
		'He did not ready any newspaper'			
	c.	*****ne****-čet-ba*		***žádných***	*novin*
		non-read$_{B/K}$		any	newspaper$_{GEN}$
		*'not reading any newspaper'			
	d.	***ne****-plavec*	*v*	*(****žádném****)*	*bazénu*
		non-swimmer$_{M}$	in	no	pool
		'non-swimmer in (*any) pool'			

Also, compare it with the agentive nominal *ne-plavec* 'non-swimmer' (371d) which tolerates the negative particle but cannot be combined with the negative polarity item. I conclude that it indicates only lexical negation. These examples confirm that only N/T nominals have a rich verbal structure with the layers embedding the sentential negation. Similar arguments have been developed in Rozwadowska (2020) for Polish nominals.

To conclude, the structure of N/T nominals in Czech is represented by the verbal layers as in (372a). However, it is worth noting that similarly to B/K nominals, N/T nominals have the potential to adopt the structure in (372b) if they lose their eventive characteristics and function as objects as we saw in examples above:

(372) **Czech N/T nominals**

a. [D … [NegP [VoiceP[ProgP[AspectP [*v*P [√root]]]

b. [D … [DivP[√root]]]]

5.4.2.3 Some Borderline Cases

N/T nominals are more complex, particularly in cases where they are on the borderline between syntactic and lexical derivations. It is important to distinguish these two types when dealing with the countability of AS-Nominals. Therefore, being familiar with the diagnostics that exclude borderline cases is highly beneficial.

Kolářová (2014) discusses such ambiguous examples, which often involve a shift in meaning from the process to the abstract result of the process. One such instance is a change in valency, which is reflected in the Case marking of their complements. For instance, the N/T nominal with a shifted meaning in (373b) changes the Case of its complement from Genitive (373a) to Dative (373b) . Additionally, it prohibits the use of Instrumental Case and the Adverb *předem* 'in advance' (373b):

(373) a. ***upozornění*** *myslivců* *předem* *Dr.Novákem*
$\text{pref}_{\text{PF.}}\text{warning}_{\text{NT}}$ $\text{hunter}_{\text{GEN}}$ $\text{in advance}_{\text{ADV}}$ $\text{Dr.Novák}_{\text{INS}}$
'the warning of hunters in advance by Dr.Novák'

b. ***upozornění*** *myslivcům* *(*předem)* **(Dr.Novákem)*
$\text{pref}_{\text{PF.}}\text{warning}_{\text{NT}}$ $\text{hunter}_{\text{DAT}}$ $\text{in advance}_{\text{ADV}}$ $\text{Dr.Novák}_{\text{INS}}$
'the warning of hunters (*in advance) (* by Dr.Novák)'

(374) a. ***varování*** *zlodějů* *předem* *Dr.Novákem*
warning$_{\text{NT.(IMPF)}}$ thief$_{\text{GEN}}$ in advance$_{\text{ADV}}$ Dr.Novák$_{\text{INS}}$
'the warning of thieves in advance by Dr.Novák'

b. ***varovaní*** *zlodějům* *(*předem)* *(*Dr. Novákem)*
warning$_{\text{NT.(IMPF)}}$ thief$_{\text{DAT}}$ in advance$_{\text{ADV}}$ Dr.Novák$_{\text{INS}}$
'the warning of thieves (*in advance) (* by Dr.Novák)'

According to Kolářová (2014), these borderline cases of N/T nominals should be treated as lexical derived nominals. However, she notes that they can still be modified by certain eventive and agentive adjectives:

(375) *úmyslná* ***varování/upozornění*** *zlodějům*
deliberate warning$_{\text{NT.(IMPF)}}$/pref$_{\text{PF.}}$warning$_{\text{NT}}$ thief$_{\text{DAT}}$
'deliberate warning of thieves'

For this reason, I propose representing these as simple event nouns with underlying verbal layers in (376), diverging from Karlík (2019), who does not attribute such a structure to N/T nominals.

(376)	[D……[*v*P[√root]]]]

5.4.2.4 Active Voice and Transitivity of Czech Event Nominals

As mentioned earlier, the adverbial tests have confirmed the existence of a Voice layer in nominalizations. Nevertheless, the crucial question now is whether this Voice layer can be active with true external arguments or whether it is passive/deficient in nature. Another related question is whether the process of passivization, for example, object preposing is possible in nominalizations. On this matter, the two linguists I am comparing hold divergent viewpoints and propose different answers.

Alexiadou (2001, 2017d) claims that nominalizations of the type (377) are either passive or unaccusative. By contrast, for Borer (2013) the example in (377a) has an active counterpart, so that (377b) and (377c) are passive. The latter derived by object preposing from (377b).

(377) a. *Kim's **formation/forming** of the team*
b. *the **formation/forming** of the team (by Kim)*
c. *the team's **formation** (by Kim)*

Although Alexiadou (2017d) introduces passive Voice in nominalizations, this functional projection is deficient and cannot introduce external arguments. The external arguments are introduced in SpecDP which results in their different interpretation. They are prone to be interpreted as Causers rather than true Agents. Also, there is no object preposing for structures such as (377c), and the theme is also situated in SpecDP directly. Thus, nominalizations rather realize ergative patterns similarly to ergative languages which have deficient *v*, and their external arguments can either surface as PPs or Possessors.

The supportive evidence for this kind of analysis can be found in Karlík (2007a) who casts doubt on the hypothesis that nominalizations are passive structure. He points out on the basis of binding relations that if syntactically derived nominals possessed a passive structure, then a genitive DP with an interpretation of A2 (internal argument) in the subject position (378b-c) should have an analogical interpretation as a DP with an A2 interpretation of passive participles (378d):

(378)	a.	***kritizování***	$_{A2}$ <u>*učitele*</u>		*žákem*	
		criticizing$_{NT.(IMPF)}$	teacher$_{GEN}$		pupil$_{INS}$	
		‘criticizing of the teacher by a student’				
	b.	**kritizování*	$_{A2}$<u>*učitele*</u>$_i$	***svým***$_i$	*žákem*	
		criticizing$_{NT}$	teacher$_{GEN}$	REFL	pupil$_{INS}$	
		*‘criticizing of the teacher by his own pupil’				
	c.	* $_{A2}$<u>*učitelovo*</u>$_i$.	***kritizování***	***svým***$_i$	*žákem*	
		teacher	criticizing$_{NT.(IMPF)}$	REFL	pupil$_{INS}$	
		*‘criticizing of the teacher by his own pupil’				
	d.	<u>*učitel*</u>$_i$	*je*	***kritizován***	***svým***$_i$	*žákem*
		teacher$_{NOM}$	AUX.BE	criticize$_{PRT}$	REFL	pupil$_{INS}$
		‘The teacher is being criticized by his own pupil.’				

These examples indicate that the object preposing operation works differently in the nominal domain than in the verbal domain.

By means of binding facts, Karlík (2007) also stresses that prenominal Genitives with the interpretation A1 (external argument) in nominalizations do not display typical subject-like properties. It is well-known fact that a subject can bind anaphors, as shown in (379a). However, neither the prenominal genitive in (379c) nor the prenominal genitive in (379d) is coreferential with the reflexive *svůj* '*self*'. The latter is a genuine Noun, indicating that prenominal genitives of nominalizations exhibit certain patterns with genuine Nouns in some cases:

(379) a. *Petr$_i$* ***kritizuje*** *svého$_i$* *učitele.*
Peter$_{NOM}$ criticize REFL teacher$_{ACC}$
'Peter criticizes its own teacher.'

b. $_{A1}$ *Petrovo$_i$* ***kritizování*** *svého$_i$* *učitele*
Peter criticing$_{NT.(IMPF)}$ REFL teacher$_{GEN}$
'Peter's criticizing its own teacher'

c. *? Petrovo$_i$* ***pobíhání*** *ve své$_i$* *pracovně*
Peter running$_{NT.(IMPF)}$ in REFL office
?'Peter's running in in his own office'

d. **Petrovo$_i$* ***křeslo*** *ve své$_i$* *pracovně*
Peter chair$_{NT.SG}$ in REFL office
*'Peter's chair in his own office'

While nominalizations in Alexiadou's theory have a deficient Voice and subjects are located in SpecDPs directly, their different interpretation is expected. SpecDP is a thematic position and can license various thematic roles. Above all, Alexiadou claims that subjects of nominalizations have different interpretation than true Agents and behave rather like Causers. On the other hand, in Borer (2013), the argument interpretation within nominalizations should be identical to the interpretation of arguments in active and passive sentences.

We can, nevertheless, employ Borer's (2013) test and try to find out whether Czech N/T nominalizations are more active-like or passive-like. Recall that in her investigation of silent subjects described in section 5.1.3, Borer (2013) realizes that silent subjects of SASNs pattern together with passive structures in having a PRO which exhibits the so-called Lebeaux effect.

Lebeaux (1984) points out that in target cases where silent subjects do not c-command each other nor is there any obvious antecedent that could control both of them, have universal/generic interpretation and hence need to refer to the same antecedent. For passive and passive nominals, Borer (2020) envisages a null indefinite pronominal $\text{pro}_{\text{indef}}$ which can have two readings: existential and generic. Whereas in their existential reading the option of the same subject construal is dis-preferred, in their generic reading the same subject reading is possible. The structural position of these silent subjects is visible in (380):

(380) a. $[_{D}\ \ldots\ldots\ldots \text{N} \ldots [_{\pi}\ \pi\ [_{e}\ \text{pro}_{\text{indef}} \ldots\ldots [_{C=V}\ \text{V}]]]]]$
b. $[_{D}\ \text{PRO N}\ [_{E} \ldots\ldots [_{C=V}\ \text{V}]]]]]$

The same effects are observed in Czech. Czech does not have gerunds as discussed in section 1.4.1, but the only available reading for infinitives in (381) is that the very same people who destroyed the work environment also reorganized the labor force. In contrast, in nominalizations as in (382), a disjoint subject construal is possible. The examples below are mine:

(381) ✗ **(Distinct Subject construal excluded)**

a.	***narušit***	*pracovní prostředí*	*znamená*	***reorganizovat***	*pracovní sílu*
	$\text{disrupt}_{\text{INF}}$	work $\text{environment}_{\text{ACC}}$	means	$\text{re-organize}_{\text{INF}}$	labor $\text{force}_{\text{ACC}}$
	'to disrupt the work environment means to reorganize the labor force'				
b.	***sjednotit***	*pracovní sílu*	*znamená*	***propustit***	*zaměstnance*
	$\text{unionize}_{\text{INF}}$	labor $\text{force}_{\text{ACC}}$	means	fire_{INF}	$\text{workers}_{\text{ACC}}$
	'to unionize the labor force means to fire workers'				

(382) ✓ **(Distinct Subject construal possible)**

a.	***narušení***	*pracovního prostředí*	*znamená*	***reorganizování***	*pracovní síly*
	$\text{disrupting}_{\text{NT}}$	work $\text{environment}_{\text{GEN}}$	means	$\text{organizing}_{\text{NT}}$	labor $\text{force}_{\text{GEN}}$
	'the disrupting of the work environment means reorganizing of the labor force'				
b.	***sjednocení***	*pracovní síly*	*znamená*	***propuštění***	*zaměstnanců*
	$\text{unionizing}_{\text{NT}}$	labor $\text{force}_{\text{GEN}}$	means	$\text{firing}_{\text{NT}}$	$\text{workers}_{\text{GEN}}$
	'the unionizing of the labor force means the firing of workers'				

Due to the fact that passive participles in Czech have a pro_{indef} a distinct subject construal is possible:

(383)

a.	*Pracovní prostředí*	*bylo*	*narušeno*	--
	work environment	AUX_{PAST}	$disrupt_{PRT}$	
---	*což znamen-alo, že*	*pracovní síla*	*byla*	*reorganizována.*
	which meant that	labor force	AUX_{PAST}	$reorganize_{PRT}$

'The work environment was disrupted which meant that the labor force was reorganized.'

b.	*Pracovní síla*	*byla*	*sjednocena*	---
	labor force	AUX_{PAST}	$unionize_{PRT}$	
---	*což vedlo k tomu, že*	*zaměstnaci*	*byli*	*propuštěni.*
	which meant that	employees	AUX_{BE}	$fire_{PRT}$

'The labor force was unionized which led to the fact that employees were laid off.'

We can conclude from this discussion that Czech nominalizations seem to be passive-like as far as implicit arguments are concerned.

Thus, if we put all pieces together, the analysis where nominalizations are intransitive or rather ergative constructions where the process of nominalization has similar consequences as passivization as suggested by Alexiadou (2017d; 2001) is most appropriate. The rationale behind this lies in the fact that ergative patterns arise due to Case considerations, and since PRO (a null pronoun) possesses a unique null Case, it remains unaffected and can display passive-like characteristics. Consequently, implicit arguments of nominalizations pattern with those of passives. When Case requirements come into play, the overt arguments behave differently from those observed in verbal passives and active structures which confirms their different point of merge in nominalizations and verbal domains.

5.4.2.5 Ergativity Patterns of Czech Nominalizations

One of Alexiadou's (2001, 2017d) statement in favor of ergativity in nominalizations comes from the case marking of argument as described in 5.2.3, which resembles that found in ergative languages. The main aim of the following discussion will be to examine the case marking of arguments in both transitive and intransitive nominalizations in Czech, to determine whether Czech nominalizations comply with this statement.

The sole argument of intransitive predicates has two options. It can appear either pre-nominally as or post-nominally:[83]

(384)	*(tatínkovo)*	***kýchání***	*(našeho tatínka)*
	$\text{father}_{\text{POSS}}$	$\text{sneezing}_{\text{NT. (IMPF)}}$	our $\text{father}_{\text{GEN}}$
	'father's sneezing/sneezing of the father'		

Transitive structures have three slots where arguments can be located, either pre-nominally as Possessives (POSS) or post-nominally in Genitive (GEN) and Instrumental (INS) Cases. There is also a strict ordering rule where the Instrumental Case can never precede the Genitive Case. Both the internal argument (A2) and external arguments (A1) can be marked as GEN or POSS and occur either post-nominally or pre-nominally when they are the sole argument of the Noun (385a-b). However, in the case of perfective Verbs, the A2 argument is forced to have a postnominal (non-subject) interpretation (385c).

(385)	a.		***napomínání***	$_{\text{A2/A1}}$ *Petra*
			$\text{talking-to}_{\text{(IMPF).NT}}$	$\text{Peter}_{\text{GEN}}$
		'talking-to Peter'		
	b.	$_{\text{A1/A2}}$ *Pavlovo*	***napomínání***	
		$\text{Peter}_{\text{POSS}}$	$\text{talking-to}_{\text{(IMPF).NT}}$	
		'talking-to Paul'		

83 There are restrictions on Czech Possessives. They must be prenominal, bare, animate and marked for +/-FEM. See Veselovská (1998, 2014).

c. ***napomenutí*** $_{A2}$ *Petra*
talking-to$_{PF.NT}$ Peter$_{GEN}$
'talking-to Peter'

When Genitive co-occurs with POSS as in (386), their thematic interpretation can be computed from UTAH. See Veselovská (1998, 2014) for more about their interpretation and the interpretation of Possessives and its complementarity with postnominal Genitives.

(386) $_{A1/*A2}$*Pavlovo* ***napomínání*** $_{A2/*A1}$ *Petra*
talking-to$_{(IMPF).NT}$ Peter$_{GEN}$
'Paul's talking to Peter'

Double Genitives are prohibited in Czech AS Nouns (389) as well as in R-Nominals (387):

(387) **obraz* *Evy* *Pavla*
picture Eve$_{GEN}$ Paul$_{GEN}$
*'picture of Eve of Paul'

We are now able to carry out a comparison with ergative structures. In order to do that we will utilize table in (388) from section 5.2.3 which compares the case marking in nominative-accusative languages, ergative languages and nominalizations. What can be observed is that in ergative languages subjects of intransitives receive the same marking as objects of transitives (absolutive case).

(388)	N/A Active	N/A Passive	E/A system	Nominalizations
A-argument (transitive)	**NOM**	**PP**	**ERG**	**PP**
S-argument (intransitive)	**NOM**	-	**ABS**	**GEN**
P-argument (transitive)	**ACC**	**NOM**	**ABS**	**GEN**

In the Czech verbal domain, this is not possible. Czech subjects receive NOM Case and objects ACC Case as table (388) summarizes. However, in Czech nominalizations subjects of intransitives as well as objects of transitives can receive GEN as in (385) and (386) respectively.

Ergative languages have special marking for subjects of transitives (ergative case), similarly to the Czech example (389) where the external argument is marked by the Instrumental Case:

(389)	***napomínání***	$_{\text{A2}}$*Petra*	$_{\text{A1}}$ *Pavlem/(*Pavla)*
	talking-to$_{\text{(IMPF).NT}}$	Peter$_{\text{GEN}}$	Paul$_{\text{INS}}$/Paul$_{\text{GEN}}$
	'talking to Peter by Paul/(*of Paul)'		

To conclude, unlike a verbal domain which does not exhibit ergative patterns, Czech nominalizations pattern with ergative structures.

5.4.3 Case Licensing

In the previous discussion, we have described morphological marking of arguments in their surface structures. In this subsection, I will assess the approaches of both linguists to their derivation in the deep structure, using Czech data for this evaluation.

Let's begin with Borer (2013) and her analysis of nominals derived from mono-transitive Verbs. She puts forward that in English, *of*-phrases in SpecAsp$_{\text{Q}}$ are a spell out of objective Case when T absent. The derivation steps for AS-Nominal in (390) are then as follows: *John* occupies SpecD but the object *city* cannot move because the subject *John* has left a copy in functional specifiers. Thus, the object must be Case marked in situ.

(390) [$_{\text{D}}$*John's* [$_{\text{F2-N}}$*painting* [$_{\text{F1-N}}$~~*John*~~ [$_{\text{N}}$~~*painting*~~ [$_{\text{E}}$~~*John*~~ [$_{\text{AspQ}}$*of the picture*[$_{\text{C=V}}$ ~~*malovat*~~]]]]]]

The problematic aspect of this mechanism for Czech data is that this mechanism involves incorporation of V-to N and then subsequent movement of N-to-D (but not as far as to D in English). I have argued in section 3.5.5 that N-to D movement is not adequate for Czech because of the surface ordering of Adjectives. They do not normally occur post-nominally, as they should if N were ever in D. Furthermore, I do not suppose that the N layer is even present in Czech. Instead, the verbal part is nominalized by nominal functional layers, either GenP or QP. Now, let's explore the implications of prohibiting N-to-D movement.

The mono-transitive structure (391) can be derived under the assumption that the complex Noun + verb (e.g., *malování* 'painting') does not undergo movement across nominal projections:

(391)

$[_{D}$ *Honzovo* $[_{F2\text{-}N}$ $[_{F1\text{-}N}$ ~~*Honza*~~ $[_{E}$ ~~*Honza*~~ *malování* $[_{AspQ}$ *obrázku*$_{GEN}$ $[_{C=V}$ ~~*malovat*~~]]]]

$[_{D}$ *John*$_{POSS}$ $[_{F2\text{-}N}$ $[_{F1\text{-}N}$ ~~*John*~~ $[_{E}$ ~~*John*~~ *painting* $[_{AspQ}$ *picture*$_{GEN}$ $[_{C=V}$ ~~*paint*~~]]]]

The system of Case licensing also correctly predicts that ditransitives are prohibited as the licensing of the third argument is pre-empted by movement of the logical subject to SpecD.[84]

(392)	**projektování*	*reformy*	*premiéra*
	projecting$_{NT}$	reform$_{GEN}$	Prime Minister$_{GEN}$
	*'designing the minister's reform'		

The derivation with two indirect objects can, of course, converge if the third argument is otherwise Case marked. In example (393) the Patient argument *dopis* 'letter' is the carrier of Genitive Case and *Eva/Eve* must be marked by Dative.

(393)	*Napsání*	**(dopisu)*	*Evě*	*trvalo dlouho.*
	on$_{PF.}$writing$_{NT}$	letter$_{GEN}$	Eve$_{DAT}$	took a long time
	'Writing *(a letter) to Eve took a long time.'			

The difficulty lies particularly in structures with a single argument. While the derivation of unaccusatives with an Asp$_{Q}$ projection seems feasible, unergatives do not, as shown in (394):

84 Two Genitives can occur only if one of them is a lexical Case: *zbavení ženy starostí/* relieving the woman of worries (Panevová 2000). Also, if the second Genitive modifies the first: *malování domu naší rodiny/painting of the house of our family.*

(394)	*časté*	***zívání/skákání/pískání***	*našeho tatínka*
	frequent	yawning$_{(IMPF).NT}$/jumping$_{(IMPF).NT}$/ whistling$_{(IMPF).NT}$	our dad$_{GEN}$
	'frequent yawning/jumping/whistling of our father'		

The analysis of unergatives would require the movement of the complex Noun+ verb across the EP projection which is not possible:

(395) a. *[$_{D}$ [$_{F2\text{-}N}$ [$_{F1\text{-}N}$ *zívání* [$_{E}$ *tatínka* ~~*zívaní*~~ [$_{C=V}$ *zívat*]]]]]
b. *[$_{D}$ [$_{F2\text{-}N}$ [$_{F1\text{-}N}$ V-C$_{N[V]}$ [$_{E}$ *of* DP1 ~~V~~ [$_{C=V}$ ~~V~~]]]]]

We can now examine the key points put forward by Alexiadou. First of all, Alexiadou (2001) follows Cinque (1980) and expects only V-to-N movement for English which complies with my analysis. Regarding the mechanism of Case licensing described in section 5.2.3, the layer *n*P has properties similar to passives, and its task is to turn a transitive verb into passive. More importantly, there is only one head for one argument to agree (presumably AspectP). Alexiadou (2017d) claims that the one argument that receives structural Case is the one which surfaces with Genitive. The only option for the other argument in case of transitive verb is to surface as *by*-phrase or escape *n*P and merge higher in SpecDP.

The proposed mechanism by Alexiadou offers an explanation for the majority of nominalization structures in Czech. However, there are some problematic cases, particularly when it comes to unergative Verbs as in (394) whose arguments might be built on Active Voice, which deviates from what is typically expected in nominalizations, as discussed earlier.

The existence of such structures is a subject of debate in Alexiadou (2001), where it is argued that process nominals are not commonly based on ergative structures cross-linguistically. In Alexiadou (2017d), this issue is revised, and it is proposed in line with Massam (2009), that subjects of unergative Verbs are introduced within the *v*P domain, at least in the context of nominalizations.

To conclude this part, both theoretical frameworks have the capability to account for various nominalization patterns, with the exception of unergative constructions in Czech. Alexiadou (2017d) proposes a solution to address this issue, suggesting that the arguments of unergative Verbs could be derived within the *v*P domain at least in nominalizations. Hence, although her analysis may be considered somewhat ad hoc, it appears to be more suitable for explaining the data in Czech.

5.4.3.1.1 Reflexivity

Another important consideration emerges when dealing with Czech reflexive Verbs, which, as demonstrated earlier, can be used for nominalizations. In the literature, the behavior of reflexive Verbs is occasionally compared to that of unaccusative Verbs. However, as previously mentioned, Alexiadou classifies them as unergative Verbs. This classification is further supported by Medova and Taraldsen's (2007) analysis, which highlights that unlike unaccusatives, reflexive Verbs do not permit *ne*-extraction from a postverbal subject.

In Czech analyses, the reflexive element originates lower in the structure (VP) and undergoes raising to a higher position. For instance, according to Panevová (2000), the reflexive clitic SE serves as an anaphoric object within VP. In contrast, Medová and Taraldsen (2007) suggest that this view poses challenges as a single element would accumulate two theta roles. Instead, Medová and Taraldsen propose that the reflexive starts as an oblique within VP and then raises to a higher position. The specific details of these proposals may vary, but the crucial observation is that the *SE*-reflexives originate lower in the structure.

In section 4.2.2, it has been illustrated that Alexiadou et al. (2015) distinguish between two types of reflexive verbs. This idea can be transferred to Czech where both semantically reflexive verb such as (396a) and anticausative in (397a) can be marked with the reflexive SE. Their syntactic structures are in (396b) and (397b) respectively. What can also be observed is that the reflexive SE 'self' is preserved in the nominalization structures in (c).

(396)	a.	*studenti*	*se*	*přihlásili*	**Semantically reflexive verb**
		student$_{NOM}$	SELF	registered	
		'students registered themselves'			
	b.	**[$_{TP}$ T [$_{Voice\ P}$ DP Voice [$_{vP}$ v REFL]]]**			
	c.	*přihlášení*	*se*	*studentů*	
		registering$_{NT}$	SELF	students$_{GEN}$	
		'registering of students'			

(397)	a.	*dveře* door$_{NOM}$ 'the door opened itself'	*se* SELF	*otevřely* opened	**Reflexively marked anticausatives**
	b.	[$_{TP}$ **T** [$_{Voice\ P}$ **REFL Voice** [$_{vP}$ ***v*** **DP**]]]			
	c.	*otevření* opening$_{NT}$ 'opening of the door by itself'	*se* SELF	*dveří* door$_{GEN}$	

With semantically reflexive verbs the reflexive SE originates lower in the structure, namely the *v*P projection. This is compatible with descriptions of reflexives in the Czech literature, see Medová and Taraldsen (2007) and Panevová (2000) as described in the previous section, leaving aside whether the reflexive *SE* starts as an oblique or not. On the other hand, reflexively marked anticausative contain expletive Voice which hosts the reflexive *SE* without its being interpreted as a thematic argument.

For the purpose of this study, I will assume that Czech has both types of reflexives illustrated in (396) and (397). For the first type the reflexive originates in the *v*P and the expletive Voice in nominalizations is also possible. Compare also its inclusion into nominalization structures in Polish by Rozwadowska (2020).

5.4.4 Morphological Issues

Another compelling argument supporting ergativity in N/T nominalizations is evident in surface morphological forms observed in Czech which will be the subject of this section. Interestingly, these forms bear a resemblance to passive participles, formed by the addition of derivational affixes such as *-(e/ě)n*, *-(a/á)n*, and *-t*. These affixes share similarities with those used in passive participles, as depicted in examples (398) and summarized in table (399).

5.4.4.1 Thematic Role Markers

Unlike most Czech deverbal event nominals that attach their derivational suffix directly to the root, derivational suffixes in N/T nominals are attached as late as after the thematic affix of the verbal stem. Therefore, I am going to analyze *thematic marker* first.[85] Table (398) below illustrates that the *-ba*

85 See Caha and Zikova (2016).

suffix is directly added to the root, whereas the *-ní* suffix is attached to the theme vowel. Caha and Zikova (2016) suggest that the presence of a theme vowel can influence the aspectual interpretation of a verb, such as semelfactivity (398c), iterativity, or signal argument structure alternations (e.g., the causative-inchoative alternation).[86]

(398)	Verb		N/T nominal	B/K nominal	
a.	'he constructed'	*stav-ě*$_{TH}$*-l*	*stav-ě*$_{TH}$*-n-í*	*stav-ba*	'construction'
b.	'he closed'	*za*$_{PF}$*-vír-á*$_{TH}$*-l*	*za*$_{PF}$*-vír-á*$_{TH}$*-n-í*	*zá-věr*	'closing'
c.	'he winked'	*mrk-nu-l*	*mrk-nu*$_{TH}$*-t-í*	*mrk*	'winking'

There are two types of thematic affixes in Czech: infinitival and present thematic affixes. These are listed in the table below in the second and third column respectively. The initial column uses the classification dividing the Czech Verbs into five 'classes'—you can see that the taxonomy is based on the present thematic vowel. By their combination, we can get all the derivational combinations of verbal Nouns in Czech, see also Čechová (2000, p. 225–226):

(399)	Infinitive thematic vowel	Present thematic vowel	VERB PAST. PART	3.SG. PRES	PASS. PART	NOMINAL	
I.i	*ɸ*	***-e***	*nes- ɸ -l*	*nes-e*	*nes-ɸ-en*	*nes-ɸ-en-í*	'carrying'
I.ii	*ɸ*	***-ne***	*tisk-ɸ-l*	*tisk-ne*	*tišť-ɸ-en*	*tišť-ɸ-en-í*	'printing'
I.iii	*ɸ*	***-je***	*kry-ɸ-l*	*kry-je*	*kry-ɸ-t*	*kry-ɸ-t-í*	'covering'
II.ii	***-nu***	***-ne***	*tisk-(nu)-l*	*tisk-ne*	*tisk-nut-t*	*tisk-nu-t-í*	'printing'
III.i	***-e***	***-e***	*tř-e-l*	*tř-e*	*tř-e-n*	*tř-en-í*	'rubbing'
III.iv	***-e***	***-í***	*sáz-e-l*	*sáz-í*	*sáz-e-n*	*sáz-e-n-í*	'setting'
IV.i	***-í***	***-í***	*pros-i-l*	*pros-í*	*proš-ɸ-en*	*proš-ɸ-en-í*	'begging'
V.i	***-a***	***-e***	*br-a-l*	*ber-e*	*br-á-n*	*br-a-n-í*	'taking'
V.i	***-a***	***-e***	*za-br-al*	*za-ber-e*	*za-br-á-n*	*za-br-á-n-í*	'$_{PF}$taking'
V.ii	***-a***	***-ne***	*po-č-a-l*	*po-č-ne*	*po-č-a-t*	*po-č-et-í*	'conception'
V.iii	***-(ov)a***	***-(u) je***	*kup-ov-al*	*kup-uj-e*	*kup-ov-á-n*	*kup-ov-á-n-í*	'buying'
V.v	***-a***	***-a***	*děl-a-l*	*děl-á*	*děl-á-n*	*děl-á-n-í*	'doing'

86 To exemplify this, the Adjective *červený- red* can be transformed into a verb by adding a theme marker; *červen-í*TH-*t* means 'to make red', while *červen-a*TH-*t* means 'to become red'.

Obviously, if B/K nominals lack the theme suffix, they are often incapable of expressing aspectual distinctions. Therefore, the *ba*-nominal in (400a) is ambiguous and can convey the meaning of the perfective (400b) or secondary imperfective (400c):

(400)	a.	*ob-haj-ob-a* pref.defence	b.	*ob-háj-i*$_{\text{TH}}$*-t* pref$_{\text{PF.}}$defend$_{\text{INF}}$	c.	*ob-haj-ova*$_{\text{TH}}$*-t* pref$_{\text{PF.}}$defend$_{\text{IMPF.INF}}$

For these reasons, I will locate the thematic vowel in this thesis in the AspectP functional projections which is missing in type II nominals.

Upon closer examination of table (399), it becomes evident that there is a significant degree of stem alternation between the present and the past participle:

- softening of the final consonant in I.ii: *tiskl> tištěn*
- *i*>e alternation in IV.iv
- vowel lengthening in V.i

As far as i>e alternation is concerned, Medová (2018) argues that this alternation is visible in contexts where the external argument is suppressed. Apart from the passive N/T participle *slaz-E-n-ý* meaning 'sweetened' from the verb *slad-I-t* 'to sweaten', she provides evidence for this alternation translatable by *-able* adjectives as below:

(401)		INF		ADJ		ADJ
	a.	*vid-ě*$_{\text{TH}}$*-t* 'see'	b.	*vid-i*$_{\text{TH}}$*-tel-ný* 'visible'	c.	**vid-ě*$_{\text{TH}}$*-tel-ný* *'visible'

The contrast between (401a) and (401b) follows if the theme E_{TH} introduces an external argument that is not a proper Agent and that the *able* adjective needs a proper [+HUM] agentive argument. The theme I_{TH} is the canonical introducer of an external volitional argument.

In contrast, we observe that there are hardly any discrepancies between the passive participle and the verbal Noun. In fact, there are only two minor alterations in theme vowels that set them apart:

- a>e alternation in the theme vowel in the class V.ii: *poč-a-t → poč-e-t-í*
- vowel shortening in imperfective stem in the class Vi: *br-á-n → br-a-n-í*

In the following section, I will put forward possible explanations for these changes. Regarding the *a > e* alternation, it can be viewed as irregular and, as mentioned by Čechová (2000, p. 231), it is historically linked to the I.i class. This parallelism provides a rationale for the characteristic transformation to *-e* observed in the I.i class.

The phenomenon of vowel shortening is more intricate. It is important to note that this change exclusively takes place in the imperfective form (e.g., *br-a-n-í* becomes *br-á-n*). Conversely, in the perfective version, vowel shortening does not occur (e.g., *za-br-á-n-í* remains *za-br-á-n*). Zikova (2016) identifies a lengthening process that is triggered by infinitives in Czech and is further conditioned by the imperfective form. In contrast, the perfective form does not undergo vowel lengthening. She compares it with *-i-e* patterns where the lengthening occurs with prefixed and unprefixed form as (402) exemplifies:

(402) lengthening

INF i/e pattern	PREF-INF	PREF-PAST PART	INF a-pattern	PREF-INF	PREF-PAST PART
CC-í-t	pref-CC-í-t	pref-CC-i/e-l	CC-á-t	pref-CC-a-t	pref-CC-a-l
tř-í-t	*roze-tř-í-t*	*roze-tř-e-l*	*br-á-t*	*roze-br-a-t*	*roze-br-a-l*
'to spread'	'to spread apart'	'spread apart'	'to take'	'to take apart'	'took apart'

It is evident that only the non-prefixed form consistently undergoes changes, either lengthening or shortening. Zikova (2016) provides an explanation for this phenomenon: theme vowels are inherently short and experience lengthening due to the prosodic constraint triggered by the infinitive template. According to Zikova, in the infinitive form, the root and the theme marker must together constitute a unit with a minimum weight of two moras. If the root already contains a vowel, the combination with the theme marker fulfills the templatic requirement without the need for lengthening. However, when the root lacks a vowel, the theme marker must lengthen to satisfy the requirement.

Looking at it from this perspective, the occurrence of lengthening in both simple and prefixed infinitives within the *i/e*-pattern can be explained by assuming that the prefix does not contribute to the infinitival template in the *a*-pattern. Subsequently, we have the two theme-alternating patterns:

(403)	*i/e*-pattern	*a*-pattern
	prefix-[root-theme]	[prefix-root-theme]

Interestingly, these patterns do not undergo initial parsing in this manner during the derivation. Instead, according to Zikova (2016) this rebracketing process occurs later in the derivation and follows prefix vocalization, where the prefix and root must form a constituent:

(404)	C-CCVC	V-CC-V
	roz-tříd-i-t	*roze-tř-í-t*
	'sort through'	'spread'

Although I will not try here to make any precise claim as for the specific stage of derivation where theme vowel shortening occurs in deverbal Nouns, I will assume that these changes are both predictable and align with the notion that nominalizations resemble passivization, given the minimal alterations from the past participle form. Additionally, this perspective is well-suited to Alexiadou's approach, which posits a passive-like/unaccusative nature for all *n*-nominals. This could explain why even forms that typically do not undergo passivization exhibit passive morphology, such as *prš-e-n-í* 'raining', *sněž-e-n-í* 'snowing' in Czech. In contrast, Borer's perspective suggests that some forms are derived from active forms, which is not supported by Czech morphology.

Consequently, I propose that the passive participle *-n/t* allomorphs in the Czech structure should be viewed as a default Gender marker rather than a passive Voice marker. It cannot be inserted under a Passive Voice because nominalizations are derived even from nominals structures that do not undergo a process of passivization. Instead, during the process of nominalization, which exhibits passive-like characteristics, the morpheme that originally functions as a passive participle marker in the verbal domain is reinterpreted as a marker of Gender.

What remains to be analyzed, is the *-í* morpheme in Czech nominalizations. It always produces stems with neuter Gender which are either count or mass. Ziková (2007) argues that it is not a Case suffix because if it were a Case marker, it would not show massive syncretism that is unprecedented in other Case paradigms.

(405)	a.	*kamen-í*	*stone*$_{\text{NT.MASS}}$
	b.	*přímoř-í*	seaside$_{\text{NT.COUNT}}$

Therefore, I will take this *í* as a portmanteau agreement morpheme for Gender and Number that is realized on the root post-syntactically.

5.4.5 More Paradigms Involving Argument Structure Licensing

Both Alexiadou (2009) and Borer (2013) concur that internal as well as external arguments are licensed within distinct functional projections. In Borer's framework the AS originates from spatial properties because AS-Nominals always include at least the event phrase (EP) node. In Alexiadou's framework, this node is not required and what is minimally needed is Aspect. These concepts were explored in section 5.2.2 and will be elaborated upon using data from Czech to reconcile these viewpoints.

The following examples show that when the N/T nominal is *imperfective* as in (406a), both the external and internal arguments can be omitted. In this aspect, there is no distinction between the N/T and the B/K nominals in (406b).

(406)	a.	*(Karlovo)*	***malov-á-n-í***	*(obrazu)*	*trvalo dlouho.*	**N/T nominal IMPF**
		Karel$_{\text{POSS}}$	painting$_{\text{(IMPF).NT}}$	picture$_{\text{GEN}}$	took a long time	
		'(Karel's) painting (of the picture) took a long time.'				

b.	*(Karlova)*	***mal-ba***	*(obrazu)*	*trvala dlouho.*	**B/K nominal**
	$\text{Karel}_{\text{POSS}}$	$\text{painting}_{\text{F.SG}}$	$\text{picture}_{\text{GEN}}$	took a long time	
	'(Karel's) painting (of the picture) took a long time.'				

The situation with internal arguments differs when the Verb is marked with the feature +/-PERF. Since B/K nominals do not have to contain this feature, their arguments can be optional. In (407b) no condition on obligatoriness is expected while N/T always require an internal argument (407a) similarly to the verbal structure in (407c). This is despite the fact that eventive contexts are induced as the modifier of events *trvat* 'took a long time' indicates:

(407)	a.	***Vy-stav-ě-n-í***	**(kina)*	*nám*	*trvalo rok.*	**N/T** nominal **+PERF**
		$\text{out}_{\text{PF.}}\text{building}_{\text{NT}}$	$\text{cinema}_{\text{GEN}}$	us	took a year	
		'Building *(a cinema) took us a year.'				
	b.	***Vý-stav-ba***	*(kina)*	*nám*	*trvala rok.*	**B/K nominal**
		pref.building	$\text{cinema}_{\text{GEN}}$	us	took a year	
		'Building (a cinema) took us a year.'				
	c.	*Radnice*	***vy-stavěla***	**(nové kino).*		**Verb**
		$\text{the authorities}_{\text{NOM}}$	$\text{out}_{\text{PF.}}\text{build}$	$\text{new cinema}_{\text{ACC}}$		
		'The authorities built *(a new cinema).'				

(408)	a.	*Po*	***ob-jev-e-n-í***	**(léku)*	*došlo*	*k poklesu úmrtnosti.*
		after	$\text{pref}_{\text{PF.}}$ $\text{discovering}_{\text{NT}}$	$\text{medicine}_{\text{GEN}}$	come	death rate decrease
		'After discovering *(the medicine) the death rate has decreased.'				
	b.	*Po*	***ob-jevu***	*(léku)*	*došlo*	*k poklesu úmrtnosti.*
		after	pref.discovery	$\text{medicine}_{\text{GEN}}$	come	death rate decrease
		'After discovery (of the medicine) the death rate has decreased.'				

Similar arguments are evident in contexts involving aspectual modifiers. Internal arguments are only required in Perfective nominals (409b). Additionally, it is notable that B/K nominals typically do not tolerate aspectual modifiers (409c).

(409) a.

čte-n-í	*(knih)*	*několik hodin/(*za hodinu)*	*nikoho nebaví*
reading$_{(IMPF).NT}$	books$_{GEN}$	several hours/in an hour	no one enjoys

'no one enjoys reading (books) for several hours/(*in an hour)'

b.

pře-čtení	**(knihy)*	*za hodinu/(*několik hodin)*	*je možné*
re$_{PF.}$reading$_{NT}$	books$_{GEN}$	in an hour/several hours	

'reading *(of the book) in an hour/(*for several hours) is possible'

c.

čet-ba	*(knih)*	*(?? několik hodin)/(*za hodinu)*	*nikoho nebaví*
reading$_{F.SG}$	books$_{GEN}$	for several hours/in an hour	no one enjoys

'no one enjoys reading (books) (??for several hours)/(*in an hour)'

Nevertheless, a few B/K examples such as (410) with aspectual modifiers seem to be natural, yet their internal arguments are not obligatory. Thus, the presence of these modifiers testifies only in favor of the feature +/- TELIC.

(410) a.

Celkové	***trž-by***	*(dodavatelů)*	*(za 1.čtvrtletí)/ (*celé čtvrtletí)*	*klesly.*
total	sales$_{F.PL}$	deliverers$_{GEN}$	in the first quarter	fall

'The total sales (from deliveries) (in the first quarter)/(*for the first quarter) have fallen.'

b.

Výro-ba	*(masa)*	*(za celý rok)/ (*celý rok)*	*klesla.*
production$_{F.SG}$	meat$_{GEN}$	in the whole year	fall

'The production (of meat) (in the whole year)/(*for the whole year) has fallen.'

The examples above confirm the following correlation: N/T nominals which are aspectually sensitive always require an internal argument. B/K nominals do not contain this feature, and their internal arguments are optional. For this reason, I propose the correlation between the feature +/-Perf and the realization of internal arguments in Czech, presumably in some form of an aspectual operator that binds them.

It also appears that the spatial dimension required in Borer's framework is not necessary, as the telicity feature, which signals Path and is spatial, does not require the presence of obligatory arguments. In Czech, what is needed is Perfectivity, and therefore, the higher aspectual component.

5.5 Chapter Summary

In this chapter, I have contrasted approaches of H. Borer and A. Alexiadou to nominalizations and assessed them with respect to Czech data. After the analysis of Czech verbal and nominalizing morphology (as presented in, e.g., 4.4.2 and 3.5), I have adopted many aspects from Alexiadou's framework because it better reflects Czech data.

In particular, I have adopted Alexiadou's *v* layer which can account for telicity and help distinguish between the function of prefixes in zero-derived B/K nominals and prefixes in N/T nominals. B/K nominals include only this layer and exhibit fewer verbal characteristics compared to N/T nominals. The latter not only project the *v*P layer but also other verbal functional projections such as AspectP, ProgP, and the NegP layer, where the negative prefix *-ne* can be assigned.

I also advocate for an ergative analysis of nominalization, following Alexiadou (2001). This position is supported by several arguments. First, external arguments in nominalizations demonstrate distinct behaviors compared to their clausal counterparts, as evidenced by binding effects explored in Karlík (2007). Second, the Lebeaux effect (1984) demonstrates that implicit arguments in nominalizations align with implicit arguments in passive structures. Third, morphological analysis of deverbal nouns in Czech reveals their formation is analogous to passive participles. Fourth, the case marking of arguments in nominalization mirrors the case marking found in ergative languages.

Subsequently, ergativity in nominalizations leads to the analysis where Voice is missing or deficient. I assume that Czech nominalizations can be associated with Passive Voice as is reflected by the presence of Adverbs and *by*-phrases.

Furthermore, I will not assume Borer's N-to-D movement in Czech and consequently adopt the mechanism of Case licensing proposed in Alexiadou (2017d). Contrary to Alexiadou, I do not attribute the nominalization function to the nominalizer *n*, as this layer is absent in my analysis. In Czech, this function is instead performed by any nominal functional projection attached to the top of verbal layers, such as GenP or QP.

These facts have enabled me to assign syntactic structures to two groups of nominals introduced in section 5.4.1: B/K nominals in (411) and N/T nominals in (412). These were carefully described by Veselovská (2001, 2018b) and Karlík in his many studies, most recently in Karlík (2019).

(411) B/K nominals

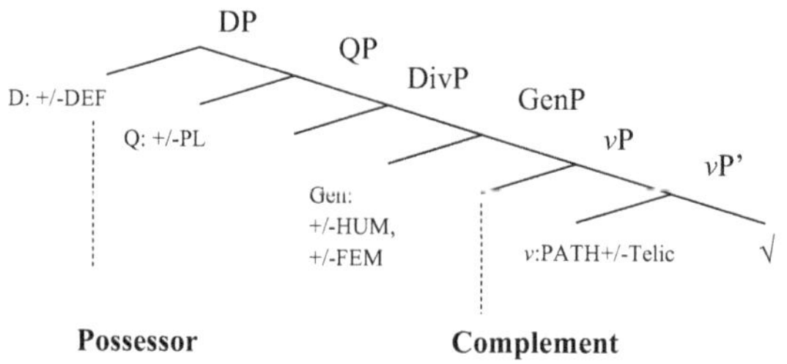

(412) N/T nominal

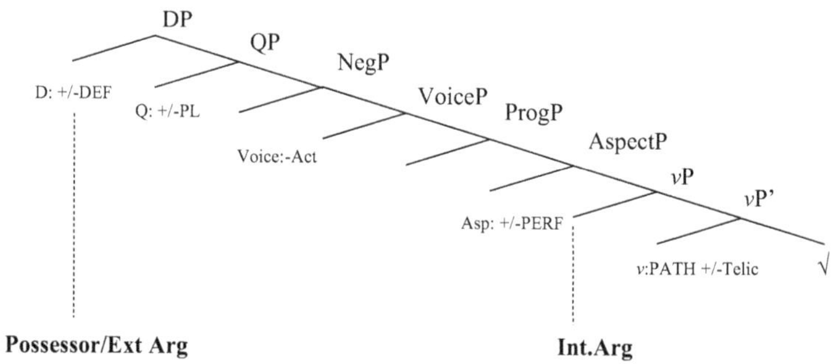

I will use these structures for nominalizations in the next chapter where I am going to investigate their nominal layers and their ability to pluralize in more detail.

CHAPTER 6

Countability of Argument Structure Nominals

In the previous chapters, I have explored issues related to a theoretical framework. Building on this discussion, I proposed structures for Czech nominal and verbal projections and conducted an analysis of the nominalization process for two distinct types of Czech derived nominals. In this final chapter, I will focus on of the features which are used to define distinctions between the two kinds of nominalizations. Namely, I will establish a theoretical foundation for the investigation of countability in derived eventive Nouns based on the parallelism between nominal and verbal domain. In order to do that I am going to include an overview of the perspectives presented by Alexiadou et al. (2010c) and Borer (2013) as they specifically address the issue of countability of CENs in English. Subsequently, the introductory framework will be tested comparing the theoretical predictions with the Czech data obtained through corpus research.

In Grimshaw's influential study from 1990, the presence or absence of plural marking serves as a significant parameter for distinguishing between Argument structure (AS) and Referential (R) Nominals, with only the latter permitting pluralization. Grimshaw's framework was properly described in section 1.3.3. She claims that the verbal character of CENs is incompatible with plural marking:

(413) a. *The **assignments** were long.*
b. **The **assignments** of the problem took a long time.*

This implies that all AS-Nominals are predominantly mass which in syntactic terms means that they have only verbal layers and insufficient nominal layers to host NumP/QP.

Recent research on AS-Nominals challenges Grimshaw's view and provides cross-linguistic counterevidence to her claims. Plural event nominals have been shown to exist in French and Italian (Roodenburg 2006; Knittel 2011), Romanian (Iordăchioaia and Soare 2009; Sleeman and Brito 2010), Dutch (van Hout 1991), Slavic and Germanic languages (Alexiadou et al. 2010c) and English (Borer 2013).

Both the authors widely cited in this study, that is, Alexiadou and Borer contribute to the discussion about countability of AS-Nominals in the English language. Both establish a correlation between the potential of AS-Nominals for countability and aspectual issues.

6.1 Borer's Countability of AS-Nominals

Borer's (2013) analysis is not extensively detailed, but she observes that telic derived nominals behave as count Nouns while atelic ones behave like mass. In view of this observation, consider her examples:

(414)

a. *the (regrettable)* ***dismissals****/(****dismissings****) of many qualified workers (by newly appointed CEOs)*
b. *the (infrequent)* ***empowerments****/(****empowerings****) of under-represented groups (by their elected officials)*
c. *the (gradual)* ***promotions****/(****promotings****) of these incompetent functionaries (by their superiors)*
d. *the (frequent)* ***replacements****/(****replacings****) of many humans with few machines (in thirty years)*
e. *the* ***appointments****/(****appointings****) of three musicians to permanent positions (by the management)*
f. *the* ***dispossessions****/(****dispossessings****) of rural land owners (by the military authorities)*

(415)

a. *a* ***dismissal*** */(*a* ***dismissing****) of a qualified worker (by newly appointed CEOs)*
b. *an* ***empowerment****/(*an* ***empowering****) of an under-represented group (by its elected official)*
c. *a* ***promotion****/(*a* ***promoting****) of an incompetent functionary (by his superior)*

d. *a* ***replacement***/(**a* ***replacing***) *of a worker with a machine*
e. *an* ***appointment***/(**an* ***appointing***) *of a musician to a permanent position (by the management)*

Although the suffix $ING_{N[V]}$ is homogeneous (atelic), the so-called ATK (*-ation* and *-kin* nominals) nominals do not share the same uniformity and can pluralize. ATK nominals refer to the set of phonological realizations associated with the C-functor, $C_{N[V]}$ in English: *-ation*, *-ance*, *-ence*, *-ancy*, *-ency*, *-ment*, *-al*.

Being homogeneous, $ING_{N[V]}$ cannot occur in the context of psychological predicates or statives:

(416) a. *#The wall's* ***touching*** *of the fence*
b. *#Kim's* ***hearing*** *of the symphony*

A non-quantity construal is not possible with achievement Verbs (which must be quantity) either:

(417) a. **Kim's* ***reaching*** *of the summit*
b. **Pat's* ***ending*** *of the flood*
c. **the* ***arriving*** *of the train*

The nominalizer *-ing* bars the projection of Asp_Q and it merges at EP. The resulting structure is in (418):

(418) [DP … [$_{NP}$ V-*ing* [$_{EP}$ DP ~~V-ing~~ <e>$_E$ … [$_{VP}$ ~~V~~]]

Interestingly, the anti-telic property of the nominalizer *-ing* is not present in verbal gerunds and progressive *-ing* forms, it seems to be neutral to telicity/anti-telicity. First of all, verbal gerunds (419) as well as progressive *-ing* (420) are compatible with achievement verbs unlike nominalizer *-ing* in (417). The examples are given in Borer (2005b, p. 164, 174, 230).

(419) VERBAL GERUND
a. *Kim's* ***reaching*** *the summit*
b. *Pat's* ***ending*** *the flood*

(420) **PROGRESSIVE**

a. *Kim **was reaching** the summit.*

b. *Pat **was ending** the flood*

Second, whereas verbal gerunds (421) are licit in the presence of telicity modifiers such as *in X-time,* nominal gerunds do not allow them (422):

(421) VERBAL GERUND

a.	*Kim **formulating** government policy*	*(for two weeks/in two weeks/ twice).*
b.	*Pat **organizing** a complex event*	*(for three minutes/in two minutes/ twice)*

(422) **NOMINAL GERUND**

a.	*Kim's **formulating** of several procedures*	*(for the past few weeks/*in a few weeks)*
b.	*Pat's **organizing** of many committees*	*(for three months /*in three months)*

Both *-ing* forms can block the culmination of events but their status is different. While the gerund assigns interpretation to (419), nominal gerund prevents such structure ever from arising (417). Thus, verbal gerund and progressive *-ing* are compatible with an Asp_Q projection but take scope over it. While the nominalizer *-ing* must be viewed in terms of inner Aspect, gerund and progressive *-ing* is an instance of outer Aspect. As an outer Aspect it takes scope over event template much like negation (e.g., *the train did not arrive* means that there was no event of a train arriving, and not that there was an event of a train not-arriving) or like the *for-X-time* phrase which is capable of leaving argument assignment intact within inner aspectual domain.

Some more compelling examples discussed originally in Chomsky (1970) and repeated in Borer (2005b, p. 240) can be provided:

(423) a. *Kim **was writing** <u>up</u> the letter.*

b. *? Kim **was writing** the letter <u>up</u>.*

(424) a. *Kim **writing** up the letter.*
b. *Kim **writing** the letter up.*

(425) a. *Kim's **writing** up of the letter.*
b. **Kim's **writing** of the letter up.*

We can see that the separation of the Verb from the particle leads to ungrammaticality when using the nominalizer *-ing* (425b). It is easily explainable if we note the contrast in (426) where Asp_Q is obligatory when the particle is separated from the verb:

(426) a. *We **ate** up sandwiches* *(for hours/all afternoon/*in three hours).*
b. *?? We **ate** sandwiches up* *(for hours/in three hours).*
Source: Borer (2005b, p. 241)

From this perspective, the nominalizer *-ing* in (425b) blocks the projection of Asp_Q which is required by the particle. Consequently, the ungrammaticality emerges, which is not observed in (423b) and (424b) with progressive and gerundive *-ing* that are neutral to the projection of Asp_Q.

To conclude this discussion, Borer (2012) assumes that that whereas nominalizer *-ing* is an inner Aspect which blocks the projection of Asp_Q altogether, progressive, gerundive *-ing* and *for-X-time* phrases are cases of outer Aspect (G-ASP) which take scope over an event template constructed independently. Telic derived nominals are also instances of inner Aspect but do not pose any constraint on countability. I will come back to this conclusion later on.

6.2 Alexiadou and Countability of AS-Nominals

Alexiadou et al. (2010c) use not only English but provide data from Romanian, German and Spanish, as well as Polish and Bulgarian AS-Nominals. Similar to Borer (2013), they accept the correlation between inner and outer Aspect and the nominal characteristics. Both the authors propose that count Nouns are similar to telic and perfective events in being BOUNDED, and mass Nouns to atelic and imperfective events in being UNBOUNDED. This explains why it is possible for telic and perfective AS-Nominals to undergo pluralization.

Alexiadou et al. (2010c) also accept Borer's analysis of the nominalizer *-ing* (their nominal gerund), referring to its being sensitive to inner Aspect (in contrast to the verbal gerund which is not). To support this claim, Alexiadou et al. (2010c) provide the following examples.[87]

(427)	a.	**the* ***arriving*** *of the train*	Nominal Gerund [+TELIC]
	b.	**the* ***erupting*** *of Vesuvius*	Nominal Gerund [+TELIC
(428)	a.	*the* ***sinking*** *of the ship*	Nominal Gerund [-TELIC]
	b.	*the* ***jumping*** *of the cows*	Nominal Gerund [-TELIC
(429)	a.	*The train* ***arriving*** *at 5 pm is unlikely.*	Verbal Gerund [+TELIC]
	b.	*John's* ***reading*** *books until late in the night worries his mother.*	Verbal Gerund [-TELIC]

In these structures, nominal gerunds inherit the inner aspect of the verb while verbal gerunds project an outer Aspect which can scope over the inner Aspect. Consequently, it follows that nominal gerunds do not have the ability to trigger an Aspect shift.

However, according to Alexiadou et al. (2010c), the inner Aspect sensitivity of the nominalizer *-ing* and the ability to pluralize also has to do with the availability of other nominal suffixes for the same structure. This can be observed in examples (430), where there are no other available nominal suffixes for Verbs like *kill* and *cross* (which are telic Verbs). In such cases, the nominalizer *-ing* is grammatically acceptable and can appropriately indicate plurality:

(430) a. *I heard of repeated* ***killings*** *of unarmed civilians.*
b. *On his frequent* ***crossings*** *of the Atlantic he has often be accompanied by his wife.*

87 Alexiadou et al. (2010c) do not discuss various sub-types of gerunds as for example Abney (1987) does. Namely Acc-ing, PRO-ing, and Poss-ing. Also, the authors claim that verbal gerund is not strictly as progressive *-ing* but leave this issue for further research.

c. *In my many/frequent **readings** of this book I failed to see its structure.*

d. *The frequent late **arrivals**/(*arrivings) of the train made me take the bus.*

In contrast, the impossibility of pluralization of verbal gerund in (431) results from the fact that it contains an outer Aspect which is in complementary distribution with Number (see also Fassi-Fehri 2005 for similar proposal).

(431) **He could not stand her **criticizings** me.*

If the outer aspect is in complementary distribution with Number, we need to explain how can perfectivity (which is defined at the outer aspectual level) tally with countability. First of all, let us have a look at some examples below quoted by Alexiadou et al. from Polish which is rich in aspectual morphology:

(432) a.

częste	*opóźnione*	***przyby-cia/odejś-cia***	*pociągu*
frequent	delayed	arrive$_{PF.CIE.PL}$/depar$_{PF.CIE.PL}$	train$_{GEN}$

'The frequent delayed arrivals/departures of train.'

b.

częste	***odkrycia***	*nowych terapii*	*raka*
frequent	discover	new treatments	cancer
	PF.CIE.PL		

przyniosly naukowcom slawe
brought researchers fame
'The frequent discoveries of cancer treatments brought the researchers international fame.'

(433) a.

**częste*	*opóźnione*	***przybywania/ odjezdzania***	*pociągu*
frequent	delayed	arrive.$_{IMPF.NIE.PL}$/ depart.$_{IMPF.NIE.PL}$	train$_{GEN}$

b.

**częste*	**odkrywania**	*nowych terapii*	*raka*	*przyniosly …*
frequent	discover.$_{IMPF.NIE.PL}$	new treatments	cancer	brought …

A first important fact to notice about the ASNs in (432) is that perfective stems tolerate a plural morphology while their corresponding imperfective pairs (433) are ungrammatical with a plural marking. It is also noteworthy that *-wa* suffix in Polish is considered as a secondary imperfective marker rather than an unmarked imperfective form. While Alexiadou et al. do not explicitly address this distinction, as they view both forms as instances of outer Aspect, it is crucial to acknowledge this differentiation. The contrast between these two types of imperfectivity has been demonstrated in the Czech language in section 4.4.1.1 and will play a significant role in our subsequent analysis and discussion.

To reconcile the issues of the simultaneous presence of countability and perfectivity, Alexiadou et al. claim that these are in fact *n*P nominalizations. The presence of an *n* head is according to these authors typically indicated by several linguistic characteristics, such as:

· Genitive PP object
· Gender features
· Adjectival modification
· Possibility to combine with all types of Determiners

What is evident from the examples in (432) is that the Polish nominals permit the modification by adjectives and the Genitive marking of their objects—both these provides clear evidence in support of the *n*-head analysis.

In contrast, verbal gerunds in English are a DP nominalization. Obviously, they are not an *n*P nominalization as they lack all these above-mentioned properties, see section 1.3 for the properties of verbal gerunds. In Emonds' (2000) terminology we could talk about the derivational and inflectional distinctions between nominalizations.

Structurally, the interactions between the verbal and the nominal domain can be explained if the projection of the ClassP can access the features within the c-commanded VP domain, which can be formalized in terms of an Agree relationship. For English AS-Nominals as in (430) a [±Count] feature on ClassP is posited which agrees with the inner Aspect that is calculated in the VP. ASNs with the telic inner Aspect have ClassP [+Count] and project NumberP, while ASNs with atelic inner Aspect have ClassP [-Count], which blocks the realization of NumberP. The verbal layers that would be projected in English telic ASNs are represented in the tree (434b) below.

The structure for verbal gerunds (421) in English is depicted in (434c). In this structure the only nominal layer is the DP projection which explains why these projections have *external* syntax of DPs. The dotted lines in (434c) mark that there can be additional verbal layers irrelevant for out discussion here. The main conclusion here is that verbal gerunds are imperfective/ unbounded and it exclude NumP projection.

For Polish examples in (432), the *n* head attaches on the top of Aspect P, which is believed to be present in Polish nominals, for example, Rozwadowska (1997). This structure (434a) is reminiscent of English telic AS-Nominals as they both host the feature [+Count] in ClassP. The distinction lies in the fact that in Polish this feature correspondents to outer Aspect while in English, it is an inner Aspect. Despite this difference, both Aspects are bounded and therefore nothing prevents from treating them similarly.

(434)

a. Polish Perfective CENs

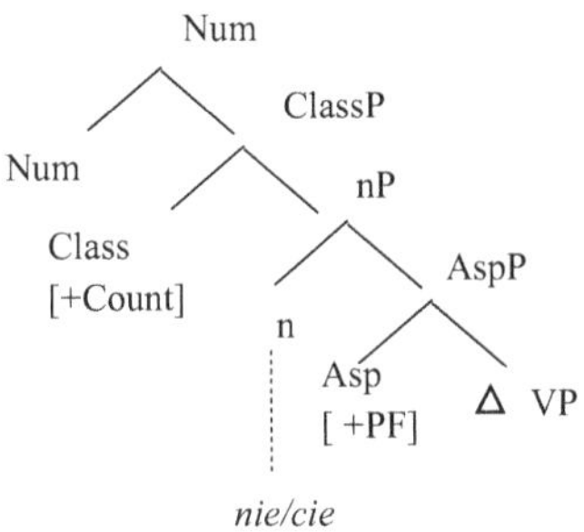

b. English telic CENs

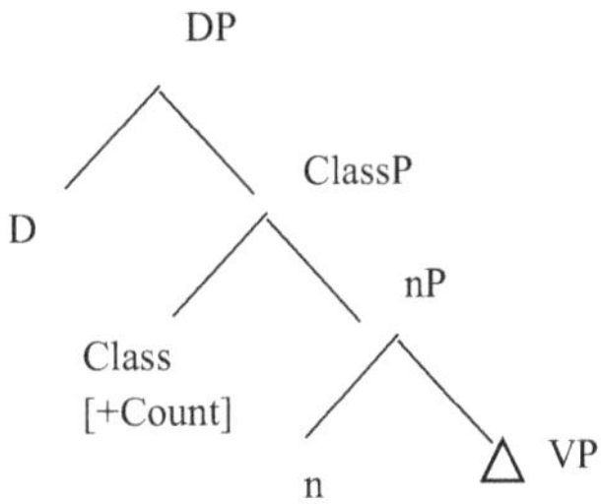

c. English verbal gerund

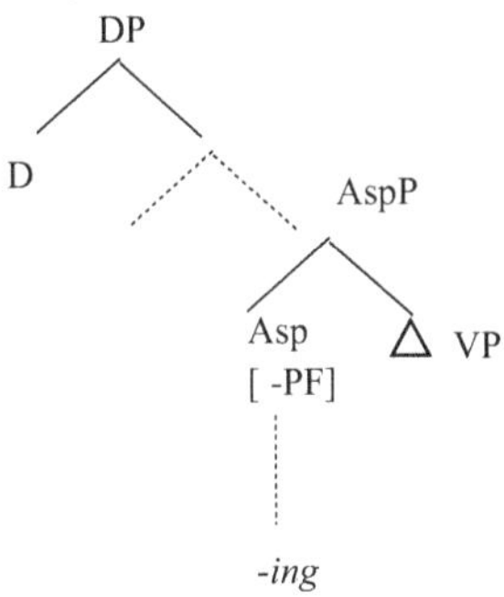

6.3 Czech Deverbal AS-Nominals and Countability

In this section, I will present the countability patterns of deverbal nominals in Czech, as extracted from corpora.[88] I will examine the correlation between aspect as proposed by Alexiadou et al. (2010c) and Borer (2013), within B/K and N/T nominals in Czech, whose structures were developed in the preceding chapter. Based on the data (and the preceding theoretical discussion) I will identify the signals of interplay between the nominal and verbal domains and propose a syntactic mechanism that will explain the countability process of nominalization. By establishing parallels between the N and V domains, I will suggest potential paths in the derivation. Crucially, I will propose the possibility of substituting layers in the nominal domain with *analogous features* in domain of the Verb. If this proposal can be confirmed, it would be able to cross-linguistically predict possible kinds of nominalizations.

We can start our description with B/K nominals. As discussed in section 5.4.1, these nominals can be classified into two distinct types, each exhibiting a specific structure as illustrated in (435). The first type is characterized by the presence of features related to telicity resulting from the presence of the projection of *v*P, while the second type refers to tangible objects and lacks these telicity-related features. Czech examples are given on the right. The relevant nominals are in bold.

(435)	a.	[D [QP [DivP [GenP[**vP**[√]]]]	*rychlá* ***stav-ba***/a quick construction
	b.	[D [QP [DivP [GenP[[√]]]]	*železobetonová* ***stav-ba***/the reinforced concrete construction

Both types of B/K nominals do not exhibit any constraints on countability, as demonstrated in the examples in (436) and (437). The latter, as already described in preceding chapter, are similar to English simple event nominals

88 For my pilot search, I used three corpora: the Czech corpus CsTenTen17, the Syn (2020) and InterCorp v16-Czech. The CsTenTen17 corpus is made up of texts collected from the Internet containing 10.5 billion words. The Syn (2020) is the Synchronic Representative Corpus, which is a part of the Czech National Corpus. This work has 121,826,797 tokens. InterCorp is a large parallel synchronic corpus containing 363,685,460 tokens and is therefore quite representative of modern Czech data.

(e.g., *the trip, concert, movie*)—both can be eventive and countable. The Czech examples below are taken from the Czech national corpus.

(436)	a.	*dvě*	*železobetonové*	***stavby***
		two$_{F.PL}$	reinforced concrete$_{F.PL}$	contructions$_{F.PL}$
	b.	*dvě*	*dřevěné*	***ná-stav-by***
		two$_{F.PL}$	wooden$_{F.PL}$	pref.additions$_{F.PL}$

(437)	a.	***Obě***	***stav-by***	*se budou odehrávat*	*na dálnici D 46.*
		both	construction$_{PL.F.NOM}$	REFL AUX$_{FUT}$ take place	on the highway D46

‘Both constructions will take place on highway D46.’

b.	*Sloužila*	*při*	***třech***	***plav-bách***	*jako*	*chirurg.*
	serve$_{PAST}$	during	three	sailing$_{PL.F.LOC}$	as	surgeon

‘She served as a surgeon during three sailings.’

c.	*Po*	***třech nebo čtyřech***	***pře-mal-bách***	*ztratil všechny půvaby.*
	after	three or four	pref.paint.$_{PL.F.LOC}$	lost all charms

‘After three or four re-paints, it lost all its charms.’

d.	*Palác*	*prošel*	***několika***	***pře-stav-bami.***
	Palace	undergo$_{PAST}$	several	pref.building$_{F.PL.INS}$

‘The palace underwent several rebuildings.’

The examples above show that B/K nominals can pluralize irrespective of their inner Aspect (telicity/atelicity) in *v*P. The reasons are as follows: First of all, they do not have an outer Aspect that would be in complementary distribution with Number. Second, they can exhibit Gender features, as exemplified by the feminine Gender in our examples. Besides, they can manifest masculine Gender, such as *jásot* ‘exultation$_{MASC}$’ and *dupot* ‘stamping$_{MASC}$’.

This latter factor stands in contrast to N/T nominals, which typically appear with a default neuter Gender marking and which are not always prone to be countable.

The literature has often discussed a correlation between Gender and Number agreement. Picallo (2006) proposes that Gender is associated with the presence of the Classifier projection ClassP and, implicitly, with the ability to trigger Number agreement. These facts imply that B/K nominals will possess a full array of nominal layers, but it will come at the expense of having fewer verbal layers.

Now let's turn our attention to the countability of N/T nominals and compare their behavior to that of B/K nominals. N/T nominals can be classified into R-Nominals or AS-Nominals as described in 5.4.2.2 and 5.4.2.3. As R-Nominals, they pluralize freely and refer either to concrete objects (438c) or simple events (438b), as previously illustrated. In their argument-taking capacity, N/T nominals (438a) are more constrained with respect to countability but under certain circumstances they can be countable. This chapter will explore these conditions.

(438) a. [D……[NegP [VoiceP [ProgP [AspectP [*v*P [√root]]]]

*Byl obviněn z **neoznámení** trestného činu.*

AUX_{WAS} $\text{accuse}_{\text{PRT}}$ of non-reporting $\text{crime}_{\text{GEN}}$

'He was accused of failing to report a crime.'

b. [D……[*v*P [√root]]]]

***Oznámení** výsledků/ o výsledcích*

announcement $\text{results}_{\text{GEN.PL}}$ about results

c. [D……[√root]]]]

*Svatební **oznámení** se stříbrným okrajem*

wedding invitation with silver trim

From the previous description, it is clear that both N/T and B/K nominals can refer to concrete objects as well as simple events, sharing the same syntactic structure. The literature has not clarified what differentiates these two types. Comments often suggest that N/T nominals are more representative of written style. Interestingly, my corpus study has shown a complementary distribution between these two types of nominals in counting contexts that is related to Telicity.

I have extracted data from Intercorp v 16 on B/K deverbal nouns suffixed with *-ba/ka* and N/T deverbal nouns that have a capacity to occur in the following structure: CARDINAL-N-GENITIVE. The total number of outcomes is visible in table (439).

(439)

	N/T nominals		**B/K nominals**	
	Concrete	Abstract	Concrete	Abstract
Telic	49	122	38	34
Atelic	50	26	307	62

I have adjusted this data to focus not on the total number of occurrences but on each deverbal noun as a representative. I then analyzed how many deverbal nouns are capable of occurring in such a structure. The outcome is visible in (440). It shows that out of 90 B/K nominals, 58 referred to concrete objects, with a frequency five times higher when the base is atelic. In contrast, N/T nominals exhibited a different pattern: out of 102 examples, 90 were abstract, and for these telic bases were five times more frequent.

(440)

	N/T nominals		**B/K nominals**	
	Concrete	Abstract	Concrete	Abstract
Telic	10	75	10	11
Atelic	2	15	48	21

On the basis of these facts, we can confirm the following hypotheses that are statistically significant with a p-value < 0.01:

- B/K nominals in countable contexts tend to select atelic bases and are inclined to form less eventive nominals
- N/T nominals in countable contexts tend to select telic bases and are inclined to form more verbal structures

The examples of B/K nominals that were extracted from the corpus are visible below:

(441)

	B/K—CONCRETE			B/K—ABSTRACT		
TELIC	*dvě*	***návrhářky***	*šatů*	*osm*	***nabídek***	*sňatku*
	two	designer$_{PL}$	dress$_{GEN}$	eight	proposal$_{PL}$	marriage$_{GEN}$
ATELIC	*tři*	*kapky*	*krve*	*pět*	*objedn**á**vek*	*jídla*
	three	drop$_{PL}$	blood$_{GEN}$	five	order$_{PL}$	meal$_{GEN}$

Similarly, the structures for N/T nominals are represented in (442) and (443):

(442)

	N/T—CONCRETE			
TELIC		*dvě*	***spřežení***	*koní*
		two	team$_{PL}$	horse$_{GEN.PL}$
ATELIC	*Vytáhla*	*dvě*	***balení***	*příčesků.*
	Pull$_{PAST}$	two	package$_{PL}$	hairpiece$_{GEN}$

(443)

	N/T—ABSTRACT				
TELIC	*Dr. Joseph Pearson*	*prováděl*	*dvě*	***vyšetření***	*nádoru*
	Dr. Joseph Pearson	carry out	two	examination$_{PL}$	tumor$_{GEN}$
ATELIC	*šest*	***hlášení***	*přepadení*	*během minuty*	
	six	report$_{PL}$	assault$_{GEN}$	in a minute	

It is important to note the difficulty in distinguishing between N/T abstract nouns that take arguments and simple event N/T nominals. In certain cases, examples in my corpus appear in eventive contexts but lack clear signals of their capacity to take arguments, leaving them ambiguous between R- and AS-Nominals with the structures described in (438b) and (438a) respectively. However, out of 90 verbal forms, 64 forms have the potential to be Argument-taking N/T nominals because they can be agentive, reflexive, or prefixed with *ne* beyond the contexts that were found in the corpus. These criteria were outlined in section 5.4.2 and will remain instrumental in distinguishing between nominals that take arguments and those that do not.

For now, we can confirm that there is a correlation between eventivity and telicity in Czech as predicted in Alexiadou et al. (2010c) and Borer (2013b).

However, a more precise analysis is necessary to confirm if this correlation holds true for AS-Nominals. To address this, I have extracted sequences from the extensive Czech corpus CsTenTen17, focusing specifically on the criteria outlined above distinguishing between argument- and non-argument-taking nominals:

- AGENTIVITY: [Cardinal numeral] [Nominal N/T] [Substantive in GEN] [Substantive in INSTR],
- Ne-PREFIXATION: [Cardinal numeral] [Nominal N/T beginning with *-ne*],
- Reflexivity: [Cardinal numeral] [Nominal N/T] [Reflexive *SE*].[89]

Upon extracting these sequences, the search yielded the following number of results:

(444)	Cardinality 1	Cardinality 2 and more	Total
1, Agentive	18	12	30
2, *-Ne* prefix	113	26	139
3, Reflexive	93	33	126

The table shows that the cardinal numeral *jedna/jeden/jedno* 'one' is the most frequently used, but in Czech, its presence does not necessarily indicate countability of Nouns. The Czech cardinal is characterized by being both [+DIVIDER] and [-DIVIDER], unlike its English counterpart, which is solely [+DIVIDER]. For a detailed analysis, refer to section 3.1.1, where the grammaticality of Czech phrase *jedno listí* is discussed, highlighting the contrast with the ungrammatical English phrase **one foliage*.

89 I used the following Corpus Query Codes to extract the concordances for the criteria in question:
Agentivity:[tag=""k4.*xC.*""][lemma="".*ní|.*tí""&tag=""k1.*""][][tag=""k1.*c2.*""][tag!=""k7.*""][tag=""k1.*c7.*""]
Ne-Prefixation: [tag=""k4.*xC.*""][lemma=""ne.*ní|ne.*tí""&tag=""k1.*""]
Reflexivity: [tag=""k4.*xC.*""][lemma="".*ní|.*tí""&tag=""k1.*""][word=""se""]
For the sake space, I only include CQL codes for the combinations with cardinal numbers. The sequences with group and kind nominals are analogous.

The second column of the table displays the results for the premodification by cardinal numerals higher than one. As we can see, these sequences are permissible. We can compare the number with standard modifiers such as *dvoje/dvojí* 'two$_{GROUP}$/two$_{KIND}$' that are recommended by Czech grammars for abstract Nouns. A visual representation of the results is below:

(445)	***Dvoje/dvojí and higher numerals***
1, Agentive	19
2, -*Ne* Prefix	27
3, Reflexive	24

Czech group and kind numerals do not directly quantify individual elements as Dočekal (2012) explains. Instead, group numerals quantify sums or groups, while kind numerals quantify sub-kinds. For example, a Noun Phrase like *dvoj-e klíče* 'two sets of keys' refers to any two sums or groups of keys, regardless of the specific cardinality within each group. On the other hand, *dvoj-í víno* or 'two kinds of wines' implies the presence of two sub-kinds of wine, such as red wine and white wine. The group and kind numerals will play a role in our discussion as there has been a tendency in Czech to replace these numerals with cardinal numerals.

We can now proceed to examine examples from the Czech CsTenTen17 corpus that demonstrate the three criteria mentioned. The first criterion, agentivity, is illustrated by examples (446a-b). We can observe that N/T nominals are pre-modified by a cardinal numeral and postmodified by direct objects in the Genitive and agentive modifiers in the Instrumental:

(446)

a.	*Dojde ke*	*třem*	***měřením***	*hluku*	*krajskou hygienou.*
	happen	three	measurement$_{(IMPF).NT.PL}$	noise$_{GEN}$	Health Station$_{INS}$

'There will be three instances of noise measurement by the National Health Station.'

b.	*Ten je složen ze*	*čtyř*	***vyprávění***	*příběhu*	*různými lidmi.*
	That is composed of	four	telling$_{(IMPF).NT.PL}$	story$_{GEN}$	various people$_{INS}$

‘That is composed of four kinds of story-telling by different people.’

This pattern provides supporting evidence for the countability of Czech AS-Nominals. I also include examples with group or kind numerals as in (447) to illustrate that AS-Nominals in Czech can commonly occur with group and kind numerals:

(447)	*Stavba … připomíná*	*dvojí*	***obsazení***	*města*	*Francouzi.*
	The building commemorates	two$_{KIND}$	pref$_{PF.}$occupation$_{NT}$	city$_{GEN}$	French$_{INS}$

‘The building commemorates occupations of the city by French two times.’

Examples (448a-b) demonstrate the criterion of *ne*-prefixation. Again, we can see that N/T nominals which are pre-modified by a *ne*-prefix and postmodified by direct objects in Genitive co-occur with cardinal numbers.

(448)

a. *příčinám vévodí … stav vozidla a ---*
causes are … condition of a car and

tři	***ne-dání***	*přednosti* ***v jízdě***
three	non-giving$_{PF.NT.PL}$	way$_{GEN}$

‘the condition of the car and the three (instances of) non-giving-way dominate the causes’

b. *Nastává až ---*
come into effect

po *dvou* ***ne-vysloveních*** *důvěry* *vládě.*
after two non-out$_{PF.}$expression$_{NT.PL}$ confidence$_{GEN}$ government$_{DAT}$
'It comes into effect after expression of no-confidence in Government twice.'

The example (449) is an example with a *ne*-prefixation and a group numeral:

(449) *Navrhli … neschválit zprávu.* ---
proposed … not approve report

Její *dvojí* ***ne-přijetí*** *znamená pád rady ČT.*
its two$_{GROUP}$ non-pref$_{PF.}$approval$_{NT}$ means fall Board ČT
'They propose not to approve the report. Its double non-approval means fall of Board of ČT.'

The *ne*-prefixation criterion in these examples confirms the claim that Czech AS-Nominals can be made countable.

Lastly, examples (450a-b) exemplify the criterion of reflexivity. What these constructions demonstrate is that the reflexive *se* 'self' collocates with cardinal numbers in N/T nominals.

(450)

a. *Termíny jsou určeny pro nejvýše* ---
deadlines are intended for at most

tři ***přihlášení*** ***se*** *daného studenta* *na zkoušku.*
three pref$_{PF}$.registration$_{NT\cdot PL}$ SELF given student$_{GEN}$ for an exam
'The deadlines are intended for at most three self-registrations of a given student for an exam.'

b. *… volby pokazila i* *dvě* ***zdržení*** ***se.***
election disrupted two pref$_{PF.}$abstention$_{NT\cdot PL}$ SELF
'the elections were disrupted by two abstentions'

In order to compare the above-mentioned examples with examples containing group numerals, the structure in (451) is provided:

(451)	*po*	*trojím*	***ptaní***	***se***	*na cestu*
	after	three$_{\text{GROUP}}$	ask$_{\text{PF.NT}}$	SELF	about the way
	'after asking three times about the way'				

It can be observed that most of the examples provided are in the perfective Aspect. However, primary imperfectives can also combine with cardinal numerals, as seen in example (446a) and (446b). In fact, out of 71 examples in my corpus five of them were based on imperfective verbs. This observation contrasts with the expectations of Alexiadou et al. (2010c). I provide an explanation for this discrepancy.

The examples that Alexiadou and her colleagues cite from Polish and that were discussed above are primarily secondary imperfectives. There is, in fact, notable distinction between these two types of imperfectivity in markedness. Primary imperfectives are considered unmarked, while secondary imperfectives bear the marked suffixes, for example, *-ova*. Being unmarked, primary imperfectives have the capacity to refer to bounded and unbounded reading.

In the domain of Verbs, a similar phenomenon can be observed where primary imperfectives can acquire a bounded reading, resulting in the plurality of the event and habitual reading discussed in section 4.4.2.2. I repeat here the example quoted by Dočekal and Kučerová (2009) in their *Bound Reading of Imperfective Verbs*. The bounded reading is achieved by the adverbial modifier za *dvě hodiny* 'in two hours':

(452)	*Když Petr studoval rychločtení, tak*	***četl***	*vojnu a mír*	*za dvě hodiny.*
	When Petr studied fast-reading, then	read$_{\text{(IMPF)}}$	war and peace	in two hours
	'When Petr took a course in fast-reading, he was reading War and Peace in two hours.'			

This becomes even more intriguing when we take into account that secondary imperfective Verbs such as *přemalovávat* 're-paint' *in* (453) can be also coerced syntactically into habitual reading with multiple instances of bounded events:

(453)

a.	*Když byl Petr malý, tak*	***přemal-ová-va-l***	*obrázky*	*za dva dny.*
	When be Peter young, then	$re_{PF.}paint_{TH \cdot IMPF}$	$picture_{GEN.PL}$	in two day
	'When Peter was young, he used to re-paint pictures in two days.'			
b.	*V minulosti stavební firmy*	***předěl-á-va-ly***	*domy*	*za kratší dobu.*
	In the past construction companies	$re_{PF.}work_{TH \cdot IMPF}$	$houses_{GEN.PL}$	in a shorter time
	'In the past construction companies used to re-build houses in a shorter time.'			

The corresponding deverbal nominal counterparts with secondary imperfectives in (454) can achieve a similar interpretation of multiple instances of bounded events if postmodified by an adverbial modifier za *dva dny* 'in two days'. Yet, the nominals with secondary imperfectives cannot be counted as the examples below exemplify and none of them were attested in my corpus:

(454)	a.		*(*dvě)*	***pře-prac-ová-vá-ní***	*textu*	*(za dva dny)*
			two	$re_{PF.}work_{TH \cdot IMPF.NT.PL}$	$text_{GEN}$	in two day
	b.	*(*po*	*dvou)*	***vy-bruš-ová-ních***	*skla*	*(za dva dny)*
		after	two	$out_{PF} \cdot grind._{IMPF.NT.PL}$	$glass_{GEN}$	in two days
	c.	*(*po*	*třech)*	***pře-děl-á-vá-ních***	*textu*	*(za dva dny)*
		after	three	$re_{PF} \cdot do_{TH.IMPF.NT.PL}$	$text_{GEN}$	in two days

This is different from N/T nominals with primary imperfective morphology, which had the ability to be made countable, as suggested above. I propose to ascribe this phenomenon to the nature of the secondary imperfective Aspect, which functions as an outer Aspect parallel to the outer Aspect found in English verbal gerunds. Recall that verbal gerunds can also take a telic modifier *in X-time,* but they cancel their culmination by taking scope over it, as demonstrated in (421). As a result, both gerunds and secondary imperfectives exhibit a lack of countability, which reinforces Fassi-Fehri's assertion that outer Aspect and Number are mutually exclusive. This statement will provide supports to the idea proposed by Borer (2013) and that is also adopted in my theory that there is a distinction between perfectivity/primary imperfectivity and secondary imperfectivity. Borer suggests that secondary Imperfectives in Czech are characterized by outer Aspect, referred to as G-ASP. However, this distinction is not made by Alexiadou et al. (2010c).

6.3.1 Factors Contributing to the Countability of AS-Nominals in Czech

In this section, I am going to introduce factors which may be plausible reasons of why Czech speakers are able to opt for cardinal premodification of AS-Nominals. First, Czech linguists notice that there is a noticeable decline in the usage of group and kind numerals in oblique Cases and in contexts that express larger numerals.

Synková (2017) claims that there has been a noticeable trend since 80s for cardinal numbers to replace group and kind numerals in oblique Cases. Oblique Cases in Czech are defined by Veselovská (2018a) as morphological Cases other than NOM or ACC, which in Czech appear after Prepositions, which select anything other than ACC. There are also NOM-ACC prepositionless Case-marked DPs selected by some Verbs, Adjectives, or Nouns. She assumes that oblique Cases are always assigned by a (possibly empty) Preposition that subcategorizes for a specific Case.

Synková's examination of the Czech national corpus data reveals that when it comes to pluralia tantum words such as (*dveře* 'door', *brýle* 'glasses', *kleště* 'pliers'), the usage of *dvoje dveře- bez dvou dveří* 'two$_{\text{GROUP}}$ doors- without two$_{\text{CARD}}$ doors' is more prevalent than using *dvoje dveře bez dvojích dveří* 'two$_{\text{GROUP}}$ doors- without two$_{\text{GROUP}}$ doors'. In spoken form, this tendency is even greater.

Additionally, Synková highlights that group/kind numerals and cardinal numerals are often interchangeable in their meaning. She provides the following example where a group, kind and cardinal numeral refers to the number of occurrences of a certain event rather than to some groups or kinds:

(455)	*dvoje/dvojí /dvě*	*střídání v poločase*
	dvoje$_{\text{GROUP}}$/dvojí$_{\text{KIND}}$/dvě$_{\text{CARD}}$	exchange in halftime

Furthermore, the forms for group numerals higher than three are rarely used. This is clearly visible in examples below with cardinal numbers such as 20 or 1,000:

(456)

a. *Celkem bylo zaznamenáno ---*
total was recorded

pět tisíc	***porušení***	*sovětských hranic*	*americkými letadly.*
five thousand	pref$_{PF.}$violation$_{NT.PL}$	soviet border$_{PL.GEN}$	American aircraft$_{INSTR}$

'A total of five thousand border violations by American aircraft have been recorded.'

b. *Podmíněná pravděpodobnost toho, že ---*
The conditional probability that

po	*dvaceti*	***nepadnutích***	*šestky,*	*šestka padne je stale stejná.*
after	twenty	non-falling$_{PF.NT.PL}$	six$_{GEN}$	six will fall, remains the same

'The conditional probability that after twenty non-occurrences of six, the six will occur, remains the same.'

Another factor contributing to the preference for pluralization of CENs is a gap in productivity of B/K nominals which results in the usage of N/T nominals as an alternative. The presence of gaps in Type II nominals was discussed in Chapter 1, section 1.4. Unlike N/T nominals, Type II nominals cannot be derived from all words. This means that while we have *pršení* 'raining', there is no corresponding form like **prš-ba*. In fact, when examining the examples used in the plural form, we observe Nouns that lack an alternative form. For instance, we have *měření* 'measuring' in (446a) but no **měřitba*, *dání* 'giving' in (448a) but no **datba*, *výslovení* 'pronouncing' in (448b) but no **výslov-ba*, and *zdržení* 'abstention' in (450b) but no **zdržba*.

6.3.2 Syntactic Mechanisms

Having described the nominals and the factors contributing to their pluralization, we can now provide their structural description. In Czech, B/K nominals with the interpretation of simple events can be categorized as either telic or atelic, while N/T nominals with the interpretation of complex event Nouns can be perfective or imperfective. Both types possess the capacity to interact within the nominal domain, which requires the feature bound.

However, unlike N/T nominals, B/K nominals are not restricted in terms of their countability and can freely form plurals and be pre-modified by cardinal numbers. One proposed explanation for this phenomenon is that B/K nominals lack outer Aspect, which would otherwise exclude the Number and the QP projection. Additionally, in Czech, B/K nominals can exhibit feminine or masculine Gender, in contrast to N/T nominals, which are limited to the default neuter Gender. According to Picallo (2006), this Gender distinction may be correlated with the dividing function within ClassP and implicitly with QP. As a result, the structure of B/K nominals would have fewer verbal layers and a comprehensive set of nominal projections, see the structure (457) for the nominal phrase *tři plavby* 'three sails':

(457) Structure of B/K nominals: *tři plavby* 'three sails'

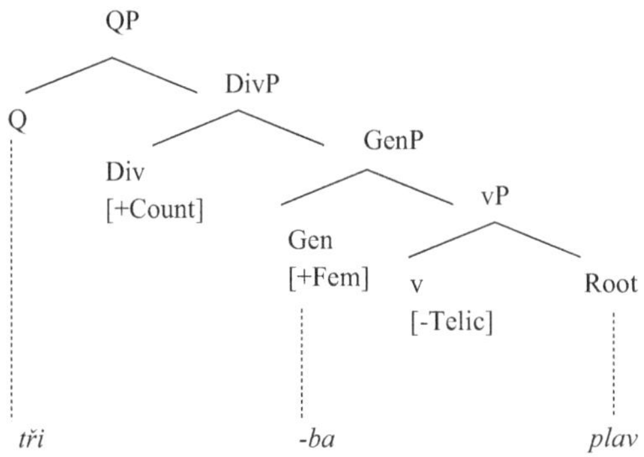

I assume that the root can raise only to *v*P as Czech has no N-to-D movement. In contrast, there is no T in nominalization and verb movement is possible. In order to get the structure with plural, the Number feature of QP has to be lowered post-syntactically.

In contrast to B/K nominals, N/T nominals are characterized as being more verbal in nature and less nominal. They do not display Gender distinctions. If we consider this lack of Gender correlation in relation to the presence of the Div function, it suggests that this particular layer might be absent, providing an explanation for the restricted pluralization of these nominals. Thus, my perspective diverges from Alexiadou et al. that DivP is present in AS-Nominals that can be made countable. Therefore, I explore alternative explanations for the dividing function in these nominals. In fact, these nominals should contain QP. The presence of aspectual adjectives *časté* 'frequent' in these nominals aligns with Alexiadou's analysis (2001), which associates them with the QP layer.

(458)	a.	***to/takové***	***časté***	*uchylování*	*se*	*k fyzické akci*
		that/such	frequent	pref$_{PF}$-resorting$_{IMPF.NT}$	SELF	to physical action
		'that/such frequent resorting to the physical action'				
	b.	***to/takové***	***časté***	*přizpůsobování*	*se*	*rozdílným lidem*
		that/such	*frequent*	pref$_{PF}$-adjusting$_{IMPF.NT}$	SELF	*different people*$_{DAT}$
		'that/such frequent adjusting to different people'				

Additionally, these nominals have the potential to be pre-modified by Determiners, which, as discussed in section 3.5.3 originate from the QP projection. Therefore, my analysis requires the QP to see the features within the verbal domain. As a result, I propose that the projection containing the [+BOUND] feature in the verbal domain can serve as a substitute for the DivP projection, eliminating the necessity for its projection.

We can now proceed to the derivation of individual structures. The picture in (459) represents Perfective N/T nominals such as *nedání přednosti* 'non-giving way'. It includes the feature [+PERF] in the AspectP layer, which may be interpreted by the syntactic structure as [+COUNT] because it is [

+BOUND]. This characteristic allows the nominal to contribute to the QP layer and be counted accordingly.

The derivation process proceeds as follows: the root can raise up to the NegP layer and undergo incorporation with the theme vowel and the negative prefix *-ne*. However, it is unable to raise any higher, resulting in the remaining nominal feature being lowered. The morpheme *-n* represents the neuter Gender, which is assigned to the structure by default. I have argued that it is reinterpreted from the *n* allomorph used in passive participles due to the fact that nominalization is akin to passivization. The portmanteau morpheme *-í* is realized on the Noun-verbal complex post-syntactically through agreement with Gender and Number features, as defined in section 2.1.2.

(459) Structure of perfective N/T Nominals: *nedání přednosti* 'non giving way'

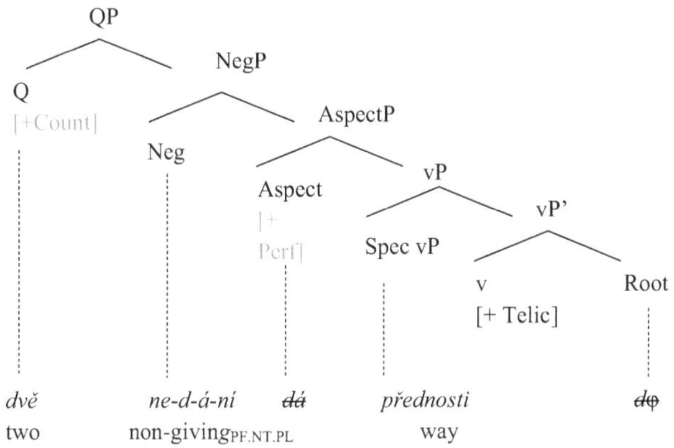

A second option is the imperfective structure in (460). As previously suggested, that the primary imperfective represents an unmarked form in Czech. We observe that the AspP layer is absent in this structure. Consequently, it has the capacity to be interpreted as both bounded and unbounded. Boundedness can be achieved at the telicity level as argued in section 4.4.2. As a result, the QP is assigned the feature [+COUNT], allowing the structure to be plural:

(460) Derivation of Imperfective N/T nominals: *měření hluku* 'measurement of noise'

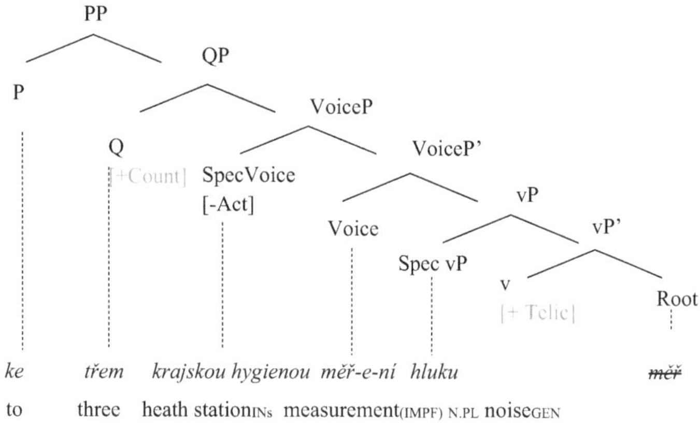

Lastly, the ungrammatical structure for Czech AS-Nominals with secondary imperfectives is * *dvě přemalování obrázku* * 'two re-paintings of the picture'. Some more examples can be found above in (454). The derivation of secondary imperfectives occurs after the perfective stage. However, the layer for secondary imperfectives is higher, as the tree in (461) illustrates, and alters the value from [+BOUND] to [-BOUND]. As a result, the structure does not possess the required [+BOUND] feature for QP and the derivation fails.

(461) The role of ProgP in the derivation

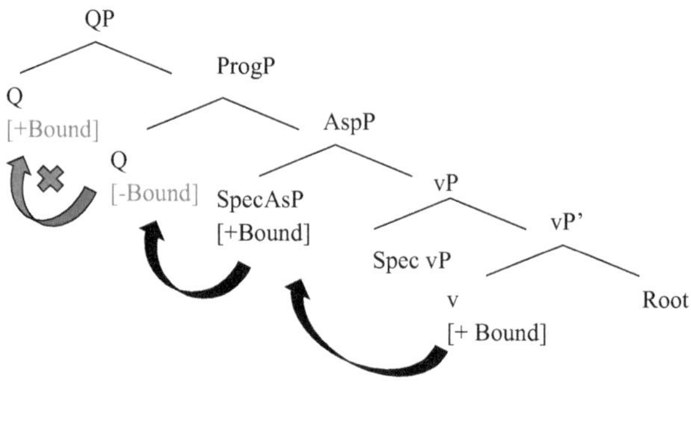

6.4 Chapter Summary

Recent research on ASNs challenges Grimshaw's view that complex event nominals are mass nouns which in syntactic terms correlates with stating that AS-Nominals have a mainly verbal internal structure (including Aspect) and insufficient nominal structure to be made countable. Scholars such as Alexiadou et al. (2010c) and Borer argue that the ability of CENs to pluralize is tied to aspectual issues. Telic derived nominals behave as count Nouns while atelic ones behave like mass. Alexiadou et al. (2010c) further emphasize the role of perfectivity as being bounded and contributing to pluralization of AS-Nominals. In contrast, Borer views perfectivity as morphological marking confined to the inner aspect level in Slavic languages.

These conclusions can be applied to Czech. Corpus research in InterCorp v16 has shown that in countable contexts, there is a correlation between eventivity and telicity, as demonstrated with B/K nominals with suffixes (*-ba/-ka*) and N/T nominals, both of which postmodified by a genitive NP. In this corpus, Deverbal B/K nominals were generally less verbal and tended to select atelic bases, whereas N/T nominals were often more verbal and typically formed from telic verbs.

Some of these N/T nominals were ambiguous between R-Nominals and AS-Nominals. Consequently, the countability potential of argument-taking N/T nominals needed to be analyzed separately through an additional corpus search in CsTenTen17 (Czech Web Corpus). It has been demonstrated that under specific circumstances, they can be made countable. Countability occurs when they are bounded by the +Perf feature or, when imperfective, they need to be bound by the +TELIC feature. Conversely, nominals based on secondary imperfective Verbs cannot pluralize due to the presence of outer Aspect, similar to the Aspect found in verbal gerunds in English, which excludes their countability in QP.

We have seen that there is a trade-off between verbal and nominal properties. B/K nominals not having higher aspectual level, can contain the full array of nominal projections. In contrast, N/T nominals possess more verbal layers and fewer nominal projections. They can, however, substitute their DivP projection by features that have similar properties in the verbal domain, supporting the hypothesized parallelism between functional layers in verbal and nominal structures. When N/T nominals contain even higher aspectual levels such as ProgP, the countability is excluded totally. It is this property which Grimshaw mistakenly took as general, and which other authors as illustrated in this work argued to be more restricted.

Conclusion

This study has analyzed nominalizations in English and Czech in terms of the functional projections which are the crux of interpretation. A central focus has been on the countability of Czech deverbal argument structure nominals and their comparison with their counterparts in English.

Since Grimshaw's influential study from 1990, there has been a prevailing assertion that argument structure nominals in English are considered mass Nouns and, therefore, not countable. This viewpoint has also been extended to Czech by Veselovská (2019) and Karlík (2019), who made similar arguments. However, more recent studies conducted by Alexiadou et al. (2010c) and Borer (2013) have challenged this claim. These researchers have presented evidence that contradicts the previous notion by investigating the relationship between Aspect and Number in argument structure Nouns. This work has shown that similar arguments can be transferred to Czech deverbal nominals.

To address this matter comprehensively, a thorough examination of both nominal and verbal functional projections and their interplay in nominalizations was essential as it has not been performed in previous studies of Czech nominalization. As for a specific framework, I have chosen the studies of two prominent linguists, Artemis Alexiadou and Hagit Borer, who have extensively contributed with valuable cross-linguistic data on nominalizations. This study analyzed and contrasted the works related to the topic of categorial projections and nominalizations in order to subsequently apply them to Czech data. In addition to some other Czech linguists, this work benefited above all from the insights found in the studies by Petr Karlík and Ludmila Veselovská since these authors made the most significant contributions to the generative analysis of Czech nominalizations.

The approach adopted in this study was the generative one. To establish the theoretical foundation, Chapter 1 presented an overview of the key principles of generative linguistics. Additionally, the study involved categorizing deverbal argument structure nominals in both languages based on the work of linguists in the field. It has previously been shown that English has at a superficial level three types of deverbal nominalizations:

(462) a. *The teacher's **examination** of the students* **Derived nominal**
b. *The teacher's **examining** of the students* **Mixed nominal**
c. *The teacher's/The teacher **examining** the students* **Gerund**

In Chomsky's (1970) study derived nominals in (462a) were relegated to Lexicon while gerunds (462c) were clearly deverbal. Mixed nominals (462b) were assumed to have intermediate properties. Grimshaw (1990) shed new light on research on nominalization and paved the way for reintegrating derived nominals within the realm of syntax.

Veselovská (2018b), who develops Emonds' (2000) model of nominalizations, and Karlík (2019) demonstrate that Czech has the types of nominals that can be compared to derived nominals in English but lacks higher verbal complexes such as verbal gerunds in (462c). Czech nominals that are comparable to English derived nominals in (462a) surface with *-ní/tí* suffixes and hence are called N/T nominals.

In Chapter 2, the fundamental principles of Alexiadou's theoretical framework of Distributed Morphology and Borer's Exo-skeletal model were established and then utilized in subsequent chapters.

In Chapter 3 more detailed analysis in both the relevant frameworks is presented focusing on the nominal projection. First summarizing the research by Borer and Alexiadou, then applying the concepts of functional domains to Czech. I concluded that the functional layers for the Czech nominal functional projection are as suggested in the Table below compared with layers used in Alexiadou's (2020) and Borer's (2005) theory:

(463)	Comparing the functional layers in the nominal domain		
	Czech model	**Alexiadou (2020)**	**Borer (2005a)**
	DP (Determiner P)	**DP** (Determiner P)	**DP** (Determiner P)
	QP (Quantifier P)	**#P/NumP** (Number P)	**#P** (Number P)
	DivP (Divider P)	**DivP** (Divider P)	**CL** (Classifier P)
	GenderP	**n** (Nominalizer P)	-

In Czech, there is a GenderP level which is associated with the features [+/-HUMAN], [+/-FEM]. Although this level is not employed by the other two linguists, Gender is important for interpretation and agreement at least at PF in Czech that qualifies it as a separate functional projection.

Moreover, I follow Borer's (2005a) work in assuming that mass-count distinction is syntactic and carried out in the DivP layer requiring the feature [+/-COUNT]. However, a noteworthy difference arises: unlike Borer's CL which hosts plural morphology and does not correspond to a canonical singular, the DivP in Czech model is by default singular. The DivP is selected by Q in QP, which hosts the plural morphology in Czech. A scenario similar to that in Czech is envisaged by Alexiadou (2021) with the Counting Plural in her NumP. In addition, she introduces the concept of Dividing plural situated within the DivP which is employed in her subsequent analyses.

I believe that the positioning of plural morphology within QP aligns with Jackendoff's (1991) notion of boundedness. According to Jackendoff, the plural function has the potential to introduce unboundedness even within structures that are inherently bounded within the DivP projection. His concept of boundedness is an integral part of this study as it enables the parallelism between the nominal and verbal domain that is central to my work.

Furthermore, I assume the presence of the DP in Czech despite the fact that Czech is an articleless language. The main arguments are presented in Veselovská (2018a) who shows that the ordering within the DP field is not completely free. Additionally, I diverge from Borer (2005b) and do not expect N-to-D movement. N-to-D movement is not supported by the ordering of Adjectives within Czech Noun phrases.

In Chapter 4 I covered the functional projection of Verbs. I followed the same method, that is, first summarizing the theories of by Alexiadou and Borer and after some comparative analysis I applied the model to Czech data. A schematic comparison of the functional verbal domains is provided below:

(464)	Comparing the functional layers in the verbal domain		
	Czech Model	**Alexiadou (2020)**	**Borer (2005a)**
	CP (Complementizer P)	**CP** (Complementizer P)	**EP** (Event P)
	TP (Tense P)	**TP** (Tense P)	**TP** (Tense P)
	VoiceP		

	ProgP (Progressive P)	**AspectP**	
	AspectP	**VoiceP**	-
	vP (telic P)	**vP** (verbalizer P)	**Asp$_Q$** (Aspect P)

The table above shows that my study has proposed in Czech three aspectual projections, *v*P responsible for telicity, AspectP for features related to perfectivity and ProgP, a site of secondary imperfectives in Czech. This treatment of aspectual projections in Czech differs from Borer, as it separates telicity and perfectivity into distinct categories rather than equating them in Asp$_Q$. The arguments for separating telicity from perfectivity in Czech was based on the length alternation of Czech prefixes developed by Caha and Ziková (2022) which would be unexplainable without these two domains. Furthermore, my proposal deviates from Alexiadou's approach, which also distinguishes telicity and perfectivity but does not specifically single out secondary imperfectives.

Moreover, I have shown that perfectives and telic predicates are bounded unlike imperfectives and atelic predicates which are unbounded. Jackendoff's (1991) boundedness helped me establish interactions and parallelism with the nominal domain in the field of nominalizations.

I have also argued for the inclusion of the Voice projection employed in Alexiadou's framework, which might or might not be projected, rather than the analogical EP layer in Borer's theory, which must be present in the verbal domain. If combined with constraints dividing verbs into externally and internally caused etc. and resolved at the level of the Encyclopedia, the Voice projections can help us avoid the massive overgeneration of structures. Also, I locate VoiceP above AspectP unlike Alexiadou (2020) where the order is reversed.

Another notable difference between my approach and that of both linguists lies in the treatment of Tense-related concepts, which are typically realized in the highest VP in Czech (my Voice P) as described by Veselovská and Emonds (2015). They argue that the TP level in Czech is not associated primarily with Tense but Mood.

Chapter 5 concentrated on the process of nominalization based on the previously established characteristics of both nominal and verbal domains. I introduced the approaches and diagnostics used by Borer and Alexiadou for detecting various functional layers. These criteria are diagnostics for

Czech nominalizations. Confirming the basic division as it appears in Czech generative tradition there are two clearly distinguishable types of deverbal nominals: Type I: the N/T nominals and Type II: the B/K nominals.

The former N/T nominals are syntactically derived with the structure in (465) and can also function as result or simple event nominals.[90] The rich verbal projection of the Czech N/T nominals explains their argument-taking capacity built on their three aspectual levels, passive Voice and negation phrase NegP. The nominal layers of the Czech N/T nominals, however, are radically impoverished when compared with B/K nominals.

(465) N/T nominals

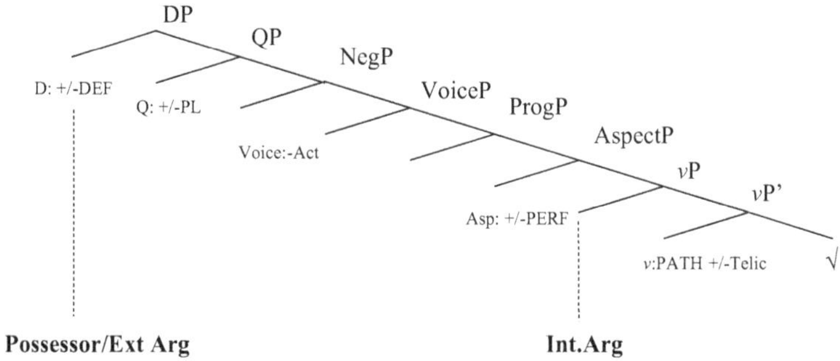

B/K nominals, on the other hand, are lexically derived nominals exhibiting characteristics similar to simple event nominals with the structure in (466) and have the ability to transform into result nominals.

(466) B/K nominals

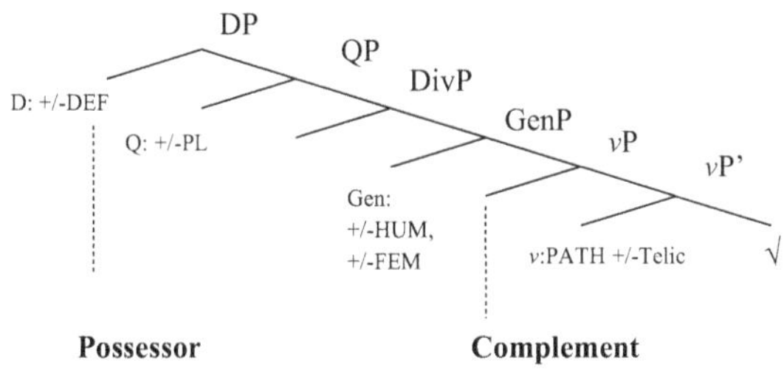

90 When N/T nominals function as result nominals, their verbal layers are impoverished. On the other hand, they can have a full array of nominal layers, allowing all determiners and Quantifiers.

Chapter 5 has also demonstrated that Czech nominalizations exhibit ergative patterns, as proposed by Alexiadou (2001) and (2017d). This was also corroborated by morphological analysis, Case marking of arguments within nominalizations and the Lebeaux effect (1984), whereby all deverbal Nouns in Czech are formed analogically to passive participles. In this respect, Czech nominalizations diverge from assumptions made in Borer (2013) for whom some nominalizations are active-like and some are passive-like.

In Chapter 6 I provided the results of a pilot study focusing on the countability of Czech derived nominals. Based on this data it has been shown that in countable contexts, N/T nominalizations, which may contain a more extensive verbal structure, tend to select telic bases. Conversely, B/K nominalizations form less complex verbal structures and more frequently opt for atelic verbs. These findings support the correlation between Aspect and countability as the greater complexity in verbal structure corresponds to an increase in telicity.

Corpus data research of CsTenTen17 (Czech Web Corpus) has also revealed that Czech N/T nominals can under specific circumstances be made countable. The data extracted from the corpora based on the three criteria (*ne*-cliticization, reflexivity and Agentivity) not only confirmed the AS-Nominal status but also demonstrated that they can be modified by cardinal numerals. To illustrate this, N/T nominal in (467) is pre-modified by a *ne*-prefix and postmodified by direct objects in the Genitive and at the same time can co-occur with cardinal numbers.

(467) *příčinám vévodí … stav vozidla a* ---
causes are … condition of a car and

tři **ne-dání** *přednosti v jízdě*
three non-giving$_{PF.NT.PL}$ way$_{GEN}$
'the condition of the car and the three (instances of) non-giving-way dominate the causes'

Similarly, in (468), it can be observed that the N/T nominal is pre-modified by a cardinal numeral and postmodified by a direct object in the Genitive and an agentive modifier in the Instrumental:

(468)	*Ten je složen ze*	*čtyř*	***vyprávění***	*příběhu*	*různými lidmi.*
	That is composed of	four	telling$_{\text{(IMPF).NT.PL}}$	story$_{\text{GEN}}$	various people$_{\text{INS}}$

'That is composed of four kinds of story-telling by different people.'

Based on these examples found in Czech corpora I demonstrated that the countability of arguments structure nominals can be correlated with aspectual issues. These proposals have been advanced by Alexiadou et al. (2010c) in their cross-linguistic studies and Borer (2013) for English whose mechanisms have been transferred to Czech data.

Countability occurs when AS-Nominals are bounded by the +Perf feature or, when imperfective, they need to be bounded by the +Telic feature. Conversely, nominals based on Czech secondary imperfective Verbs (469) cannot be made countable due to the presence of outer Aspect, similar to the Aspect found in verbal gerunds in English, which excludes the manifestation of their countability in QP.

(469)	*(*dvě)*	***pře-prac-ová-vá-ní***	*textu*	*(za dva dny)*
	two	re$_{\text{PF.}}$work$_{\text{TH·IMPF.NT.PL}}$	text$_{\text{GEN}}$	in two day

In this chapter I also mentioned other factors that allow the rare but attested countability of Czech N/T nominals, noting a decline in the usage of group and kind numerals in oblique Cases and their replacement by cardinals (468) as well as in contexts that express larger numerals (470). Moreover, there is a gap in productivity of Czech B/K nominals which seems to be compensated by the extensive use of N/T nominals as their alternative.

(470) *Podmíněná pravděpodobnost toho, že ---*
The conditional probability that

po	*dvaceti*	***nepadnutích***	*šestky,*	*šestka padne je stale stejná.*
after	twenty	non-falling$_{\text{PF.NT.PL}}$	six$_{\text{GEN}}$	six will fall, remains the same

'The conditional probability that after twenty non-occurrences of six, the six will occur, remains the same.'

The analysis of countability of argument structure nominals have confirmed that there is a trade-off between verbal and nominal properties. B/K nominals not having higher aspectual level, can contain the full array of nominal projections. As a result, they can be made countable without any constraints. In contrast, N/T nominals possess more verbal layers and fewer nominal projections. They have only the QP layer but lack the DivP layer responsible for mass-count distinction in nominalization. They can, however, substitute their DivP projection by features that have similar properties in the verbal domain, namely bounded features. When N/T nominals contain even higher aspectual levels such as ProgP, the countability is excluded totally, presumably because outer Aspect is mutually exclusive with Number as proposed by Fassi-Fehri (2005).

In spite of the fact that the corpora search was only a pilot one, its results supported the parallelism between functional layers in verbal and nominal structures which is the core of this study. Apart from the theoretical discussion, this study of Czech data, paradigms and proposed analyses has also demonstrated a more general and not always obvious fact: the present-day Generative Grammar linguistic models are applicable for the analysis of entirely current Czech language, and, moreover, the detailed analysis of Czech complex overt morphology can contribute to the development of the formal generative framework in a new and revealing way.

Bibliography

Aarts, B. (2001). *English syntax and argumentation*. Palgrave.
Abney, S. (1987). *The English Noun phrase in its sentential aspect*. [Doctoral dissertation, MIT]. MIT Libraries. <https://dspace.mit.edu/handle/1721.1/14638>
Adger, D. (2003). *Core syntax: A minimalist approach*. Oxford University Press.
Alexiadou, A. (2001). *Functional structure in nominals: Nominalization and ergativity*. John Benjamins.
Alexiadou A. (2004). Inflection class, Gender and DP internal structure. In G. Müller et al.
(eds.), *Exploration in nominal inflection* (pp. 21–50). Mouton de Gruyter.
Alexiadou, A. (2005). Gerund types, the present participle and patterns of derivation. In C. Maiernborn & A. Wöllstein, *Event arguments: Foundations and applications* (pp. 139–152). Max Niemeyer Verlag.
Alexiadou, A. (2007). *On argument supporting nominals and the mass vs count Noun distinction*. Syntactic Variation and Interfaces Grand Meeting at Lake Myvatn.
Alexiadou, A. (2009). On the Role of Syntactic Locality in Morphological Processes: The Case of (Greek) derived nominals. In A. Giannakidou & M. Rathert, *Quantification, definiteness, and nominalization* (pp. 253–280). Oxford University Press.
Alexiadou, A. (2010a). Reduplication and doubling contrasted: Implications for the structure of the DP and the AP. *Linguistica Linguística – Revista de Estudos Linguísticos da Universidade do Porto, 5*, 9–25.

Alexiadou, A. (2010b). Nominalizations: A probe into the architecture of grammar, Part I: The nominalization puzzle. *Language and Linguistics Compass, 4*(7), 496–511.

Alexiadou, A. (2012). The syntactic construction of two non-active Voices: Passive and middle. *Journal of Linguistics, 48*(1). 1–34.

Alexiadou, A. (2014a). *Multiple Determiners and the structure of DPs*. John Benjamins Publishing Company.

Alexiadou, A. (2014b). Active, middle, and passive: The morpho-syntax of Voice. *Catalan Journal of Linguistics, 13*, 19–40.

Alexiadou, A. (2014c). Roots don't take complements. *Theoretical Linguistics, 40*(3/4), 287–297.

Alexiadou, A. (2017a, May). *Nominalization structures across languages*. [Paper presentation]. Queen Mary University of London, London, UK.

Alexiadou, A. (2017b) Gender and nominal ellipsis. In L. Nicholas, K. Moulton & A. M. Tessier, *A schrift to fest Kyle Johnson* (pp. 12–22). Universtiy of Massachusetts Amherst.

Alexiadou, A. (2017c). On the complex relationship between deverbal compounds and argument supporting nominals. In M. Bloch-Trojnar & A. Malicka-Kleparska (eds.), *Aspect and valency in nominals* (pp. 53–82). De Gruyter Mouton.

Alexiadou, A. (2017d). Ergativity in nominalisation. In J. Coon, D. Massam & L. D. Travis (eds.) *The Oxford handbook of ergativity* (pp. 355–372). Oxford University Press.

Alexiadou, A. (2019a). Morphological and semantic markedness revisited: The realization of plurality across languages. *Zeitschrift für Sprachwissenschaft, 38*(1), 123–154. <https://doi.org/10.1515/zfs-2019–0004>

Alexiadou, A. (2019b). On plurals and plurality. In N. Topintzi, N. Lavidas & M. Moumtzi (eds.), *23rd International Symposium papers on Theoretic–l and Applied Linguistics - Selected Papers*. (pp. 3–18). Thessaloniki: School of English, Aristotle University of Thessaloniki.

Alexiadou, A. (2020). D vs. n nominalizations within and across languages. In A. Alexiadou & H. Borer. *Nominalization: 50 years on from Chomsky's Remarks* (pp. 87–110). Oxford University Press.

Alexiadou, A. (2021). Syntactic representation of plurality. In P. C. Hofherr & J. Doetjes, *The Oxford handbook of grammatical number* (pp. 251–256). Oxford University Press.

Alexiadou, A., Anagnostopoulou, E. & Schäfer, F. (2006). The properties of anticausatives crosslinguistically. In Frascarelli (ed.), *Phases of Interpretation* (pp. 187–212). Mouton de Gruyter.

Alexiadou, A., Anagnostopoulou, E. & Schäfer, F. (2009). PP licensing in nominalizations. *Proceedings of NELS 38*, 39–52.

Alexiadou, A., Anagnostopoulou, E. & Schäfer, F. (2015). *External arguments in transitivity alternations.* Oxford University Press.

Alexiadou, A., Haegeman, L. & Stavrou, M. (2007). *Noun phrase in the generative perspective*. Berlin: Mouton de Gruyter.

Alexiadou, A., Iordachioaia, G., & Soare, E. (2010c). Number/Aspect interaction in the syntax of nominalizations. Distributed approach. *Journal of Linguistics, 46*(3), 537–574.

Alexiadou, A., Rathert, M., & von Stechow A. (2003). Introduction: The modules of perfect constructions. In Alexiadou, A., Rathert, M., & von Stechow A., *Perfect Explorations*. Mouton de Gruyter.

Alexiadou, A., Rizou, V., Karkaletsou, F., and Tsokanos, N. (2021). Gender mismatches in Heritage Greek. *Languages, 6*(3). <https://doi.org/10.3390/languages6010003>

Alexiadou, A. & Schäfer, F. (2010). On the syntax of episodic vs. dispositional -er nominals. In A. Alexiadou & M. Rathert (eds.), *The syntax of nominalizations across languages and frameworks* (9–38). Mouton de Gruyter.

Bach, E. (1986). The algebra of events. *Linguistics and Philosophy 9*, 5–16.

Baker, M. (1988). *Incorporation: A theory of grammatical functional changing.* University of Chicago Press.

Borer, H. (2005a). *Structuring sense volume I: In name only.* Oxford UP.

Borer, H. (2005b). *Structuring sense volume II: The normal course of events.* Oxford UP.

Borer, H. (2013). *Structuring sense volume III: Taking form*. Oxford UP.

Borik, O. (2002). *Aspect and reference time*. [Doctoral dissertation, University of Utrecht]. LOT Publications.

Borik, O. (2006). *Aspect and reference time*. Oxford UP.

Bošković, Ž. (2005). On the locality of left branch extraction and the structure of NP. *Studia Linguistica, 59*(1), 1–45. <https://doi.org/10.1111/j.1467-9582.2005.00118.x>

Bošković, Ž. (2008). What will you have, DP or NP? In *Proceedings of NELS 37* (pp. 101–114).

Bruening, B. (2013). By phrases in passives and nominals. *Syntax 16*, 1–41.
Caha, P. & Ziková, M. (2016). Vowel length as evidence for a distinction between free and bound prefixes in Czech. *Acta Linguistica Hungarica 63*(3), 331–377.
Caha, P. & Ziková, M. (2021). *Deverbal nominalizations and prefixes in Czech*. In Ph.D. Seminar, KAA FF, Palacký University Olomouc.
Caha, P. & Ziková, M. (2022). Prefixes in Czech zero-derived nominalizations and Verbs. In P. Karlík & L. Taraldsen Medová (eds.), *Nominalizations and participles in Czech and beyond* (pp. 3–61). Lincom.
Chierchia, G. (1998). Reference to kinds across languages. *Natural Language Semantics*, *6*(4), 339–405. <https://doi.org/10.1023/A:1008324218506>
Chomsky, N. (1957) *Syntactic Structures*. The Hague: Mouton.
Chomsky, N. (1965). *Aspects of the theory of syntax*. MIT Press.
Chomsky, N. (1970). Remarks on nominalization. In J. A. Roderick & P. S. Rosenbaum, *Readings in English transformational grammar* (184–221). Ginn and company.
Chomsky, N. (1975). *Reflections on Language*. Random House.
Chomsky, N. (1986) *Barriers*. The MIT Press, Cambridge, Mass.
Chomsky, N. (1995) *The Minimalist Program*. Cambridge, Massachusetts: The MIT Press.
Chomsky, N. (1999). *Derivation by phase* (MIT Occasional Papers in Linguistics No. 18). MA: MIT. [Revised version appeared as Chomsky, 2001].
Chomsky, N. (2000). Minimalist inquiries. In M. Roger, D. Michaels, & J. Uriagereka (eds.), *Step by step: Essays on minimalist syntax in honor of Howard Lasnik* (89–155). The MIT Press.
Chomsky, N. (2001). Derivation by phase. In M. Kenstowicz (ed.), *Ken Hale: A Life in language* (pp. 1–52). The MIT Press.
Chomsky, N. & Lasnik, H. (1993). The theory of principles and parameters. In J. Jacobs, A. von Stechow, W. Sternefeld & T. Vennemann (eds.). *Syntax: An international handbook of contemporary research* (pp. 209–569). Walter de Gruyter.
Cinque, G. (1980). On Extraction from NP in Italian. *Journal of Italian Linguistics*, *1*, 47–99.
Cinque, G. (1994). On the evidence for partial N-movement in the Romance DP. In G. Cinque, J. Koster, J-Y. Pollock, L. Rizzi, & R. Zanuttini, eds.,

Paths towards Universal Grammar: Studies in Honor of Richard S. Kayne (pp. 287–309). Georgetown University Press.

Cinque, G. (1999). *Adverbs and functional heads: A cross-linguistic perspective.* Oxford University Press.

Cinque, G. (2002). *Functional structure in DP and IP. The cartography of syntactic structures, Vol. 1.* Oxford University Press.

Čakányová, M. (2018). *The grammar of the English infinitive.* [Unpublished doctoral dissertation]. Palacký University in Olomouc.

Čakányová, M. (2022). Deverbal nominals in Czech: Stem and root nominalization. In M. Janebová, Emonds, J. & Veselovská, L. (Ed.), *Language use and linguistic structure: Proceedings of the Olomouc linguistic colloquium 2021* (pp. 34–49). Palacký University in Olomouc.

Čechová, M. (2000). Pojmenování a slovo, In. M. Čechová et al., *Čeština, řeč a jazyk* (pp. 225–242), Praha: ISV nakladatelství.

Davidson, D. (2007). *Truth-Theoretic Semantics.* Oxford University Press.

DeSwart, H. (1988). Aspect shift and coercion. *Natural Language & Linguistic Theory 16*, 347–385.

Dočekal, M. (2012). Atoms, groups and kinds in Czech. *Acta Linguistica Hungarica 59*(1–2), 109–126.

Dočekal, M. & Kučerová, I. (2009). Bound ability readings of imperfective verbs: A case for presupposition. In M. Dočekal & M. Ziková, *Czech in Formal Grammar* (pp. 39–51). Lincom.

Dvořák, V. (2014). Case assignment, aspect, and (non-)expression of patients: A study of the internal structure of Czech verbal nouns. In O. Spevak, *Noun valency* (89–111). John Benjamins Publishing Company.

Embick, D. (1988). *Syntax and categories: Verbs and particles in Latin perfect.* MIT.

Embick, D. (2004). On the structure of resultative participles in English. *Linguistic Inquiry 35*, 355–92.

Embick, D., & Noyer, R. (2001). Movement Operations after Syntax. *Linguistic Inquiry 32*(4), 555– 595.

Emonds, J. E. (1976). *A transformational approach to English syntax: Root, structure-preserving, and local transformations.* Academic Press.

Emonds, J. E. (1978). The Verbal Complex V'-V in French. *Linguistic Inquiry 9*, 151–175.

Emonds, J. E. (1991). The autonomy of the (syntactic) lexicon and syntax: Insertion conditions for derivational and inflectional morphemes. In C. Georgopoulos & R. Ishihara (Eds.), *Interdisciplinary approaches to language: Essays in honor of S. Y. Kuroda* (pp. 119–148). Kluwer.

Emonds, J. E. (2000). *Lexicon & grammar: The English syntacticon*. Berlin: Mouton de Gruyter.

Emonds, J. (2012). Which is the Extended Projection above N? In L. Brugè, A. Cardinaletti, G. Giusti, N. Munaro & C. Poletto (eds.), *Functional heads*. Oxford University Press.

Emonds, J. E. (2013). Universal default right-headedness and how stress determines word order. In T. Biberauer & M. Sheehan, *Theoretical Approaches to Disharmonic Word Order* (pp. 139–161). Oxford University Press.

Emonds, J. E. (2022). *The syntax and morphology of English Verbs*. DeGruyter Mouton.

Fassi-Fehri, A. (2005.) Verbal and nominal parallelisms. *Documents & Reports*, *8*, 1–22.

Filip, H. (2000). The quantization puzzle. In C. Tenny & J. Pustejovsky, *Events as Grammatical Objects: The Converging Perspectives of Lexical Semantics and Syntax* (39–96). Stanford, CA: CSLI Publications.

Giorgi, A. & G. Longobardi. (1991). *The syntax of Noun phrases: Configuration, parameters, and empty categories*. Cambridge University Press.

Giusti, G. (1991). The categorial status of quantified nominals. *Linguistische Berichte 136*, (438-454).

Grimshaw, J. (1990). *Argument structure*. MIT Press.

Halle, M. & A. Marantz (1993). Distributed morphology and the Pieces of Inflection. In K. Hale & S. J. Keyser (eds.), *The View from Building 20* (pp. 111–176). MIT Press.

Harley, H. & Noyer, R. (2000). State-of-the-article: Distributed morphology. *Glot International 4*(4), 4–9.

Harris, Z. S. (1957). Cooccurrence and transformation in linguistic structure. *Language 33*, 283–340.

Haspelmath, M. (1990). The grammaticalization of passive morphology. *Studies in Language 14*, 25–72.

Havranová, K. (2020). *The Nominalization process in English, Dutch, and Czech*. [Unpublished doctoral dissertation]. Palacký University in Olomouc.

Hendrick, R. (1991) The Morphosyntax of aspect. *Lingua 85*, 171-210. <https://doi.org/10.1016/0024-3841(91)90021-V>

Horrock, G. & Stavrou, M. (1987). Bounding theory and Greek syntax: Evidence for wh-movement in NP. *Journal of Linguistics 23*, 79–108.

Hudousková (Volencová), Andrea. 2009. Reflexive Verbal Form. [Unpublished doctoral dissertation]. Palacký University in Olomouc.

Iordăchioaia, G. (2020). Categorization and nominalization in zero nominals. In A. Alexiadou & H. Borer. *Nominalization: 50 years on from Chomsky's Remarks* (pp. 231–254). Oxford University Press.

Iordăchioaia, G. & Soare, E. (2009). Structural patterns blocking plural in Romance nominalizations. In E. Aboh, E. van der Linden, J. Quer & P. Sleeman (eds.), *Romance Languages and Linguistic Theory 2007* (pp. 145–160). Amsterdam: John Benjamins.

Jackendoff, R. (1977). *X-bar syntax: A Study of phrase structure*. The MIT Press.

Jackedoff, R. (1991). Parts and Boundaries. *Cognition 41*, 9–45.

Kamp, H. & Reyle, U. (1993). *From Discourse to logic; Introduction of model theoretic semantics of natural language, Formal logic and discourse representation theory*. Kluwer Academic Publishers.

Karlík, P. (2002). Ještě jednou k českým deverbálním substantivům. *Čeština– univerzália a specifika, 4*, 13–23.

Karlík, P. (2003). Poznámka k rozboru dějových jmen. In M. Tichý, *Sborník prací filozoficko-přírodovědecké fakulty SU v Opavě D3* (pp. 154–167). Slezská univerzita v Opavě.

Karlík, P. (2004). Mají dějová substantiva slovesný rod? In Z. Hladká & P. Karlík, *Čeština univerzália a specifika 5* (pp. 33–46). Masarykova univerzita.

Karlík, P. (2007a). Mixed nominals in Czech. In Dočekal, M., Karlík, P. & Zmrzlíková, J., *Czech in generative grammar (eds.)* (pp. 105–118). Lincom.

Karlík, P. (2007b). Několik drobných poznámek k dějovým jménům. *Sborník prací Filozofické fakulty brněnské univerzity - Linguistica Brunensia A 55.* (pp. 235–246). Masarykova Univerzita.

Karlík, P. (2008). Věčný spor lexikalismus vs. transformacionalismus. In A. Jaklová (eds.), *Člověk - jazyk – text* (pp. 45–50). Jihočeská univerzita.

Karlík, P. (2019). Škála nominalizací. In P. Karlík & Malčík, P. *Svět podle Grepla* (pp. 91–110). Host.

Karlík, P. & Nübler, N. (1998). Poznámky k nominalizaci v češtině. *Slovo a Slovesnost 59*, 105-112.

Knittel, M., L. (2011). French event nominals and number-inflection. *Recherches Linguistiques de Vincennes 40*, 127–148.
Kolářová, V. (2010). *Valence deverbativních substantive v češtině.* Karolinum.
Kolářová, V. (2014). *Valence vybraných typů deverbativních substantiv ve valenčním slovníku PDT-Valex.* ÚFAL MFF UK.
Kopečný, F. (1962a). *Základy české stavby.* SPN.
Kopečný, F. (1962b). *Slovesný vid v češtině.* Nakladatelství Československé akademie věd.
Kramer, R. (2015). *The morphosyntax of Gender.* Oxford University Press.
Kratzer, A. (1996). Severing the external argument from its verb. In J. Rooryck & L. Zaring (eds.), *Phrase structure and the lexicon* (pp. 109–137). Dordrecht & Boston: Kluwer.
Krifka, M. (1989). *Nominalreferenz und Zeitkonstitution. Zur Semantik von Massentermen, Pluraltermen und Aspektklassen.* Wilhelm Fink Verlag München.
Křen, M., Cvrček, V., Henyš, J., Hnátková, M., Jelínek, T., Kocek, J., Kovářiková, D., Křivan, J., Milička, J., Petkevič, V., Procházka, P., Skoumalová, H., Šindlerová, J. & Škrabal, M. (2020). *SYN2020: reprezentativní korpus psané češtiny.* Ústav Českého národního korpusu FF UK, Praha. <http://www.korpus.cz>
Landau, I. (2016). DP-internal semantic agreement. A configurational analysis. *Natural Language and Linguistic Theory 34*, 975–1020.
Lebeaux, D. (1984). Anaphoric binding and the definition of PRO. *North East Linguistic Society, 14* (1), 253–274.
Lees, R., B. (1960). *The grammar of English nominalizations.* Mouton.
Lieber, R. (1983). Linking and compounds in English. *Linguistic Inquiry 14*(2), 251–285.
Longobardi, G. (1994). Reference and proper names: A theory of N-movement in syntax and logical form. *Linguistic Inquiry 25*(4), 604–665.
Marantz, A. (1997). No escape from syntax: Don't try morphological analysis in the privacy of your own lexicon. In A. Dimitriadis, L. Siegel, C. Surek-Clark, & A. Williams (eds.) *UPenn Working Papers in Linguistics 4*(2), 201–225.
Markopoulos, G. (2018). *Phonological Realization of Morpho-Syntactic Features.* [Unpublished doctoral dissertation]. University of Thessaloniki, Thessaloniki.

Massam, D. (2009). The structure of (un)ergatives. In *Proceedings of the 16th Meeting of the Austronesian Formal Linguistics Association* (AFLA16) (pp. 125–135).

Mathieu, E. (2014). Many a plural. In A. Aguilar-Guevara, B. Le Bruyn, & J. Zwarts (eds.), *Weak referentiality* (pp. 157–182). John Benjamins.

Medová, L. (2018). The Czech able. *Linguistica Brunensia, 66* (2), pp. 37–46.

Medová, L. & Taraldsen, T. (2007). 1, 2, Se. In Dočekal, M., Karlík, P. Zmrzlíková, J., *Czech in generative grammar (eds.)* (pp. 119–139). Lincom.

Mourelatos, A. (1978). Events, processes and states. *Linguistics and Philosophy 2*, 415–434.

Nash, L. (1996). The internal ergative subject hypothesis. *Proceedings of NELS 26*, 195–209.

Newmeyer, F. J. (1986). *Linguistic theory in America*. Academic Press INC.

Newmeyer, F. J. (2009). Current challenges to the lexicalist hypothesis. An overview and a critique. In W. D. Lewis, S. Karimi, H. Harley & S. O. Farrar (eds.), *Time and again* (pp. 91–117). John Benjamins.

Norris, M. (2014). *A Theory of Nominal Concord* (1564215936) [Doctoral dissertation, USCS]. ProQuest Dissertations Publishing.

Panagiotidis, P. & Grohmann, K. (2009). Mixed projections: Categorial switches and prolific domains. *Linguistic Analysis 35*, 141–161.

Panchewa, R. (2003). The aspectual makeup of perfect participles and the interpretations of the perfect. In Alexiadou, A., Rathert, M., & von Stechow A., *Perfect Explorations* (pp. 277–306). De Gruyter Mouton.

Panevova, J. (2000). Poznámky k valenci podstatných jmen. In Z. Hladká and P. Karlík, eds. *Čeština – univerzália a specifika 2* (pp. 173–180). Brno: Masaryk University.

Pesetsky, D. (2013). *Russian case morphology and the syntactic categories*. Cambridge, MA: Massachusetts Institute of Technology Press.

Pesetsky, D., & Torrego, E. (2001). T-to-C movement: Causes and consequences. In M. Kenstowicz, ed. *Ken Hale, A Life in language* (pp. 355–426). The MIT Press.

Pesetsky, D., & Torrego, E. (2007). The Syntax of valuation and the interpretability of features. In S. Karimi, V. Samiian, & W. K. Wilkins, eds. *Phrasal and clausal architecture: Syntactic derivation and interpretation* (pp. 262–294). John Benjamins.

Picallo, M. C. (1991). Nominals and nominalization in Catalan. *Probus 3*, 279–316.

Picallo, C. (2006). Some notes on grammatical gender and l-pronouns. In K. von Heusinger, G. A. Kaiser, & E. Stark (eds.), *Proceedings of the workshop 'Specificity and the evolution / emergence of nominal determination systems in Romance'* (Arbeitspapier Nr. 119). Fachbereich Sprachwissenschaft, Universität Konstanz.

Pollock, J. Y. (1989). Verb movement, Universal Grammar, and the structure of IP. *Linguistic Inquiry 20* (3), 365-424. < http://www.jstor.org/stable/4178634>

Ramchand, G. (2004). Time and the event: The semantics of Russian prefixes. *Norlyd, 32*, 323–361.

Ramchand, G. (2008). *Verb meaning and the lexicon*. Cambridge: Cambridge University Press.

Rappaport, G. C. (2004). The syntax of possessors in the nominal phrase: Drawing the lines and deriving the forms. In J.-Y. Kim, B. H. Partee, & Y. A. Lander (Eds.), *Possessives and beyond: Semantics and syntax* (pp. 243–261). GLSA Publications.

Ritter, E. (1991). Two functional categories in noun phrases: Evidence from modern Hebrew. In S. Rothstein (eds.), *Syntax and semantics 25: Perspectives on phrase structure: heads and licensing* (pp. 37-62). Academic Press.

Ritter, E. (1992). Cross-linguistic evidence for number phrase. *Canadian Journal of Linguistics, 37*, 197–218.

Ritter, E. (1993). Where's Gender? *Linguistic Inquiry 24*, 795–803.

Roeper, T. (2020). Where are thematic roles? Building the micro-syntax of implicit arguments in nominalizations. In A. Alexiadou & H. Borer, *Nominalization: 50 years on from Chomsky's Remarks* (pp. 87–110). Oxford University Press.

Roodenburg, J. (March–April 2006). The role of number within nominal arguments: The case of French pluralized event nominalizations. In the *36th Linguistic symposium on Romance languages*, Rutgers University.

Rozwadowska, B. (1997). *Toward a unified theory of nominalizations*. Wydawnictwo Uniwersytetu Wrocławskiego.

Rozwadowska, B. (2020). Polish psych nominals revisited. In A. Alexiadou & H. Borer. *Nominalization: 50 years on from Chomsky's Remarks* (pp. 337–362). Oxford University Press.

Sleeman, P. & Brito, A., M. (2010). Aspect and argument structure of deverbal nominalizations: A split vP analysis. In A. Alexiadou & M. Rathert (eds.), *The Syntax of Nominalizations across Languages and Frameworks* (pp. 199–229). Mouton de Gruyter.

Smith, C. (1997). *The parameter of aspect: Studies in Linguistics and philosophy.* Kluwer.

Stowell, T. (1981). *Origins of phrase structure.* [Doctoral dissertation, MIT]. MIT Libraries. <https://dspace.mit.edu/handle/1721.1/15626>

Suchomel, Vít (2018). csTenTen17, a Recent Czech Web Corpus. In *Twelveth Workshop on Recent Advances in Slavonic Natural Language Processing* (pp. 111–123). Brno: Tribun EU. <https://www.sketchengine.eu/cstenten-czech-corpus/#toggle-id-2>

Svenonius, P. (2004). Slavic prefixes inside and outside VP. *Norlyd 32*(2), 205–253.

Synková, P. (2017). O tom, jak se v češtině spojují jména jako dveře, ponožky, víno nebo cinkání. In Adam, R. et al., *O jazyce bez hranic a další zajímavosti ze současného zkoumání češtiny.* Praha: Nakladatelství Lidové noviny.

Štícha, F. (2018). *Velká akademická gramatika spisovné češtiny. I. Morfologie: Druhy slov/Tvoření slov Část 1.* Academia.

Travis, L. (1984). *Parameters and effects of word order variation.* [Doctoral dissertation, MIT]. MIT Libraries. <https://dspace.mit.edu/handle/1721.1/15211>

Van Hout, A. (1991). Deverbal nominalization, object versus event denoting nominals: implications for argument and event structure. In F. Drijkoningen & A. van Kemenade (eds.), *Linguistics in the Netherlands 8* (pp. 71–80). Amsterdam/Philadelphia: Benjamins.

Verkuyl, H. J. (1972). *A theory of aspectuality.* Cambridge UP.

Verkuyl, H. J. (1993). *A theory of aspectuality: The interaction between temporal and atemporal structure.* Cambridge University Press.

Verkuyl, H. J. (1998). Tense, aspect and aspectual composition. *UiL OTS Working Papers*, February.

Veselovská. L. (1998). Possessive Movement in the Czech Nominal Phrase. *Journal of Slavic Linguistics*, 6 (2), 255–300.

Veselovská, L. (2001). K analýze českých deverbálních substantiv. In Z. Hladká and P. Karlík, eds. *Čeština – univerzália a specifika 3* (pp. 11–28). Brno: Masaryk University.

Veselovska, L. 2008. The extended verbal projection in Czech: Three variants of the verb be. In G. Zybatow, L. Szucsich, U. Junghanns & R. Meyer (eds.) *Formal description of Slavic languages: The fifth conference, Potsdam 2003* (pp. 555–569). Peter Lang.

Veselovská, L. (2011). Inversion and fronting in English: A cartography of discourse in generative framework. *Czech and Slovak Linguistic Review 1*, 53–72.

Veselovská, L. (2014). Possessives and their equivalents in English and Czech: A comparative study. In L. Veselovská & M. Janebová, *Nominal structures: All in complex DPs* (pp. 110–133). Palacký University Press.

Veselovská, L. (2018a). *Noun phrases in Czech: Their structure and agreements.* Peter Lang.

Veselovská, L. (2018b). Morphological taxonomy in the present-day generative framework: A case study of English and Czech nominalizations. *Topics in Linguistics 19*(20), 1–21.

Veselovská, L. (2022). The features of null subjects: A case study of Czech. In G. Dalmi & E. Tsedryk & P. Ceglowski (eds.), *Null Subjects in Slavic and Finno-Ugric. Licensing, Structure, and Typology* (pp. 133–177). De Gruyter.

Veselovská, L. & Emonds, J. E. (2015). The cross-linguistic homes of mood and Tense. In Henk Riemsdijk a Marc van Oostendorp *(eds.), Representing Structure in Phonology and Syntax* (pp. 277–314). Berlin: de Gruyter.

Veselovská, L. & Emonds, J. E. (2016). Morphology, divided and conquered? *Linguistica Brunensia 64*(1), 143–162.

Veselovská, L. & Karlík, P. (2004). *Analytic passives in Czech. Zeitschrift fur Slavische Philologie 2*(49), 163–235.

Williams, E. (1981). On the notions "Lexically related" and "Head of a Word." *Linguistic Inquiry 12*(2), 245–274.

Williams, E. (1987). *The Thematic-structure of derived Nominals.* Proceedings of the Chicago Linguistic Society.

Zikova, M. (2007). Why Czech case markers sometimes get lost. In Dočekal, M., Karlík, P. Zmrzlíková, J., *Czech in generative grammar (eds.)* (pp. 193–203). Lincom.

Zikova, M. (2012). Lexical prefixes and templatic domains: Prefix lengthening in Czech. In M. Ziková & M. Dočekal (eds.), *Slavic Languages in Formal Grammar* (pp. 325–338). Peter Lang Verlag.

Zikova, M. (2016). When Prosody Follows Syntax: Verbal Stems in Czech. *Linguistica Brunensia 64*(1), 163–185.

Zubizarreta, M. L. (1979). *Extraction from NP and a reformulation of subjacency.* (unpublished manuscript). MIT.

Potsdam Linguistic Investigations
Potsdamer Linguistische Untersuchungen
Recherches Linguistique à Potsdam

Edited by/Herausgegeben von/Edité par
Peter Kosta, Gerda Haßler, Teodora Radeva-Bork, Lilia Schürcks,
Nadine Thielemann and/und/et Vladislava Maria Warditz

Band	1	Peter Kosta/Lilia Schürcks (eds.): Linguistics Investigations into Formal Description of Slavic Languages. Contributions of the Sixth European Conference held at Potsdam University, November 30–December 02, 2005. 2007.
Band	2	Lilia Schürcks: Binding and Discourse. Where Syntax and Pragmatics Meet. 2008.
Band	3	Christiane Hümmer: Synonymie bei phraseologischen Einheiten. Eine korpusbasierte Untersuchung. 2009.
Band	4	Svetlana Friedrich: Definitheit im Russischen. 2009.
Band	5	Matthias Guttke: Strategien der Persuasion in der schriftkonstituierten politischen Kommunikation. Dargestellt an Parteiprogrammen der Neuen Rechten in Polen. 2010.
Band	6	Peter Kosta/Lilia Schürcks (eds.): Formalization of Grammar in Slavic Languages. Con-tributions of the Eighth International Conference on Formal Description of Slavic Languages – FDSL VIII 2009. University of Potsdam, December 2–5, 2009. 2011.
Band	7	Roman Sukač (ed.): From Present to Past and Back. Papers on Baltic and Slavic Accentology. 2011.
Band	8	Diego Gabriel Krivochen: The Syntax and Semantics of Nominal Construction. A Radically Minimalist Perspective. 2012.
Band	9	Teodora Radeva-Bork: Single and Double Clitics in Adult and Child Grammar. 2012.
Band	10	Anja Hennemann: A Context-sensitive and Functional Approach to Evidentiality in Spanish or Why Evidentiality needs a Superordinate Category. 2013.
Band	11	Diego Gabriel Krivochen/Peter Kosta: Eliminating Empty Categories. A Radically Minimalist View on Their Ontology and Justification. 2013.
Band	12	Christina Behme: Evaluating Cartesian Linguistics. From Historical Antecedents to Computational Modeling. 2014.

Band	13	Kathleen Plötner: Raum und Zeit im Kontext der Metapher. Korpuslinguistische Studien zu französischen und spanischen Raum-Zeit-Lexemen und Raum-Zeit-Lokutionen. 2014.
Band	14	Marion Eva Ernst: Produktnamen der Lebensmittelindustrie. Eine empirisch-strukturelle Untersuchung. 2014.
Band	15	Stefanie Wagner: Eine „unbekannte" Sprache lesen *oder* Von der Entdeckung des Nissart durch Interkomprehension. 2015.
Band	16	Nataša Todorović: The Indicative and Subjunctive da-complements in Serbian: A Syntactic-Semantic Approach. 2015.
Band	17	Vladislava Warditz / Beatrix Kreß (eds.): Multilingualism and Translation. Studies on Slavonic and Non-Slavonic Languages in Contact. 2015.
Band	18	Nadia Varley: Optionality and overgeneralization patterns in second language acquisition: Where has the expletive ensconced *it*self? 2015.
Band	19	Verónica Böhm: La imperfectividad en la prensa española y su relación con las categorías semánticas de modalidad y evidencialidad. 2016.
Band	20	Roland Wagner: Reflexivität im tschechisch-deutschen Sprachvergleich. Möglichkeiten und Grenzen einer Prognose. 2016.
Band	21	Ray C. H. Leung: Institutional Construction of Gamblers' Identities. A Critical Multi-method Discourse Study. 2017.
Band	22	Markéta Ziková: Licensing of Vowel Length in Czech. The Syntax-Phonology Interface. 2018.
Band	23	Ludmila Veselovská: Noun Phrases in Czech. Their Structure and Agreements. 2018.
Band	24	Carmen Conti Jiménez: Complejidad lingüística. Orígenes y revisión crítica del concepto de lengua compleja. 2018.
Band	25	Nadine Thielemann / Nicole Richter (eds.): Urban Voices: The Sociolinguistics, Grammar and Pragmatics of Spoken Russian. 2019.
Band	26	Udo Mai: La modalité et ses réalisations en français. 2019.
Band	27	Davide Fanciullo: Temporal expression in nominals: tripartite deictics in the Bulgarian Rhodope dialects. 2019.
Band	28	Olga Flug: Russisch und Ukrainisch im Wandel. Eine korpusbasierte Untersuchung zur Destandardisierung am Beispiel der Anglisierung in der Werbesprache nach 1985. 2019.
Band	29	Teodora Radeva-Bork / Peter Kosta (eds.): Current Developments in Slavic Linguistics. Twenty Years After (*based on selected papers from FDSL 11*). 2019.
Band	30	Anja Hennemann: Topic and Focus Markers in Spanish, Portuguese and French. 2020.
Band	31	Peter Kosta: The Syntax of Meaning and the Meaning of Syntax. Minimal Computations and Maximal Derivations in a Label-/Phase-Driven Generative Grammar of Radical Minimalism. 2020.

Band 32 Magdalena Lipinski: Wortbildung Polnisch und Deutsch: Integrative Darstellung ausgewählter Wortbildungsprozesse. Mit einem Anhang von Hans-Heinrich Lieb. 2020.

Band 33 Peter Kosta / Katrin Schlund (eds.): Keynotes from the International Conference on Explanation and Prediction in Linguistics (CEP): Formalist and Functionalist Approaches. Heidelberg, February 13th and 14th, 2019. 2021.

Band 34 Steven L. Franks / Alan H. Timberlake / Anna W. Wietecka (eds.): Selected Proceedings of the 14th Meeting of the Slavic Linguistics Society. In Honor of Peter Kosta. 2021.

Band 35 Viktor Tichák: Aspekt und Erfolg: Eine kontrastive Analyse aspektualer Relationen von tschechischen und deutschen Verbpaaren. 2022.

Band 36 Helle Metslang / Miina Norvik / Andra Kalnača (eds.): Insights into the Baltic and Finnic Languages. Contacts, Comparisons, and Change. 2022.

Band 37 Michaela Čakányová: The Grammar of English Infinitives with Czech Comparison. 2022.

Band 38 Markéta Blažková; Nominalization: Exploring Aspect and Countability. 2026.

www.peterlang.com

www.ingramcontent.com/pod-product-compliance
Ingram Content Group UK Ltd.
Pitfield, Milton Keynes, MK11 3LW, UK
UKHW041826100926
8556IPUK00002B/37

9 783631 934562